Beyond

The Elfin Book of the Dead, Ascending towards the Faerie Realms through Progressive Incarnations

The Silver Elves

Dedication

We would like to dedicate this book to all the soulful spirits who have passed on to the Between due to the Coronavirus Pandemic 2020 and we hope you awaken onto the realization of the life eternal.

"It should be clear to nearly everyone that life in the world will eventually kill your body, but life in Elfin will ultimately awaken you to the immortality of your spirit."

— The Silver Elves

"The end of the world lies on the border of Eternity."

—The Silver Elves

Table of Contents

"Life begins through replication and continues through diversity. The Source is the same but the experience different and the possibilities nearly infinite. The deepest necromancy doesn't call to the dead but to the source that connects us all." —The Silver Elves

The Elfin say: "While our bodies may grow old, our spirits remain eternal."

"Some people think Life and Death are opposites, Elves know they are the same."
— Old Elven Knowledge

"The Voices of the ancestors rise from the land, waft through the trees, sing from the water, the incessant song of Necromancy."

"Immortality is a function not of the body but of the consciousness."

The Elves Say: "In the end, we die as we were born and as we elves have ever lived, embracing the Mystery."

"The beginning holds all that comes after. The End contains all that came before. Time is Eternal and it is always Now."
—Ancient Elven Wisdom

Introduction

Beyond Death: The Elfin Book of the Dead is a guide for those who are dealing with the recently deceased or dying, as well as for anyone who would like to begin consciously preparing for their own demise. There are two parts to *Beyond Death* — the first part explores the theoretical aspects concerning death and the Between worlds from an elven perspective, and the second part of this book has practical admonitions and spells based on the Elven Star (7 pointed acute hexagram) that can help a person who is in the process of transitioning from one incarnation to another. We purposely put the 14 day spells and admonitions (ritual) for the recently deceased loved one as the Part Two in this book so it may be easy to find when you need it for guiding your loved one through the Between (see more on this in the second introduction on page 293).

Part One of *Beyond Death* explores death and the Between states as it relates to a variety of topics including: elven magic, immortality of elves, raising the dead, lucid dreaming, the experience of the between state, the Death card in the Tarot, the stages of grief and dealing with death, death and amnesia, the fae descent into matter, Faerie and the Nether-realms, elven perspectives on how various myths and religions view death, the wild hunt, banshees and black dogs, Day of the Dead, Sitting Shiva and Shiva, astral travel and the relationship of death to teraphim, nature spirits and animism.

We elves don't say 'the Dead' in general because if someone has been dead for a year or more, it is likely they have already been reincarnated, although the time of reincarnation is more an individual phenomenon than a fixed one, despite what anyone says. There are tendencies to be sure, just as it is a tendency for most people to sleep for eight to ten hours a night, but there are exceptions to that as well. Still, using the spells of this book, one could help those who are currently incarnated to progress through the life they are now living. For, in a sense, we are all dying every day, and surely every one of us has died at some time, perhaps many times, life after life, which is really to say incarnation after incarnation since Life is eternal. Death and Life are not opposites, as some seem to think, but all part of one process and that process, the process of learning, developing and evolving, is Life.

We Silver Elves see ours'elves as being elven spirits born into humanoid bodies. We look similar to Men and Women, but while we elves are male and female or, for some elfae, a variation thereof, we are not really of the same spiritual race as Man and are something quite other, something else entirely, in a sense, while still being related to all things. According to legend, we elfae are something much older, yet still here upon the Earth (that is those of us who are earthborn, for surely some have advanced into the realms and dimensions of the Shining Ones) and thus not entirely unrelated to Man and all others currently incarnating here. For the Universe and all in it are One. We are a part of it, although a very individualized, you could even say eccentric, part of the Whole. We elves are the glimmer in a lover's eye, the smile on lips sweetly kissed, the sigh after a great bout of lovemaking.

Having faith in our own elven nature and spirit, we cannot help but believe in re-incarnation, which to us is rather like putting on a new suit of clothes from time to time, a 'meat suit' as they sometimes say in films and shows, although actually, the body is just energy in the form of light, just atoms formed into a sort of mobile sculpture. It seems solid, but isn't really. It is all a matter of perception as the sorcerers like to tell us.

We cannot prove to others that reincarnation exists, and as far as we know, despite the plethora of experiential and anecdotal accounts and case histories of those who remember previous lives and so forth, no one seems to have definitive proof of what happens after death, other than the most technical descriptions of what occurs to the body after the spirit, which is to say the cohesive lifeforce, leaves the material body on its own to disintegrate into the essential energetic particles that composted it. That lifeforce, by the way, is not necessarily a conscious thing, as people in comas demonstrate. It doesn't require our thought or intention to be and keep the body alive, at least it doesn't require our surface consciousness in order to animate the body. Otherwise, we'd die every time we went to sleep.

But this lack of proof is also the case for those who believe that there is an afterlife of heaven and/or hell, or that there is one life only and we are obliterated completely thereafter. What proof do they have but faith and sometimes obstinate denial of the alternatives that those ideas are true? While we Silver Elves don't believe in either of these possibilities, oblivion or an afterlife in heaven or hell as permanent states of being, we do acknowledge that there is truth to both of these beliefs, if only in a transitory and temporary fashion.

It is easy to see how the idea of oblivion arises. We fall asleep and except when we are dreaming we are totally unconscious, or so it seems. And yet, the unconscious is a consciousness as well. A deeper and more subtle consciousness, but consciousness, none-the-less. Otherwise, why would we wake up when someone calls to us or shakes us or when there is a loud noise? If we are totally unconscious and oblivious, as we seem to be when anesthetized, we would only wake up when we were done with our requisite sleep. And people who are under anesthesia sometimes experience what they believe to be out of the body experiences. How is that possible if there is no deeper consciousness? One that is not necessarily directly connected to the body and its awareness and certainly not dependent upon the surface mind of our day to day lives and awareness.

Death is thought by some to be a state of permanent unconsciousness, also bodiless-ness, and yet how is it that we arise into life in the first place? Where were we before we were conceived? How did we awaken into consciousness in the first place and having done so once why, in the infinity of time and possibility, wouldn't we do so again? Born once, why not twice, thrice and so on? If life is just an accident, what stops it from happening a number of times? Lightning does strike twice in the same place. Maybe not often, but it happens and in the infinity of time and space it is surely bound to do so. We are variations on a theme. Unique, yes, but not entirely, and becoming individualized more by experience than creation directly. We are made very similar, all from the same source, the energy of the Universe, but we become very different through the lifetimes.

And as far as the existence of Heaven and Hell, there are people who live in hell on this Earth and others who seem to be living in heaven, and there are times that feel hellish in our lives and other times that seem heavenly and sometimes there are periods that seem to be a little of both as when someone falls deeply in love but doesn't know as yet if their love is reciprocated. What horrible and delicious torture that is.

To we who are elven, people who live their lives dominated by hate and prejudice seem like they are in hell, but those who are prejudiced or ignorant don't experience it that way at all, usually. Most of the time, they consider themselves quite knowledgeable and illuminated, quite justified and righteous in their judgments concerning others. In the same way, alcoholics often see their lives as simply wonderful and they think it is the people around them that really have the problem with their drinking until the alcoholic finally becomes aware of the reality of their own suffering and addiction and the painful consequences for themselves and others that their addiction causes in their lives.

There are *Between* incarnation states, as well, (the Buddhists call them Bardos), after death of the body and before a new incarnation, that can be heavenly or hell-like but those are really just illusions or, in a sense, dream states that seem real at the time as a dream does while we are in the process of dreaming it. And so they are, in that sense, real, which is to say real to us as an experience until we wake up into a different reality or different perceptual state and we accept this new waking experience as reality.

But these are not permanent states of being except in so far as they affect our choices for a new incarnation or shape our future in our current incarnation. We will awake from these dreams, that we experience in the *Between*, into another life just as we awake into the world after sleep. Still, we experience these states, live through them, and that is what we are talking about, isn't it, conscious experience and the effect it has upon us? Many people dismiss their dreams as irrelevant but we elves embrace our dreams and view them with the same intent and seriousness that we encounter life. They have meaning for us, when we can decipher them, and evoke the mysteries when we can't, and they represent experiences that can affect our lives when we can integrate the message they present to us with the world we consciously live in day to day. It is all about integrating our reality and experience as a whole.

So, all these possibilities of between incarnation states have truth to them, but just not always in the way, certainly not in the permanent fashion, that many folks imagine them to manifest. We are spirits learning, developing, growing and evolving through time, which is to say via successive phenomena and experience, and we are in the process of becoming, which is to say individualizing and developing uniqueness, due to those experiences and due to an inherent destiny within us manifested or honed or chiseled, perhaps, through that experience. We ever gravitate toward becoming whom we truly wish to be, which is, in fact, who we are destined to be. We are destined always in the long run to become our own true s'elves, no matter how much we may strive to be otherwise at times in response to the pressure of others in the world. But what is that s'elf? It is the being you truly wish to be. Always, in the long run, we become ours'elves. Who else could we be?

The Elves Say:

"Every time we come near death we hear our ancestors say, hang on, cling to life, cherish every moment. This perhaps is the most common necromancy there is and nearly everyone experiences it."

Part One. . .

Musings on Life, which is to say Death,
which is to say Life

"DEATH IS NOT THE OPPOSITE OF LIFE, IT IS THE MEANS LIFE USES TO CHANGE."....
. . .

Chapter 1:
Magic

This is a book of magic, or enchantment really, because Elven magic is nearly always essentially enchantment. But then, in some ways, we use those terms, magic and enchantment, interchangeably, enchantment being a form of magic, just as sorcery, wizardry, weather witchery, hedgewitchery, ceremonial magic, necromagery, thaumaturgy and other magic ways are sub-divisions of the greater category of Magic or Magick if you will.

We seek to distinguish enchantment not from Magic overall but from the sort of manipulative and power over, domination magic that is commonly seen in books, television shows and movies (see our book *The Keys to Elfin Enchantment*) and is therefore part and parcel of the mistaken notion that a person needs to dominate thems'elves, Nature, their environment and all those around them like some petty tyrant god.

Still, nearly all our Silver Elves books are books of magic and enchantment. They are books on the elven philosophy of magic, books on elven culture, which at its very heart is magically enchanting, and books of practical elfin magic with spells that can be used to achieve your goals whatever else the book may be about, and books on the various ways of divination, another category of magic, that we elves utilize. Our books are all about magic and enchantment even when their principle subject seems elsewise. But then, we are an Elsewise folk, we elven, are we not?

So, it is that you can use the spells in this book to help someone who is dying, or even someone who has recently passed on and is already beginning to transit the Between. Yet, even if you are an atheist or someone who simply doesn't believe in reincarnation, you could still use the spells in this book to help inspire those who are struggling in this life to achieve what they desire and to become greater beings, for really, there is only Life and it is eternal. Beyond life there is only nothingness, and in that nothingness lives infinite potential not yet expressed and it springs into being because there is absolutely Nothing to stop it from doing so. Life is born of its own inherent possibility.

Although, it should be pointed out that at times and at its heart, magic is so subtle that it would be invisible to most people's eyes and thus non-existent to those who only believe in the material world and its manifestation. But then, those strictly materialistically oriented folks are unlikely to read this book, or much of it, and are even less likely to believe in the power and efficacy of magic and enchantment or the value of developing thems'elves as individual spirits other than to succeed in their transitory lives in the material world, which they believe to be the only world existent or possible. But then, perhaps they are right. Perhaps they are only extras, on the stage and off again quickly, in the eternal sagas of the rest of us. Although, we don't actually believe this to be so. They have their heroic tales and quests to fulfill as well.

However, in the end, no matter what petty things we may seem to desire in the short run of an individual incarnation, in the long run, we all strive to fulfill the two essential drives of incarnate beings. The first of which is survival and from that naturally a movement toward longevity and by means of that the fulfillment of our efforts to eventually achieve immortality. One arises from the other as the kundalini snake ascends the spine igniting the chakras as it does so.

And the second primal directive is the inner urge to achieve happiness, which is usually perceived as success and power in the world or sexual satisfaction and love through the manifestation of our individual being and the interaction of our souls in communion and congress with others. The Universe is interconnected by its nature, we are just enhancing the power of the links that connect us.

Life is magic and thus magic rules this book, which is about Life and its eternal movements. We call it *Beyond Death: The Elfin Book of the Dead*, but really, we could have called it The Elven Book of Life Eternal (but that is too much like the title of our book *The Elven Tree of Life Eternal*) or maybe we might have entitled it The Elven Book of Mastering the Magic of the Between and the Techniques for Passing from One Incarnation to Another. However, *Beyond Death: The Elfin Book of the Dead*, despite its failure to accurately describe the nature of Life, lets the reader know it is along the lines of the *Egyptian Book of the Dead* and the *Tibetan Book of the Dead* in as much as it is a source book for those who have assumed or accepted the task of helping someone progress through the Between states from one incarnation to the next or for preparing ones'elf for one's own inevitable transition from one incarnation to the another.

Note that Timothy Leary, Ph.D., Ralph Metzner, Ph.D., & Richard Alpert, Ph.D (also known as Ram Das) wrote *The Psychedelic Experience* and based it on the *Tibetan Book of the Dead*, as a manual for guiding individuals through psychedelic states of being. Life is life in all its forms most particularly in its tendency to continually change and, in many ways, the

Psychedelic Experience is surely more like the Between than mundane reality. Faerie is an enchanting realm and, in its way, much like a Psychedelic experience, but then don't they warn those venturing into Faerie not to eat or drink anything offered there?

This book isn't really about dying or being dead, it's about using those states of experiential being to ascend toward greater realization and power as an elfae spirit and fae enchanter and as an elfin magic wielder or whatever you may happen to be or call yours'elf. Death, in that sense, is a staircase. Going up? Going down? Getting off on the same level? It's up to you, which is to say utterly dependent upon your individual power to use magic to master your own being on every level of manifestation and consciousness. Life is like a school where you take every class until you thoroughly master it. Failure just means you take the class again ... and again ... and perhaps again. Getting better and better at it, as you do so. You never get kicked out of school, in fact as the Buddhists tell us, it's impossible to be kicked out of school until you finally graduate and graduation only leads to another, higher, level of education. We never stop learning, for life is experience, experience is education and education is eternal. The important thing is to learn all we can, while we can, whenever a lesson is offered to us.

You will find spells in this book and exhortations that you may read to the dying or the dead to help them progress and navigate through the *Between* incarnation phases, the stages of transition that the Tibetans refer to as the Bardos. Those are worlds where, like dreams, we tend to be less thought oriented and more feeling experiential. Our consciousness is not our ideas, as some people seem to suppose, but something much deeper, an inner sentient awareness that is more like our dreams than our conscious thoughts, opinions and ideas.

But these stages of being are the same in their way as the things and situations we face while we are incarnated, while we are conscious, but also while we dream and while we float or fly through the netherworld, the liminal realms of transmutation or transubstantiation or, for some folks, transmogrification. For some individuals progress up the scale of evolution, some digress or devolve, seemingly downward, but all eventually, in the course of time, will find their way toward the magic of their own true being. It is all life; and life moves ever on and we are forever becoming our own true s'elves guided by our instincts and desires.

The spells in this book are in English and Arvyndase (see our books *Arvyndase [SilverSpeech]: A Short Course in the Magical Language of the Silver Elves* and *The Complete Dictionary of Arvyndase*). While one certainly may wish to know what the spell is saying, for we elves surely would not wish to do magic blindly, chanting it in Arvyndase gives it an extra touch of enchantment (see Aleister Crowley's *Magick: In Theory and Practice* on the use of The Barbarous Names of Evocation, except we elves use a tongue not barbarous but one both fair and sublime). Using Arvyndase is like sprinkling faerie dust upon your spell, or wrapping it up in starlight enchanted with elfin magic and the wondrous possibilities of the Faerie worlds. Using Arvyndase connects your magic to Elfin and Faerie and brings the blessings of those realms upon your efforts. It helps establish our elfae culture as a living culture and a vibrant magical tradition in the world.

Thus, when we write spells in our books including this one that you hold in your hands, we also add the phonetic pronunciations of Arvyndase words so you may be as clear as possible about how it is supposed to sound. But remember, however it may seem to you and with whatever accent you may pronounce it, making it sound beautiful and as flowing as possible is the most important thing. Use your best understanding of what we've offered you and make it lovelier. In that way, also, make it your own. But if you think you've made a mistake in pronunciation or are uncertain, don't worry, the elven spirits understand full well and so do we. It is your conscious intent and motivation that are most important here. Plus, just do it. Magic is in the doing.

In the long run, it is not the words the spirits pay heed to the most but the power with which you express them. It is your true heart's intent that really counts. Words can be false or mistaken. Emotions can be faked or mimicked. But true feeling resonates through the Universe and touches the hearts of all that it encounters unfolding wonders as it does so.

Some think that the letter of the law, or the exactness of a spell is vital, as it may be in combining elements and ingredients in chemistry in which if you do the formula incorrectly things could explode in some cases or go very wrong, or as in math where a formula off by but a fraction can lead to the wrong conclusion. But for elven magic, the intent of the law or spell, is most important. Our magic is less like chemistry and more like cooking. You may not wish to stray too far from the recipe but individual tastes are to be expected and they provide variety and delight to a meal. Spice according to your own taste. So, use the spells in this book without fear or hesitation. Doing your best is what is really vital, and feeling the depth of your intent most efficacious for making them work. Doing your best, in many ways, is the true magic. Shall we get started?

Spell of Sealing:
By this spell my fate I seal
My destiny doth make it real

Arvyndase:
La wyr moja el'na El daba
El'na lawath båver kord ter alth

Pronunciation:
Lah were moe - jah eel'nah Eel day - bah
Eel'na lay - wayth bah - veer cord tier ale-th

ॐ

Chapter 2:
Are Elves Immortal?

ost stories about the fae folk say that we are immortal or very long lived. Of course, that's also what is said about vampires (what we Silver Elves think of as dark elves, sometimes but not always of an unseelie variety) until someone plunges a stake through their heart or binds them into the sunlight and the light turns them to ashes and dust that blows away with the wind. This destroys their body, surely, but where does their spirit go?

Elves, too, as we say, are sometimes seen as being immortal up until the point when we, like vampires, get killed, although the methods for killing us are often less idiosyncratic than it is for vampires. Still, if your body can be killed, it's not exactly

Beyond Death.... 21

immortal as a cohesive unit, just potentially long lived and we each strive for immortality not only of the spirit but of the body as well.

There is a reason that, while we know ours'elves to be spirits, we think of our bodies as our own and a part of us. It is true that we have, in a sense, commandeered energy from the Universe and formed it into our body and that body changes, shedding skin, hair and other things, all its cells being replaced periodically throughout our lives, and yet it still remains one unit while we are in it. Our body may change utterly through the course of a life and yet still we remain ours'elves. We are learning through the vehicles of incarnation how to construct bodies that will last and endure and become a part of us in a more permanent fashion. In a certain sense, the union of our spirit and our body is a marriage of sorts. The fact that for most of us, as yet, that marriage ends in divorce/death is only to say that we have much to learn about magic and need a good deal more time and effort in order to increase our own powers of endurance, healing and manifestation.

As it is, most of us elves currently incarnated into human bodies do not have immortal material bodies. We die, like everyone else, but often, but not always, we do have a basic tendency to live a bit longer than normal human beings and to appear younger than our age as compared to most of the normal folk around us. But that may have less to do with us being elven than the fact that we also are inclined to have better diets, to exercise more and in general take better care of ours'elves and our bodies than Men often do theirs. But those things, in themselves, are surely elven traits, and it wouldn't hurt Men at all to follow our example in this regard and in that way potentially live longer while becoming just a bit more elven. Of course, toning down their aggressive tendencies and their inclination to go to war with nearly everyone about nearly anything, would probably serve to extend their lives as well.

Although, it is rather paradoxical that Men, who frequently think that they have only one life to live, so often treat their bodies with such rough disregard, while we elves, who know ours'elves to be essentially spirit, nurture, value and do our best to preserve our bodies in each incarnation even knowing that we will get another fresh one when our current one is done. Men often take better care of their cars than they do their own bodies. We elves see our bodies as a part of our spirit family, you might say, and we take care of our family, for all our kindred are beloved to us.

And yet, though we do incarnate into fragile human bodies, there is an immortality to the elven, but that is really the case for all beings and is not something that is exclusive to we who are elven as some seem to suppose. It is just that some folks, like Men, have not realized the essential nature of their own immortal being. All of life is eternal. Our bodies are immortal, actually, or really the energy that we have used to formulate these bodies is, although the forms themselves are temporary and changing even as we inhabit them. But once the form dissolves the energy that composed it simply goes elsewhere. Energy can neither be created nor destroyed, it merely transforms. The key is in learning and achieving the ability to guide that transformation as best we may. Life after life, we develop our abilities, including our ability to successfully inhabit a material body and do so in a way that it will endure, heal and revitalize itself for as long as possible. Trees can live for thousands of years, why can't we? And the answer is, of course, that we can, but we are still learning how to do so.

Our spirits are immortal, even though they are not exactly the same thing as the transitory personalities that we use to express ours'elves any more than we are actually our thoughts, emotions or opinions. Our ideas, feelings and points of view may change, hopefully will, as we grow more experienced and potentially wise, but our essential nature, the core of our inner being, remains forever the same, although hopefully deepening, in a sense, as our experience, power and potential wisdom increase. We are always ours'elves even when we are not aware of who precisely that may happen to be.

We may go through a period of finding ours'elves, as the expression goes, when we are very young, but finding ones'elf really is a quest for lifetimes and what most people mean by finding oneself is finding one's place in the world, finding where one fits in or how one wishes to fit into society as it already exists. We may settle on some rather simple notions of our being as we develop into maturity, often falling back into the example that our parents set for us but we are always more than we may seem to be in any particular lifetime and continually evolving toward the greater realization of our beings, whether it seems that way or not. We may go down a lot of dead-ends in our search for enlightenment but those are an education, too. We may wander and meander but when we finally arrive in Elfin we will see that we got there just when we were meant to do so, and the journey, however inconsistent it may have seemed at times, was our path and no other's.

And certainly, the higher spirits, the Shining Ones who live upon higher dimensions, or more expansive dimensions, you might say, so that they are able to live in our world and yet beyond it, are immortal as compared to our limited incarnations, but even they are in the process of change and transformation, ever in the process of becoming. And while death may be different for them, chosen perhaps, rather than thrust upon them, they still are subject to change. Only it is something they embrace and use, like driving a car we might say, rather than to experience fearfully as most of us tend to fear death as though we are sitting in the backseat as our drunk and half blind grandfather races down the highway. We are, after all, energy formulated by a deep magical consciousness and attaining that consciousness in a more persistent and constant fashion is to obtain immortality. Continuity of consciousness from life to life or body to body or incarnation to incarnation, however you may wish to express it, is immortality in the sense that most of us deem it to be and strive toward achieving.

The old Tooke, as we sometimes called her, one of the original Elf Queen's Daughters, once said to us that all fear at its core was the fear of death. But what is there to fear in death, if death is oblivion? Not pain, nor suffering, that all has passed, just the fear of not being. Should we fear sleep? When we Silver Elves are exhausted we look forward to it and life, in the long run, can be very exhausting. Most of us cling to life with a fierce passion and there is a reason for us doing so because we are spirits manifesting through the world and we do not desire to let go until we have completed ours'elves and our destiny and our destiny is to live forever consciously and fulfilled, which is to say to Live Happily Ever After, just as so many of the faerie tales about us indicate by their endings.

There is truth in the faerie tales, although not always the truth that some presume. Like a tarot reading or other divination from an oracle such as the *I Ching* (see our book *The Elven Book of Changes* for our elfin version of the *I Ching*), fairy tales take some interpreting. One needs to understand them from the perspective of the dimensional realms of Elfin and from the perspective of one's own life, one's experience and one's individual, personal understanding of magic, enchantment and the reality of elvish being, or being elvish, in the world, arising out of one's own experience and comprehension thereof. Magic is universal in that it adapts itself to every person and circumstance. Like water it shapes its'elf to whatever it rests within. Like fire, it spreads readily wherever nature is disposed. Like air, it goes nearly everywhere and like earth it makes all things real and manifest, supporting them and giving them what they need to grow unto their own s'elves.

Of course, there are those individuals who believe in an afterlife of heaven or hell and fear that they may be punished for the wickedness they have done in their lives, and yet, that doesn't seem to stop them from doing wicked things, harming others, being greedy to the point of pure selfishness while undermining everyone else around them including their own kin. It makes one wonder if, indeed, they truly believe in that afterlife, but then such individuals also often smoke, eat to excess, drink with no moderation at all, knowing it will harm their bodies eventually and yet pretending otherwise until it is far too late to change their ways and have the doing so alter their fate for the better. They have yet, it seems, to truly understand the nature of life, karma, which is to say cause and effect, and their own power to shape their lives through their actions, which is to say use magic to make a better world for themselves and all their others around them. Instead they have accepted, through their actions and failure to change for the better, the cruel judgments that Life and Nature declare on those who violate its basic conditions and requirements. These folks tell us they believe in an afterlife dependent upon their behavior in this life but their actions belie their declarations of faith.

But what of those folks who commit suicide? Did they fear death? Apparently not. What they feared, it seems, was the horrible inner agony that life can bring. Is it death we really fear? Or is it suffering? And yet, most of us will endure nearly anything to live just a few moments longer while the fear of a distant and yet to be experienced hell is but a vague haunting usually brought forth only by impending death.

What is it that you really fear? What would be so terrible that you'd rather be dead? Which is really to say, so bad you'd wish to give up upon your current body and incarnation and take a chance on a new unknown situation that might be better but could be much worse or could be nothing at all. And how much would you suffer and endure just to stay alive a little bit longer? And whatever some might say or think about this, what they do or think when they are faced with reality when it is being so hard and cruel, or really when they are caught in the clutches of cruel and uncompromising fate, may be quite different than they presumed. As we elves say, Reality can change your mind.

In such situations, our opinions fade and reactions become less mental and more instinctual. And, so it is in the Between states for most of us, just as it is in dreams, the decisions we make are made instinctually from our inner being and from our deeper awareness and directed by our true nature as expressed by our instinctual inclinations. The Between is a world where the etheric aspect of our gut brain, so to speak, thoroughly takes charge (see the book *What's Behind Your Belly Button? A Psychological Perspective of The Intelligence of Human Nature and Gut Instinct* by Martha Char Love and Robert W. Sterling for more on this) and we are guided by our instincts and true feelings rather than any notions we might have held in our last incarnation. Of course, we don't really have a gut in that body except in the most imaginal sense. Let us thus call it our instinctual brain, or our subconscious mind.

Is it death people fear the most? Is it suffering? We don't know the answer to that but we suspect that, like nearly everything else, it really depends upon the individual. Like most things in life, there isn't just one answer for every question. People are different and the ways through life multitudinous. Life is a forest and we are creating new pathways as we go along and when we stop using those pathways, the elfin forest reclaims those paths behind us. Faerie is a protean realm that is forever in process, forever redesigning itself, forever growing, changing and becoming.

But if we know we are immortal really, know it as an idea at least, if we believe in an afterlife either as a new incarnation, or an afterlife of spirit in the heavenly realms, or even the blessed sleep of oblivion where we won't have to put up with all this trauma drama (also known as bullshit) of the world anymore, why do we fear death at all? Because, of course, it is our nature to do so, which is to say, Nature's way of telling us to live as long as possible, for we are, after all, not simply immortal spirits in transitory bodies, but immortal spirits in the process of creating more effectively enduring and permanent material bodies or bodily forms. We're growing sick of all these rentals; we desire a home of our own. We are tired of living in other people's worlds. We're here to create Elfin upon the Earth and among the Stars and to live together in love, joy and happiness forever more.

The Spell:

Death's icy grip brings me no fear
For Elfin's love does hold me dear

Arvyndase:
Fanth'na lasath fit curalu el kon mak
Fro Êldat'na feln ba gosp el fysa

Pronunciation:
Fane-th'nah lay - sayth fight cur - rah - lou eel cone make
Fro L - date'nah feel-n bah go-sp eel fiss - sah

❧

Chapter 3:
Raising the Dead, the Balance of Life

It is quite common in films and television shows about magic or the occult that the idea of bringing someone back from the dead is a dreaded thing. And the individuals who desire this to happen are often told that there is a balance to life and in order to bring the person they desire back to life, someone or something else will have to die. This is repeated so commonly that many people unthinkingly accept this idea without questioning it at all. But is this really the case? Let's consider it together.

If death is not the opposite of life, then your life goes on even after you have abandoned or been forced out of a body. You are still there, which is to say still alive, you still exist, you are just no longer in that body. In order to reanimate the body, it isn't about someone else dying. If that was the case there would be an exact ratio of people being born for every person who died and we'd have no need to ever fear overpopulation. But that isn't the case at all.

If we get seriously sick and then heal, does someone else need to get sick in order for us to do so? That's the same basic idea and that idea is ridiculous. Coming back to life really is about our ability to heal the body. We don't need to vampirically suck someone else's lifeforce to reanimate ours'elves, although a bit of borrowed energy might help jump start the process, rather like jump starting a dead battery in your car. You don't kill someone else's battery when you jump start your own. Their battery starts yours but their battery still works perfectly. You are just borrowing a bit of energy. There isn't some other car in another city whose battery goes dead automatically just because yours has been revived.

The problem with being reanimated, coming alive again in the same body, isn't that someone else needs to die for you to come back and re-inhabit your old body, but that the body itself is usually no longer adequate to support your lifeforce, which is probably why you died in the first place. It's not a body that you'd want to inhabit again unless you could revitalize and heal it as well. Otherwise, you're essentially a zombie walking around and falling apart at the same time like they tend to do in movies.

Let's think of your body as if it were a car. If your car breaks down to the point where it no longer works at all and can no longer be fixed, it doesn't do you any good really to jump in the driver's seat and make engine noises, like a little kid, as you haul the steering wheel back and forth. The car is not going anywhere, unless you have it towed to the junkyard or you leave it to eventually rust to the point it returns to the earth. Although, in the child's mind and imagination, it can go tremendous distances, and that is not entirely unlike our life in the Between, which in many ways is an imaginal world decorated and populated by our own inner being and consciousness.

Or, let's think of it as a radio or television. If your radio or television set, or even your computer breaks down and can't be fixed, that doesn't mean that the radio waves (our spirits) aren't still out there being broadcast or that the internet doesn't still exist, nor does it mean in order to get your television to work you need to break someone else's television set to do so. Must someone else's computer break down if you have yours repaired, thus bringing it back to life, so to speak?

Clearly, when you begin to think about it in those terms, the assumptions that people have made concerning reanimation of the body are simply false. Although, as we say, most people have merely accepted what they have seen in stories and have never bothered to think about it for thems'elves. After all, despite their religious beliefs, they think reanimation is essentially impossible and for the most part, they are right. At least, impossible for a decayed body, but the spirit lives on.

What do you do if your television or computer breaks beyond repair? You go get another one as soon as you can afford to do so. And hopefully a better one with all the upgrades and new advanced features and programming. That is essentially what we do with the material body. If it breaks down beyond repair, we get another and optimally a better one that provides greater opportunities for spiritual and magical realization and advancement. At least, that is the hope, although some people may temporarily have to make do with an inferior product because of their karmic debts, which is really to say their own inner direction to evolve and their own choice to select an incarnation that will give them the opportunities that will help them best do so. In the long run, we will discover we are creating our own lives in all that we do.

If we reanimate your body, we don't need to take someone else's lifeforce to do so. It's your lifeforce we're trying to put back into the body, but your spirit may not be able to revive the body, which is why you abandoned it. It's not about using someone else's lifeforce, but the current inadequacy of our own powers to heal the material plane. That's what we are here to achieve. Increasing our resiliency, endurance and our capacity for s'elf healing on this plane of reality is one of the ultimate goals of evolution. We don't need to take lifeforce from elsewhere to do that, we just need to increase the potency and power of our own lifeforce and our own powers for energizing a body to the point where it may heal and be fully revitalized and functional again. In other words, we need to increase our own powers and mastery upon the material plane of manifestation.

Now, it is said in the *New Testament* that Jesus brought Lazarus back after he had been dead for four days, and Lazarus' wife warned Jesus before he opened the tomb that Lazarus might be pretty ripe by then, as a result of being fairly well decayed. Some people believe that Lazarus was probably just in a coma and simply woke up when Jesus called him to come out, but even if that was true, waking someone from a coma on command is no mean feat, but a pretty nice bit of Thaumaturgy (see our book *Creating Miracles in the Modern World*). We'd like to be able to do that.

But supposing that Lazarus was actually dead and brought back from the Between, is that what he truly wanted? We suppose so. We get attached to our old lives but the fact is that some of the Between states can be quite marvelous to behold and had he been experiencing one of those, he may not have been so eager to return to his more limiting manifestation in a human body, for our powers on the astral planes of the Between are vast and quite magnificent, quite like what people imagine the Faerie and Elfin realms to be and our magical powers in the Between are similar to those we are told we would have in Faerie; and our life on the material plane, with all its challenges and obstructions, pales in comparison to our life in those wonderful realms.

The other idea that often comes with the notion of bringing someone back from the dead (other than zombies, vampires, etc.) is that the person we bring back into the body may not be the person we intended to revive. Rather, the notion is that some demon or other nefarious spirit will answer our evocation and insert themselves into the body while the original occupant has moved on. This is an idea found in the old play *The Monkey's Paw*, in Stephen King's *Pet Cemetery* and other tales. This is rather like the idea of possession, except in this case the original spirit has moved on and it is only the body that is being possessed, rather like homeless people squatting in an abandoned house or apartment building.

We Silver Elves, for our part, are open to believing that Jesus actually brought Lazarus' spirit back into his own body (and not some other entity or that Lazarus was in a coma), but had Lazarus determined himself to go on, it is possible that another spirit, finding an opening there, may have inserted itself into that body. The fact that the spirits who do this are usually seen as demonic spirits is a product of drama.

Such insertion into another body may be possible but would be quite rare, we think, and there is no reason to assume that the being taking over the body is necessarily wicked, although the idea of possession by demons is another common form of the same notion with all the stories and literature about exorcisms and so forth that go along with this idea. Only with possession the individual didn't die and leave their body thus providing an opening for another spirit but had another spirit push itself into the body, like some unwanted guest coming to live in your home and taking over. Home invaders that don't just steal and leave but move in with you, holding you captive.

The idea of another spirit, this one more congenial, taking over another's body, can be found in the books of T. Lobsang Rampa who claims to have been a Tibetan monk who awakened in the body of an Englishman who willingly abandoned it, because that previous occupant was, according to Rampa, bored with his current life. But, as we said, such occurrences, if they do exist would be rather rare, but not beyond the realms of possibility. After all, are we the only ones who could drive our car?

Still, in the case of T. Lobsang Rampa, who supposedly took over another's body, where did the previous occupant go? Why, inevitably off to another life and another body, being the same spirit with all its accumulated karma, and the need to develop and work out all the challenges and karmic obligations that he was previously faced with. So, he changed bodies but didn't escape his fate. We remain ours'elves no matter what body we may inhabit. We may escape our current body and life but we cannot escape our fate, karma or destiny. We simply cannot escape being ours'elves, although we may try very hard to be someone else at times. And yet, our essential nature is extremely protean, ever in the process of changing and developing, constantly becoming. We ultimately become what we truly wish to be. The details of that wish may change from time to time, or from lifetime to lifetime, but every permutation with its consequent experience eventuates in the realization of our true being.

Abandoning your body is like changing the place where you live but you will still be getting bills from your previous creditors (karma) and you still have to pay the bills in your new residence (fate). Death may free us from a body temporarily, but we are still spirits striving to become our true s'elves, which is to fulfill our destiny. Our spirits will find a way to manifest in order to do so.

The Spell:

Lifetime after lifetime my magic does increase
Growing ever stronger my powers never cease

Arvyndase:
Filym låka filym el'na êldon ba memarn
Lythdas vari mythfa el'na eldroli konzar orz

Pronunciation:
Fie - limb lah - kay fie - limb eel'nah L - doan bah me - mare'n
Lith - dace vair- rye mill-th - fah eel'nah eel - drow - lie cone -
zair oars

❧

Chapter 4:
Lucid Dreaming,
Astral Travel, the Body of Light

In some ways, it can be very helpful for achieving a favorable rebirth to spend some time in our current life learning and developing our ability to lucid dream, to astral travel and formulating and developing our body of light or energetic body, which is what we will be living in when we are traversing the Between. You might call this the imaginal body, which it is in a sense, although it really is pure energy and it becomes formed and shaped through the use of our consciousness and our imaginations. It is still form, and still material in the sense that light is material, but much more subtle than our more mundane material bodies but still unified by our consciousness.

Some people are very adept at lucid dreaming and astral travel, being able to have these experiences at will, whenever they desire to do so, but some of us have only had these experiences occasionally and often quite unexpectedly at that. For our own part, while we Silver Elves have had lucid dreams, we found that when we tried to control them, instead of just watching what was going on, we woke up immediately. It would have been better, we think, certainly at those early stages, to simply observe and go along with the dream. After all, our unconscious was trying to communicate with us using its own symbolic language and we were like individuals who, instead of just listening, were trying to interject our own unsolicited opinions into a conversation.

Yet, from what we understand, most people don't lucid dream or astral travel at all, and if you are one of these, don't worry. Lucid dreaming and practice with astral travel, while they can be helpful, are not vital to effectively moving through the Between. There is something natural and instinctive going on in our progress through the Between, and it doesn't really require our thinking mind to do what it needs to do. But then, in a certain way, that is like just floating down a river where instead of trying to steer one's boat as one goes along, we just drift along and the place we come ashore will depend upon happenstance. However, who's to say that consciously choosing a place to land would be all that much better for us. Sometimes, you just have to trust in the magic of Elfin and in the power of your own elvish being.

In fact, while we Silver Elves think developing these powers of lucid dreaming, astral travel and developing one's body of light are good things to do, it is our deeper inner consciousness, our instinctual consciousness that makes most of the decisions in the Between and guides us toward our next incarnation and if we allow it to do so, we will surely find the way, the next life, that is right for us.

This instinctual sense is similar to the scene in *The Fellowship of the Ring* when Boromir attempts to persuade Frodo to give him the ring and Frodo responds that all Boromir's arguments sound very logical and reasonable on the surface but that there is something deep in his (Frodo's) heart that tells him it is the wrong thing to do. It is just that *something within* that exists in each of us that guides us in the Between.

Some folks might question the existence of this deeper consciousness, thinking only the conscious mind exists, just as they question the reality of the Between, but this deeper inner consciousness is also the consciousness that guides people around when they are sleepwalking. They are not in their normal waking consciousness and yet they find their way around quite instinctively. It is this inner consciousness that guides us in the Between most of the time, a sort of sleepwalking that gets us to where we need to go.

So, if that is the case, what is the value of developing lucid dreaming, practicing astral travel and formulating the energetic body of light? If they are essentially unnecessary, why bother to develop these abilities at all? The fact is that we are in this life to learn to master the material world and create enduring bodies that will not die, at least not so quickly at first, and which later will become immortal. Part of the process of doing this is infusing ours'elves and our lives and our worlds and thus our bodies with that very light that we use to create our imaginal bodies, our illuminated bodies. We are becoming enlightened. We are becoming bright. Not just mentally, as this notion is usually taken to mean, not just in our minds, our thoughts, opinions and points of view, but also in our bodies so that we, like the pictures of saints with halos, radiate light all around us affecting the world for the better through our mere presence. We are becoming radiant beings and in doing so mastering the material world.

Part of the process of creating immortal bodies is also the transformation of those bodies into forms that are more and more composed of light, which is to say made of matter in its illuminated essence, and thus, in more than one way, less dense, closer to the source of the energy which composes these bodily forms and thus more enduring. We expand thereby into the fourth dimension, that is we learn to consciously live in four dimensions and not just in three as we currently do Most of us usually live in three dimensions utterly unaware of the potential of our fourth dimensional reality or of our possible and we might say eventual or even destined existence there.

Elfin and Faerie are frequently seen as being parallel worlds that live alongside of what most people call the "real" world but as worlds that exist but are more ephemeral in nature. This is what we are speaking of. Entering Faerie or Elfin isn't about stepping through a portal into another realm almost exactly like this one but which is elsewhere in space as you might travel from Japan to China and back, although death is that portal in a certain sense. But the goal is to become able to live permanently in that world by making ours'elves and our lives more light-filled, thus vibrating upon the same frequency as the Faerie and Elfin realms. And it is this harmony of vibration that allows us to enter or live within those realms. In vibrating on the same frequency as Elfin, we become attuned to Elfin, which in effect means that we enter Elfin and can live there.

Entering Elfin or Faerie by becoming more illuminated is our quest and becoming more illuminated is also the means for succeeding in that objective. Becoming more elfin is increasing the power and vibrancy of one's aura, the radiated inner light of our being, which is also to say our aura and our powers of enchantment. And it is by becoming more elfin, more filled with the light of Elfin enchantment, that we create Elfin around us. It is a paradox of Faerie magic that Elfin exists and yet our own existence there depends upon us creating it, or making it real in our own lives.

Suicide will not avail us in achieving this. We can't skip the steps that lead to realization any more than we can force someone to truly love us. If we kill our bodies, we will just return to this mundane world again in another body. In fact, suicide pretty much ensures that we will have to do so.

In trying to escape from the world in that fashion, we just strengthen our bondage to it. The body and situation we next inhabit will be similar, if not a bit worse, by which we mean more limiting, than the one we attempted to escape from. It is like one of those Chinese finger traps, the harder you pull to get away the more it entangles you. You may flee from a particular incarnation and the circumstances around it, which is to say your current fate, but you can never escape from yours'elf, which is your destiny, and your destiny will only be attained through the mastering of your karma and the fulfillment of yours'elf as a unique being in the Universe expressing its'elf in the purity of its being-ness. But then, as you will realize in the long run, that is all to the good. Everything in the long run leads to the realization, fulfillment and empowerment of your true and essential s'elf. Karma isn't really a punishment, although it can surely seem that way, but the method by which we learn, through cause and effect, that our actions have consequences in this life and through the lifetimes. Every life is designed to lead us closer to the realization of our true s'elves and our subsequent powers that manifest from being the unique elves that we are.

It is the development of our capacity to live in our light bodies and to travel through the astral planes and planes of energetic spirit that enables us to grow accustomed to life there, in that more expansive dimension, while at the same time transforming, or spiritualizing if you will, the world around us here. We are transforming a mundane world into a world vitalized with wonder, making it, in that way, even more energetic. It is not just ours'elves that we are illuminating but all the world around us and in doing so we create Elfin, which ever exists in potential but is, as we said, realized through our beings.

So, do all you can to increase your power to live energetically, and empower your body of light by doing so. And yet, at the same time, don't worry about it. This is not something that you need to stress over. Your destiny, which is your own true s'elf in motion, will carry you to where you need to be and we have forever to accomplish our designs. Our destiny is a like a powerful magnet attracting us to the realization of our true s'elves. And our destiny always lives within us even as it calls to us from Beyond, which is both our past and our future. The past in the sense that our potential has ever existed within us waiting to be realized, and our future in the sense that this is the realization we are destined to achieve. Thus, we elven often refer to ours'elves as the People of the Ancient Future or the People of the Future Past.

There are many books on methods for developing lucid dreaming and on astral travel. We've read quite a few of them, tried the techniques and none of them have worked for us. When we lucid dream, it just happens. Trying to make lucid dreaming occur hasn't been effective for us, although we know others who are quite proficient at it. Curiously, most of these are college professors with Doctorates, but that just may have to do with the people we have happened to know and have had conversations with about this subject. Still, we seek to increase the power of our bodies of light and we do this in the easiest and most enjoyable ways possible. That is the elven way of education after all, the way of play, taking the path of least resistance by utilizing our natural motivations and integrating them with our everyday habits.

For the elves, education is best when it is fun and also when it is natural. Therefore, in using our imaginations to help empower our body of light, we link those efforts to things which we do quite regularly and naturally, and you might even say instinctively, like daydreaming. When we daydream about having sex, or winning the lottery or whatever we may happen to delight in imagining, success or happiness in some form, usually in ways that are near impossible, surely improbable or would take a miracle to achieve, we also add to our musings our images of our body of light, adding our pointed ears and everything about us that we envision as being a part of our ideal magical body. Some might add their faerie wings, and others their faun or satyr horns and furry legs, and still others may imagine thems'elves in their various other animal forms, as wolves or centaurs or whatever. But make it a body of light, somewhat like an image projected upon a screen, or perhaps, even more so, as a sort of hologram.

See your body as light, formed as you desire, and move in that body. This is just like Olympian athletes who imagine themselves doing their particular sport to increase their skill and performance. Going through the motions in our minds increases our ability to do it in physical space, only in this case, the Between is a very subtle form of physicality. It is form composed of very fine substance.

Now, we Silver Elves like to have fun while we work on our magical powers. Yet, we know that there are others, of a more serious and concerted nature (often quite young), who will dedicate thems'elves to developing their light body with fervor and unbending intent, striving hard to achieve what they desire. That's okay as well. There are different styles of learning, so use the style that works best for you. Just, if you don't mind, don't look down on others, as some serious folk tend to do, just because those others don't happen to share the fanatical fervor with which you may happen to approach things, if indeed that is your style. We are not deriding those who are extremely seriousness in their approach. None-the-less, whatever your learning style may happen to be, pursue your studies, and increase your powers thereby, whichever way works best for you. For doing it the way that is most attuned to your own nature, whether it is being very serious or through play, is taking the way of least resistance. Whatever way you proceed, make it real through consistent and continual action.

The Spell:

In a body formed of light
My elfin spirit soars in flight

Arvyndase:

Ver na miwa qumïn u lun
El'na êldat tari roflu ver fosd

Pronunciation:

Veer nah my - wah que-m - in loon
Eel'nah l - date tay - rye row-f - lou veer foes-d

಄

Chapter 5:
Necromancy and Necromagery

* m*ancy is a suffix that indicates divination. Necromancy involves divination through communication with the dead. Pyromancy involves divination using fire, as often happens when people stare into a campfire or a fire burning in a hearth at home or elsewhere as though hypnotized or entranced, which they are, and various inspirational thoughts occur to them. Geomancy has to do with oracles that in ancient times involved the observation of the movements of creatures and things on the Earth, but in the course of time, Geomancy developed into a system of a number of dots dashed intuitively and randomly upon a piece of paper (see our book *Elven Geomancy*), thus evoking the individual's psyche and unconscious in the process, and then these dots are conjoined in a prescribed fashion and used to derive a reading.

We find Geomancy a quite interesting process, really, and we Silver Elves, for our part, added a means of deriving a series of magical movements (using your body) from the oracle that one can use to increase the power of the prophecy one receives if one likes the reading they got or avert unwanted consequences if the oracle is less favorable or not to one's liking. In deriving a Geomantic oracle from our book, one also receives a mini magical ritual.

When we call to mind our ancestors, the founders of our country or others who formulated our culture but who are long since deceased from the bodies in which they did so, and we evoke their wisdom to guide us, we are performing

Necromancy. When people use the Bible or the Koran or some other book whose author or authors died ages ago to help them find inspiration in their current lives, they are also using necromancy to find answers to the questions that confront them. Although they, of course, believe they are reading the inspired words of their particular god. Who is, naturally, the one true, best, most powerful and only real god, unlike all those other gods including the other monotheistic ones, or so they tell us.

Still, the words were written down by and believed in by their ancestors and thus again, it's actually a form of necromancy. Which is to say, these are words of the dead used as an oracle (see our book *Ruminations on Necromancy*) in order to guide or often dictate our actions and our lives according to the adherents of a particular religious philosophy. If we are to believe the philosopher Friedrich Nietzsche and his proclamation that God is Dead, then prayer in any form in which the individual hopes for some guidance or response from their chosen or inherited god would be a form of Necromancy.

History, and thus history books, and stories and tales of the great people of the past, the heroes who saved the nation or the great inventors and prominent statesmen or women, whose lives are meant to help guide our own, are also a form of necromancy. Whenever we are deriving wisdom and thoughts from reading books written by those who are dead, we are essentially practicing necromancy, especially when we seek some knowledge and understanding of our current lives and situations by doing so or wish a glimpse at what the future might bring to us by paying heed to history.

The Ouija board is, of course, the most popular and famous, although in many ways the least understood form of necromancy. The only people we Silver Elves have ever encountered who actually knew what they were doing in using the Ouija board, and were quite effective in using it, were our sisters of the Elf Queen's Daughters, who upon occasion would withdraw, in pairs (for Elf Queen's Daughters always did the Ouija board in two person teams who were closely linked and connected spiritually and psychically), into seclusion to speak with certain individuals they had known previously who had died in such a manner that enabled them to ascend to the higher or more ephemeral and expansive dimensions of spiritual manifestation. For those individual spirits had sacrificed their own lives willingly in order to save the lives of others and had, according to the occult and esoteric beliefs of the Elf Queen's Daughters, been automatically elevated by doing so.

Thus, in speaking to the dead, they weren't speaking to demons, as popular horror movies like us to believe, or as certain religious folks proclaim, nor were they speaking with the shards or energetic echoes of those who have gone on and are currently incarnated into another human life, but they were, in fact, speaking with one of the Shining Ones, a living being vibrating at a higher frequency upon a dimension where their powers are both vaster and greater and where they have a wider view and greater understanding of reality. This illumination of being is, in part, what the Buddhists encourage the spirit traversing the Between to waken to and thus free thems'elves from the limitations of mere and very limiting earthly existence.

Another form of necromancy, although it is not practiced so much anymore and certainly not used as much as the Ouija board, although usually it is utilized by those who are more adept than the majority of the folks who experiment with the Ouija board, is the séance. Holding séances was once a very popular practice, or pastime, about a century or so ago, but not so much today. Today, most folks, who in the past would conduct séances, now simply act as channelers for the dead or enlightened spirits from other dimensions, allowing them to speak through them. But it is really the same thing, although usually without as much ceremony or as many props or accouterments. They used to do séances around a table in a secluded room, now they tend to channel from a stage in an auditorium. However, we have seen a channeler simply sit on a bed to give a private reading to an individual.

On the other hand, when Jesus raised Lazarus from the dead, he wasn't doing necromancy. After all, he didn't raise Lazarus in order to talk to him and gain some information from him. Jesus was performing *Necromagery* (a word that we Silver Elves created in order to distinguish this form of magic from the magic of necromancy, since the two are so frequently confused in the common mind). He was communicating with the dead but not for the purpose of getting an oracle by doing so.

The magic that was done in Stephen King's book *Pet Cemetery* was also Necromagery not necromancy. They weren't bringing their pet dog back from the dead so it could tell them about their future and make predictions in a series of barks. One bark means yes, two means no, a low growl means maybe or ask another time. They just loved their pet deeply and missed its company and wanted its return.

Aragon, in the *Lord of the Rings* books, when he compels the dead to fight for him out of an ancient obligation they owed to his ancestors is also performing necromagery. You could say that he performed necromancy when he called them forth in order to speak to them to demand their help, but he wasn't doing that in order to receive an oracular prophecy from them. Rather, he was calling on them in order to remind them of their oaths given in the past and to require the fulfillment of their obligations pledged to his ancestors and his bloodline, which they, to their disgrace and regret, had neglected during their material lives. So, again, as we said, that is necromagery not necromancy. Only he wasn't bringing them back into their physical form, as Jesus did Lazarus, but calling forth their action in their ghostly or otherworldly forms as they were suspended in the Between unable to go on to higher dimensions or return to the world of the living, trapped, as it were, by their karmic debt.

But the problem with necromancy and necromagery, as we've hinted elsewhere is that the dead, in most cases, if we wish to call them that, may not be dead anymore, they may very well have moved on to another incarnation and all that you are hearing from them if you ask for their advice, like when you read a book, is a sort of recording or record of their thoughts and opinions that they left behind. And echo left by the shards or echoes of their lives and actions in some previous incarnation.

In their current incarnations, it is quite possible, even probable, that they have changed their minds and think quite differently and, hopefully, at the very least, their ideas will have developed and matured. That is the goal of spiritual evolution, after all.

The Spell:

Life after life the ancestors light the way
For I was them and they are me alive this very day

Arvyndase:
Ela låka ela tae doreldåli lun tae yer
Fro El daïn tam nar tam da el alsaru wyr lefa lea

Pronounciation:
Eel - lah lah - kay eel - lah tay door - eel - dah - lie loon tay year
Fro Eel dah - in tame nair tame dah eel ale - sayr - rue were lee
- fah lee - ah

೭

Chapter 6:
As Above, So Below (or "As Within, So Beyond") and Vice Versa

There is a common occult adage that goes "As Above, So Below," or as we elves sometimes say "As Within, So Beyond," or other things to that effect. The whole idea is that Nature in the microcosm is a reflection of Life in the macrocosm and in looking at one we can get some idea of the other and vice versa, which is not all that different from the expression Like Father, Like Son.

For instance, we know we are composed of atoms and these atoms have electrons, protons and neutrons spinning around their nucleus and that is similar in its way to our solar system, with the Sun being the nucleus of the atom and the planets and asteroids, comets or meteors and so forth being electrons and protons, perhaps, and maybe moons being neutrons. So, in attempting to understand death it behooves us to examine other things in life that seem similar to or remind us of death. Examples of this are the cycles of being awake and being asleep and even the sub-cycles or stages of sleep to give us some comprehension of what goes on when we die and what happens in the process of death, which is to say in the Between, the liminal realm that can lead from one life to another but also can bring us to the threshold of and the potential to obtain mastery of vaster dimensions. This is what life, which encompasses death, is about, gaining mastery over ours'elves and thus successfully living in and navigating through the various realms and dimensions of manifestation.

The problem with using reflection to understand reality is that most of us as individuals like things neat and orderly and we tend to overextend such reflections as though they were exact rather than similar. For instance, our reflection in a mirror is rather exact, except that it is a reverse image. Our calendar and year in the Western world is based upon a rather exact system even through the year is not exactly 365 days (although many may wish it would be) but 365+ days and we add a day every four years to account for this.

Many Asian peoples have a lunar calendar that is based upon the phases of the moon and this is surely a more accurate way of doing things except then the New Year's day jumps around from year to year, which seems confusing to those in the West who have less flexible minds. And even though, for most people in the West, the New Year seems to really begin with the Winter Solstice, when the light begins to increase again, (although the Celtic tribes and their Druids apparently began it on Samhain or Halloween), we don't celebrate the New Year until over a week after the winter solstice (summer solstice for beneath the equator). But that's probably so we can have a week to recover after our Yule/Christmas celebrations before we party again on New Year's Eve. Still, we elves would agree it is wise to take a bit of a break between all that eating and drinking so we can have another celebration separate from Yule. Indulgence is always best when tempered with a bit of abstinence.

The fact that Christmas and Yule have been merged is a function of religion rather than Nature and if we in the West were a more sensible people we'd begin the New Year and celebrate Yule on the Solstice or join the Asian folk in following a lunar year, which is the way we elves generally do it. Of course, being elves, we have no problem celebrating Solstice, Yule, Christmas, Western New Year and Lunar New Year, as well. Plus, any other holidays you'd like to throw in, as long as they involve celebration and not fasting or pious religious rigmarole. All holidays work for us as long as there's a bit of feasting involved and kindred coming together in love and harmony.

Our point here is that while it can be helpful to observe Nature with an eye to understanding the Between and the stages of Death, keeping the principle of As Above/So Below in mind, we need to be a bit flexible in doing so. Things are not exactly the same from dimension to dimension, although they may be very similar, and things change from individual to individual. There is no guarantee that my Between experience will be of the same duration as yours or that we will encounter exactly the same things as we pass through those states. In fact, we can pretty much guarantee that they will, at least in part, be very different, just as we are each likely to have different dreams at night.

In fact, having the same dream on the same night, instead of one unique to ones'elf, would be the notable exception, not the other way around. Still, there are dreams that have common themes, such as falling, being chased or suddenly realizing one is naked before an audience, that many people share in common but with each individual having the dream at different times and with details that may be unique to them as an individual but the central theme of fear or embarrassment, helplessness or whatever is the same.

So, also, the Between, and our experience there, has a commonality to it, although it is not usually an exactness of form. Yet, there is a similarity to what one will encounter while passing through those realms and it is of these things that we will deal with in the second part of this book as we offer readings that one may use to guide those who are progressing through the Between and to help ones'elf understand and thus prepare for what one is likely to experience in those realms.

So, it is that the force of gravity that is so powerful upon the Earth is not exactly the same on the Moon and is different in vast space as well. Things change and there are differences between a manifestation in a particular material incarnation and our manifestation and experience in the Between realms. And just as we can walk with a bounce to our step on the Moon, or float around if we are on a ship in space, so in the Between the powers of the gravity, we might say, of material incarnation have a good deal less influence over us. We can fly in the Between without need of a plane, jet or faerie wings (although if you are a faerie it is likely you will experience them anyway, since they just add to the magic for you and are part of your destined s'elf). In the Between, our imaginal powers begin to take immediate effect. What we wish becomes instantly true. Our magic there manifests as powerfully as it does or is shown to do in fictional tales and stories about magic.

There is the principle of Occam's Razor that cautions us about continually and overly extrapolating from limited data and information. This notion is then refined into the idea that the simplest and most elegant scientific theory that accounts for all the facts is to be preferred over a more complicated theory, since Nature, in its essence, tends to be direct and simple while at the same time being less exact and often seemingly more random than we might wish it to be. This, really, is the central principle of Chaos Magic where there is an understanding that the Universe is so vast that things appear utterly random at times, but beneath that apparent randomness there is an implicit order. However, the order is not so easily perceived. It is just this random order, so to speak, that almost all oracles seek to tap into by the sort of haphazard methods of their evocation. It is by doing things randomly that we tap into the implicit order that exists beneath the seemingly random.

So, in considering the world that we know in order to understand the world, the Between, that we know so little about, it is helpful to be flexible in our considerations. Things that are similar like those things that appear the same such as products that are made on an assembly are not always exactly the same. Even identical twins are different people, individuate so to speak, as they encounter different circumstances in the course of their lives. Life is the process of change.

And yet, if we consider the cycles of the year upon the Earth and the seasons, and watch plants and other things grow, die and come back again, we may use Autumn's harvest or the first frost as a symbol of dying and Winter as an indication of the Between or even to represent life in the womb, or first one and then the other, for they are connected. And we can then view Spring as the season of rebirth. Nature its'elf gives us the notion of reincarnation in its cyclic manifestations.

This same idea is presented by those cartoons that often appear around the time of the approach of the New Year that show a very old man, bent over and hobbling along, holding a scythe (like the image of the grim reaper) and carrying an hourglass whose sand has nearly run out, followed in his wake by a baby in diapers, often wearing a top hat that is too big for him (or her).

The top hat would be an indication of one's previous life, development and the sophistication, in a sense, through time and experience of one's spirit incarnated into a new fresh body and manifestation. We carry over from incarnation to incarnation the deep spiritual lessons that we've learned, or earned you might say, for we often go through hell to achieve these lessons that advance us in the spirit realms. Death is followed by rebirth, in the cycles of the year and in the cycles of our lives and lifetimes. But again, the timing may not be exactly precise and may differ for each individual.

This inclination toward exactness may very well stem from the dualistic thought patterns that come from Zoroastrianism, with its subsequent influence upon Christian and Islamic thought and its juxtaposition of light and dark, good versus evil and from that our tendency to think that death is the opposite of life and good cannot exist without there being evil in the world and other such nonsense. There is light in the Universe and dark, but there are also grays in their variations from the intermingling of the two and beyond that a wondrous color spectrum, as well. The world isn't just black and white and our thoughts about Life and the passage from one incarnation to another shouldn't be based upon such simplistic dichotomies (see our book *Faerie Unfolding*). Such notions are convenient for a quick understanding of things, maybe for explaining things to children, but we must go deeper and farther afield to truly understand Life overall.

And yet, the existence of day and night is surely the primary source of this dualistic thought. Most people would be inclined to think that the sun comes out in the day and the moon always comes out at night, if it wasn't for the obvious reality of the moon in the day sky from time to time denying this notion. There is more to life and the world than it often seems to superficial perception and if we are to determine on a scientific theory as truth, we need to do our best to uncover and account for all the data and facts that we have discovered and to be ever open to rethinking our theories when new information, new data arises to expand our understanding. Especially, those facts that would question our theories and that compel us to think more deeply in order to account for them.

So, let the rainbow of possibility into your thoughts concerning Life and about the processes and stages of death, which is to say the rather dreamlike states of the Between, and you may find yours'elf crossing the Rainbow or Bifröst bridge, as they called it in Norse Mythology, and ascending into the realms of the Shining Ones and quite possibly discovering a pot of gold at the end of it. Wouldn't that be nice.

The Spell:

As Above, So Below and round and round
And round we go
As Within and So Without
Elfin wakens with a shout

Arvyndase:
Tat Usel, Re Yana nar ond nar ond
Nar ond eli tas
Tat Enåver nar Re Enåkon
Êldat siltålu ena na ontar

Pronunciation:
Tate You - seal, Re - Yeah - nah nair oh-nd nair oh-nd
Nair oh-nd e - lie tace
Tate E - nah - veer nair Re E - nah - cone
L - date sile - tah - lou e - nah nah oh-n - tair

❧

Chapter 7:
Hebrews, Christians and Muslims,
Celts and Vikings

The Hebrew view of the afterlife is rather vague, as far as we can tell. It is the other side of the veil and it is shrouded in mystery. It seems to revolve around the idea that good things happen for good people and bad things happen to bad people, and perhaps mediocre things occur to those who were a little good and a little bad, or good sometimes and bad at other times, but we're not sure of that part.

Maybe like the old Catholic idea of purgatory, those who were not entirely bad suffer for a while until they've paid their debt of sin/karma and then go to heaven but that's very close to the idea of karma in terms of our successive purification of ours'elves through lifetimes of effort and 'right living' as the Buddhists would put it.

In many ways, the material world that we currently abide in is a form of purgatory or realm of purification for most of us, and as we clear away our karma and gain greater awareness as we do so, we are thus able to ascend or expand to vaster dimensions in which there are less limitations/karma/fate upon us and we have increased power to achieve what we wish and obtain all that we desire in harmony with the Universe. Our life in the Between is just a preview of those worlds.

The Christians and Muslims are a bit more precise about their afterlife, but the situation is essentially the same, the good join their god in heaven, and the evil folk, which is usually those who didn't believe in their particular faith, suffer for their lack of belief and for their ill deeds. Although, in some sects it is more for the former than the latter, although we Silver Elves think it should be, and really is, in fact, the other way around or really the latter and not the former at all. Which is to say that belief in and obsequiousness to a particular demi-god, no matter how powerful his (it's almost always a his) followers claim him to be, has no part in our karmic quest and destiny really.

Christians in heaven, we are told by fundamentalist, get to sing their god's praises forever, which sounds a bit boring, and makes their god appear to suffer from a Narcissistic Personality Disorder but we Silver Elves expect there's a bit of romance and hanky-panky going on in the heavenly choir (there just has to be), just as we've heard there is in church choirs on Earth. Otherwise, how could it be considered heaven?

And Muslim men, we suppose, get a wonderful afterlife surrounded, as they were in life, by women to serve them. Things don't seem to change much for their women, unless they don't obey their men folk and then they get to join the non-believers and the wicked ones in hell, which they call Jahannam, although we suppose their thoughts on these matters will evolve in time as social conditions and expectations change in their societies. Some of them would like to keep things forever the same (both Muslim and Christian) but that just isn't going to happen, or not for long. Sooner or later, change, which is to say Life, has its way and its way is ever evolving.

Like *Dante's Inferno*, there are circles of hell in the Jahannam of Islamic thought, and one's place in hell is determined by the nature and degree of one's evil deeds. This is not entirely unlike the ancient Greek story of the afterlife where Sisyphus was punished for his cruelty and tyrannical rule during his life, by having to push a large rock up a steep hill, only to find it rolling back down to the bottom as it was almost to the top, and this over and over again for eternity. This is an endless torture, rather like working in the world doing seemingly pointless things to make people who are already rich even richer. Will some rich people after they die go to hell and have to work eight hours or more a day for minimum wage forever, doing mindless things that never end? Now that would be poetic justice!

Are people working in the world really in hell? It sometimes feels that way to them. However, their torture isn't eternal, eventually they will escape to a new incarnation and if they have purified their karma and endeavored faithfully to improve their own true s'elves and their personal powers without incurring additional karmic debt by interfering with the destiny of others, it may very well be a better incarnation where they get to work for thems'elves doing what they love to do. Which is probably some sort of arts or crafts but it could be nearly anything. We elf folks have varied tastes and interests, just like, perhaps more so than, everyone else. Certainly, working for ours'elves and supporting ours'elves by doing what we enjoy doing is surely the ideal for most people in the world. This is especially true for those of us who are elven, elfae or other of some sort.

However, not all Islamic scholars agree upon the eternal nature of hell, some see the possibility of redemption after a period of suffering (punishment for the individual's ill deeds) and purification and that again suggests the idea of purgatory or the clearing of one's karmic debt and, therefore, of the possibility of reincarnation or rebirth. At the very least, a rebirth into a heavenly life.

Muslims, for their part, are encouraged to think and debate about the meaning of the Koran whereas most Christians are most often simply taught to obey unthinkingly and accept the interpretation of those who present themselves as being holy and thus above them, those who are designated as the authorities of their particular church or creed. This, of course, bodes better for Islamic societies in the long run than it does Christian ones, even though in many ways the Christian folk, for the most part, seem more socially advanced and aware at this juncture in time. But that can all change in a few generations.

For Christians, life in hell is eternal and one can never be redeemed there. One is condemned to be in hell forever. Although, according to modern fiction you apparently can escape from hell for a while if you are really clever. Or, if you become an advanced demon, you can come to Earth to tempt others, entice them to make deals and draw them down to perdition and by doing so slowly work your way up the ladder of the demonic hierarchy (which apparently exists in Christian thought just as there is an angelic hierarchy), much like obtaining successive career advancement in modern corporations or in organized crime, which are sometimes the same thing.

The Celts seemed to have a somewhat similar belief to Christians, except that their Summerlands were sometimes seen as heavenly and paradisiacal versions of this world only more Faerie-like and often on islands just removed from this world across the seas. Although, sometimes these realms were underground domains (again a similarity to Faerie lore as well as to Greek mythology). However, it seems that in Celtic lore, one didn't have to spend one's afterlife eternally praising some god, of which the Celtic tribal peoples, like most ancient peoples, had quite a few. Like the Greeks, Romans, Norse, Egyptians and many, many others, the tribes that we now refer to as Celtic had whole families of gods.

Of course, one might argue that the Christians with their god the father, the son and holy ghost have a family of gods, but we are told that they are all one god even though they/he are/is manifesting in separate ways. It would make it seem as if their god has Dissociative Personality Disorder or Multiple Personality Disorder as it was once called. However, we might also take it as an analogy for our lives. Our past incarnations would be symbolized by god the father (or mother for females), our current incarnation by god the son/daughter and god the holy spirit or ghost would be our transition through the Between and the connective spirit that manifests in each incarnation and through them and on to the possibilities that our destiny moves us toward realizing.

In the realms of the spirit, we are not really male or female but potentially both. This accords with the Depth Psychology notion that we each have an inner aspect of ours'elves which is opposite to our manifest gender. Thus, an inner female for males and an inner male for females. But what about hermaphrodites?

However, the Celtic tribal peoples had an oral tradition, as many ancient folks did, and didn't write things down, so we who have come after them, or are reincarnated from them, are forced to theorize about them and their beliefs and practices from the writings of outsiders, often the Greeks and Romans, who lived contemporaneously to Celtic tribal folk, and who did keep accounts of their own lives and the cultures they encountered in the world (and often killed, enslaved and destroyed).

Alternatively, we may use our psychic powers and understanding to reach into the Collective Unconscious of our own elven spiritual race in order to intuit ideas about them or at least sense what is true and differentiate it from what seems false to our instinctual understanding and perception. In that way we are sensing, as we Silver Elves often do about various faerie tales, legends and lore, that something just doesn't feel right and using our inner elfin sight to understand it from our own heart's perspective and correct it in our own minds if not, also, in the thinking of our kindred and others in the world at large.

Plus, there are scientists who make some educated guesses about the various Celtic tribes and the cultures they shared based upon archaeological evidence that they have so far discovered. Although, these scientific theorists don't always agree about the meaning of what they have unearthed and there is an unfortunate tendency for individuals, eager for notoriety and social advancement in academia and the pressure to 'publish or perish', as we've heard them call it, to interpret the evidence to fit their pet theories.

There is, as well, a danger of attempting to understand things from our own modern perspective without really comprehending the life perspective of peoples who actually lived in those times. Or, we might put it, our own s'elves as we saw and experienced life in those particular incarnations. It is easy to forget and hard to remember; and yet every important experience is emblazoned upon our spirits like luminous badges or tattoos or perhaps sigils of magic that affect our lives thereafter seared into our deep unconscious manifesting sometimes in the form of a blessing or seeming grace upon our lives and at other times in what seems to be, for some people, a sort of curse or doom upon their lives.

There is a sometimes a tendency for people who have abandoned one viewpoint of life upon taking on a new perspective to act as though they never held the previous point of view at all. In embracing the new, we sometimes forget the old and surely there is some value in erasing the past that would otherwise haunt us and to go fully into the new. That, in great part, is the value of death and our movement from incarnation to incarnation. Our past, in a certain sense, it erased, although our karma still lingers.

Much as criminologist profilers seek to understand the minds of serial killers and other villains and to think as these miscreants do in order to catch them, so we need to try to understand the perspective of the ancients, as much as possible, from their own experience and understanding of life and nature. And sometimes, that means looking within ours'elves. Not at our enculturated opinions and notions but at our own deep inner feelings to view things from the same viewpoint we did when we were very young.

For our previous lives are reflected and encapsulated, according the elven occult theory, in the first 28 to 29 years of our current life before our first Saturn return, which is to say when Saturn completes its transit through the Zodiac and returns to the place on our astrological chart where it was situated at the time of our birth. Thus, if we examine our early life in this incarnation we are able to see a recapitulation, in brief, of our former incarnations; much like those scenes before television shows that say "Previously on ..." and show us clips from the past that are relevant to the show that is about to begin.

This is just a more esoteric view of Haeckel's theory that *Ontogeny*, the development of an individual organism and its anatomical and behavioral features from its earliest stages into maturity, *Recapitulates Phylogeny*, the evolutionary development of a species or group of organisms particularly as they diversify in form and behavior from each other and become unique beings. We carry our previous incarnations within us, in a sense, imprinted in our spirits, or at least we carry indications, like inner histories, of our own process of evolutionary development through our incarnations.

At the same time, we are saying to you, while we are doing our best to understand these various beliefs, we Silver Elves are not Muslims, Christians, nor are we the ancient Celtic folk, although it is possible that we are, in part, descended from them or spent a few lifetimes as Celtic tribal folk or possibly Christians, Jewish or Muslims and many other things as well, having experienced various religions and cultures in the course of our incarnations. We were certainly, at one time, ancient Taoists, before Taoism was turned into a religion.

We elves have the grace to be born into whatever body will best serve our purpose in a particular lifetime and are not compelled, as some people seem to be or they assume that they must be, born in a particular genetic bloodline. Therefore, interpret, as much as possible, what we are telling you from your own life and experience and from your own interaction with the faerie realms and the worlds of the Between, which are very similar as you will see, and search inside yours'elf for the truth as you know it to be.

Shed most of the ideas and notions that were given to you by your religious upbringing (if you were raised with a religious doctrine) and just feel your way into the past. Look into your past incarnations which are often reflected in your early life, and through those events see into the future. For knowing the past and the present gives us an idea of the direction we are headed, although for elfin folk that is nearly always and eventually to Faerie and Elfin. We know where we are going, we just don't always know in a particular situation or set of circumstances the best path to take to get there.

This idea of an otherworldly afterlife paradise on Earth that we are told the Celtic folk held is much like Tolkien's mythology in which there are separate islands for the Valar (high angels), Maiar (lower angels or maybe saints), and the Elves (potential angels? or advanced or evolved humans? or very lowly angels?) and a land for Men and others all on the same planet, in a sense, and yet somewhat like different planets or perhaps different dimensions on the same planet. It's not entirely clear.

When the elves sailed west to the Blessed Lands in Tolkien's lore and thus left the worlds of Men, which is to say left Middle Earth, did they sail across the seas or across the stars and the heavens, or both? This is similar to the tales where the Sisters of Faerie carry King Arthur's body away in a boat after he is killed in battle and that craft sets out from the shores of Britain but sails into the Mists of Avalon where he abides forever or until the time of his return when Britain truly needs him. Is Avalon an island close to Britain as some people presume, or is it a mystical land in a parallel world?

We expect that the Celts also believed the wicked got their just deserts after life and suffered for their ill deeds for this seems a commonly held view and one which most of us in life wish to be true unless we've been particularly wicked ours'elves. Those who have done evil deeds may still very much believe in their inevitable punishment but will wish to put it off as long as possible, or bargain it away if they can, which they can't. Although, some think that if they confess at the last moment and embrace Jesus as their Lord and Savior or perhaps one of the other 'one true gods' then all their ill deeds will be forgiven. And, surely, they are not mistaken as far as that goes. But while karma will forgive, it does not forget, which is to say, we can't escape from the worlds that we have, by our own actions, created. We, as human beings or spirits in human bodies really, are often eager to see other people get their comeuppance, but most of us are less inclined to have to face the consequences of our own actions. But the reality is that we have absolutely no choice but to do so. We might delay facing them, but in the long run we cannot help but deal with those things that stand between us and the realization of our true s'elves, which is whom we are destined to be.

Karma may seem like punishment but really it is just the nature of reality. It's like lifting weights in a way. If you can bench press only 50 lbs. and you wish to press 200, you simply have to keep training until you are able to do so. Life isn't primarily about retribution for our ill deeds, but about training ours'elves in things that will increase our powers and abilities, life by life, and decrease the amount of resistance and the number of obstructions we encounter due to our past deeds, which is to say karma.

Doing wicked things just makes it harder in the long run to obtain what we truly want and delays our realization of those things our spirits truly wish and desire by creating resistance from Nature and others in the Universe, especially those we have harmed by our actions. The Path of Least Resistance, which is a basic principle in Nature, is also what we wish to obtain as magical spirits. We wish to flow through life unobstructed and in fact aided by others as much as possible and we can only do that by decreasing the deeds that inevitably led to people seeking to hinder our success.

It is not so much that others necessarily will hold us responsible for our actions, although many would surely be eager to do so, but that it is our own spirits that confront us to face the facts of what we've done in any particular incarnation for it is only by doing so that we may advance to those dimensions where our true power is unleashed. As they indicate in *Step Programs* for addicts, it is not just about giving up the alcohol or drugs to which one has become addicted but making amends for the harm that one has done.

We might get away with wicked deeds in the sense that no one may ever know about them or may know of the deeds but don't know that we did them and thus we are never caught for those ill deeds in that particular incarnation. But those deeds live within us, are really a part of our magic, and we cannot escape that fact and though we might try to hide from our wicked actions, repressing them into our subconscious, denying that we did them to others or even to ours'elves, they will surface sooner or later.

We hunger for our true power, which stems from being in touch with our own true natures and thus attuned to Nature and the Universe overall, of which we are an intimate part and we can only develop our true natures by being able to fully accept ours'elves as integrated spirits and move through the Universe as best we are able to do so in harmony with others.

There is something in human nature, whether we are elves or others, which makes us rejoice to see people get their just due whether it is for good deeds or bad, although we elves are especially fond of poetic justice. It just seems special and so perfectly apt to our minds. We love it. And, if truth be told, we have experienced it in our own lives from time to time, and learned many lessons therefrom and changed our lives accordingly. To fail to heed the warnings of fate is to suffer accordingly.

And as you grow wiser as a spirit you come to realize it is just folly to do things that will bring suffering to yours'elf and others and that therefore obstruct your progress toward the realization of your true being unless destiny and honor dictates that you endure suffering to promote what is right and fair in the world. And doing that, by its very nature, uplifts us in future incarnations. If we harm others, we owe them, until our debt is paid in one incarnation or another, or over multiple incarnations. But if we willingly sacrifice for others, they don't owe us precisely, but they are very inclined to promote our success, prosperity and wellbeing, lifetime after lifetime. For our success is their success.

Much like in Faerie, in the Celtic Summerlands one never ages, there is no sickness or disease and even the weather is wonderful all the time, much like Hawaii where we Silver Elves currently abide. We'd think that we live in the Elfin paradise realms, if it wasn't for our Dentist periodically reminding us of the evident mortality of the bodies into which we're currently incarnated.

Celtic afterlife can be heavenly and paradisiacal without all the Christian rigmarole and praising God that some take for granted. When religious fanatics come around us blabbering their praise god banter, we find it utterly boring. We imagine that even their own god must tire of it in time. After a while, it just becomes so much white noise in the background of our lives.

In the Celtic Summerlands, on the other hand, you apparently just enjoy the afterlife forever (if you are not, as is also the case with the Viking folk, battling much of the time). In the Celtic afterlife otherworld, you are on what seems to be a more permanent version of retirement or an eternal vacation without having to age or get sick or ever go back to work. Sounds good to us. Cocktails, anyone?

These various views of the afterlife are not that different, in their way, from the Egyptian and Greek myths of afterlife existence and the weighing of one's soul (what we'd call one's spirit) to determine its purity and goodness. The dead usually go to underground realms according to their beliefs, perhaps because they would bury their dead in caves or, for the higher social classes, in Mausoleums or Pyramids but then, what are those but manmade caves? A Pyramid is just a type of barrow, we might say. And actually, most modern residences are really just artificial caves when you think about it. Most of the people in the world are, for the most part, just a bunch of cavemen, only with bits of technology. This must make our dwarven kin happy, however, and those elfae who like to live in caverns, but we Silver Elves wish we were able to live deeper in the woods. Still, being in Hawaii, there is a lot of beautiful nature all around us and the ocean is just a five minute walk away.

This underground afterlife is just another bit of lore that is reflected in tales about the underworld realms of Faerie and is similar in a way to the underworld realms of Hades in Greek mythology. His name comes from the Greek Aïdes, which means the Unseen One but he was also called Pluto or Pluton, and this is translated to mean the Giver of Wealth or the Wealthy One. Think about that for a moment. What unseen or hidden wealth is the god of the dead offering? What wealth awaits us in the hidden worlds of Faerie? Why the true wealth of happiness and eternal bliss that comes from loving each other and being with those one loves forever. With the added bonus of the possibility of the pot of gold on the other side of the Rainbow Bridge. Not that you need gold in the hereafter or could even use it for anything. Perhaps, it is not a pot of gold but golden pot (see our book of short stories and modern elfin faerie tales *Elven Silver*).

In just such mounds, according to faerie lore, abide the Aos Sí, as they are sometimes called. But this is an older form of Aes Sídhe, which is the Irish term for the supernatural race of faerie folk that may be found in their mythology and also in Scottish lore and legend (where the word Sidhe [she] is written as Sith, but the pronunciation is the same). But then the Scots came to Scotland from Ireland and merged with the Picts, or pixie peoples who were already there (see *Fairy Faith in the Celtic Countries* by Evans-Weitz for the linguistic connection between Picts, pixies, piskies [Cornwall] and others). These fae are said to live in fairy mounds beneath the earth and may draw you or lure you, or enchant you down into their realm, where if you eat their food you will be trapped in Faerie forever or so the legend goes.

Note that this idea of eating the food in the otherworldly realms is the same myth as that of Persephone and Hades where Persephone ate the food of the underworld and had to stay there for half the year. An allusion to the seasons surely and the hibernation of plants in winter but perhaps it is also an allegory of re-incarnation? Of going into the otherworld, or Between and then returning again?

From our elven point of view, it isn't that one eats faerie food and has to stay in Faerie but that the food is so delicious, or perhaps so enlightening and revelatory and the world it reveals so enchanting, that one desires to stay there forever or come back again and again as was the case with Persephone. We are not forced to stay in Faerie; we are eager to remain eternally. This may account for the tales where someone leaves the faerie realms and feels an intense and never-ending longing for it ever after. Faerie food is not physically addictive, like certain drugs, but psychologically compelling and attractive like some beautiful person we cannot help but want to gaze upon totally fascinated as we do so.

The Vikings had a somewhat different view of the world, of life and the afterlife. Like Tolkien's world, and the Greeks for that matter. The gods existed in the same world as Man, only higher on the tree of life or world tree or Yggdrasil tree, but lived mostly apart from Men. For Tolkien, the Valar are on different islands. For the Greeks, the gods were on Mount Olympus, and for the Egyptians, seeing as they were a little bereft of mountains, their gods lived mostly among the stars but upon the Earth and out in Nature as well, manifest, at least in part, in the form of the Pharaohs. Monarchs as representatives of the Divine on Earth. An idea carried on in the notion of the Divine Right of Kings and the Divine Appointment and Anointment of Royalty that the nobility were once so fond of believing in and some perhaps still are.

The Vikings, which is really to say the Danes, Norse and other folk who would go Viking as a practice, and therefore raiding other lands and peoples to kill, steal, pillage, rape and take slaves, had worlds for the gods, worlds for the elves, dwarves and others, and a world for men, as well (called Middle Earth, or Midgard). When one died, if one died a heroic death with sword in hand fighting, one joined the gods in Valhalla. This is a rather different idea than the Christian one about what constituted being good, which seems to center mostly upon obedience to god as defined by one's designated social and spiritual superiors.

However, for the Vikings, if one failed to die with sword in hand, one went to the Goddess Hel's realm since dying without sword in hand was deemed a dishonorable death. Note that the Greek god Hades and the Norse and Danish god Hel have both had their names used to designate the torturous underworlds of the Christians.

And yet, one could also, according to Scandinavian lore, ascend to the realms of the elf folk through the accomplishment of significant deeds in one's life, (see scholarly work *Elves in Anglo-Saxon England: Matters of Belief, Health, Gender and Identity* by Alaric Hall) becoming more elven thereby, which has ever been the preference of we Silver Elves, obviously, with the hope of living in those realms permanently as we achieve the power and thus earn the right to do so.

We are eager to imbibe the food and drink of Faerie (and have done so numerous times). This is what we elfae folk pursue in our lives, traveling toward the Elfin and Faerie realms, by the means and magic of creating them in and through our own lives, thus manifesting Elfin in reality or the material world that most people consider reality, although we elves know that it is, in its way, just as real and as illusionary, as our life and experiences in our dreams and in the Between states.

If you made it to Valhalla, it is said you would spend your days fighting and killing the other warriors there, often your old enemies, only to be reborn at night to feast with them, your comrades and with the gods and sleep with willing women, day after day after day or night after night after night.

This myth not only reminds these elves of the idea of reincarnation, of dying and being born again and dying again, on and on, but it also reminds us of when we were very young and would spend our days playing *Cowboys and Indians* (as we called it then) with our friends and whenever one of us got shot and killed, that one would fall down dead, lay there counting to ten and then get up and keep on playing, day after day after day. That is until the world came to force its own peculiar and limited notion of reality upon us and sought to beat, preach, and/or educate (which usually meant bore) the elvishness or faerie nature out of us. Obviously, that didn't work so well.

The Spell:

From this world we ever go
Life after life, the truth to know

Arvyndase:
An wyr telth eli vari tas
Ela låka ela, tae lodver va ken

Pronunciation:
Ane were tealth e - lie vair - rye tace
E - lah lah - kay e - lah, tae load - veer vah keen

☙

Chapter 8:

Ghosts and Shards

We Silver Elves love ghost stories (and zombie movies and television shows, and magic stories, stories of the occult and the supernatural and well, all of that otherworldly stuff, really). We are especially fond of the tales where the ghosts are clever and kindly and full of fun and sometimes up to a bit of charming mischief, particularly when it results, as it often does in such stories, in someone getting the justice they so deserve. For elves, fae and faeries are called the Fair Folk not only because our glamour can make us seem beautiful and because we certainly view each other as being lovely, but because we believe in and promote fairness in all things and situations. A fair world is a beautiful world.

An example of these types of ghosts is found in Thorne Smith's novels *Topper*, which was also called *The Jovial Ghosts*, and its sequel, *Topper Takes a Trip*, which inspired a number of movies and a rather delightful television show. In these stories, the amiable ghosts of George and Marion Kerby come upon and decide to haunt a rather staid banker named Topper, much to his chagrin, amazement and occasional delight.

Another interesting ghost story that we love is the *Canterbury Ghost*, which was made into a movie or two and based upon a story by that great faerie writer, and quite surely faerie lord, Oscar Wilde. Much like the ghosts in *The Return of the King* that Aragon summons to fight for him, the *Canterbury Ghost* was a coward in a previous life and therefore due to this he became stuck in a castle, doomed to haunt it until his cowardice was overcome. In this case, however, it is a direct descendent of his that would redeem him through his (the descendant's) bravery rather than the ghost itself overcoming the karmic debt of his past neglect and cowardly actions, or lack of action, perhaps. For in many ways, cowardice is a quite natural thing. It is the will to survive by running away and it takes a love of one's family and kindred to overcome this natural tendency, or in the case of Men, the fear of social approbation or the harsh punishment one is threatened with if one doesn't fight.

In both the above stories, the ghosts are, for the most part, really kindly individuals, and seemingly conscious, thus thinking beings, only stuck in a ghostly or ephemeral form and are thus invisible unless they choose to make their appearance known. Although, they could affect things on the physical plane if they decided to do so, as in the sort of poltergeist activity that has been mostly associated with highly emotional pubescent teenagers, in the form of things flying around, being knocked off shelves and so forth.

In most current ghost stories, however, with the emphasis in our current times on horror (and we Silver Elves for the most part are not really horror fans), the ghosts are usually demonic in nature wishing to harm people and are dispersed, as they are in the *Supernatural* television series, by pouring salt over their remains or over some physical object that is anchoring them to the material plane and then torching the remains or object to ash, forcing the ghostly form to depart the physical plane altogether.

This presents the idea that even ghosts need an anchor, or a sort of body of some sort, in order to manifest, even in their ghostly form upon the material plane. This is not entirely unlike the idea of teraphim, or spirits that can abide in statues or spirit houses of the sort that the Thais have all over their country and the Shinto folk sometimes have around Japan. And this is essentially the same idea as that of churches, mosques, shrines, temples and so forth, providing a material resting place and home for nature spirits and demi-gods. Although, instead of a house, sometimes the shine is a figurine or statue of some sort providing a body that typifies the spirit of the deity that is being invoked and invited to dwell therein in order to draw it closer to one and create a feeling of connection between the spirit and a particular people living in its area of manifestation.

These sorts of threatening demonic ghosts are tied to the material plane due to a hunger for revenge. They have a form of consciousness but that consciousness is usually totally focused on exacting justice (from their point of view), although often their fury is taken out upon those who don't really deserve it and who merely have the misfortune to be in the wrong place at the wrong time, which is the area of the ghost's range of haunting. For an example of this type of revenge haunting, see the Swedish movie *Draug*, which is set in the 11th century, and is about just such vengeful ghosts, called Draugr, as those we are describing here.

But then, we Silver Elves have met living beings who display the same sort of fixated focus on getting back at those they believe have harmed and humiliated them or keep them down in their lives. These folks are also incredibly territorial and controlling about what they regard as their personal domain and will terrorize anyone they don't like who enters their space. It is not that they wish power over others in general, usually, but that they seek a domain for themselves in which they can wield absolute power and control. We suspect that these individuals were brought up in situations where someone, most often a parent, wielded such absolute power over them and where they felt that they had no control whatsoever and have been psychologically driven to achieve it ever since.

This is not entirely different from the idea in ceremonial magic where one seeks to be the 'god' of their own magic circle, except in this case the ghost's motives are purely focused on vengeance. And, like the currently incarnated beings that we've encountered who are like this, where the individual often takes offense even when the person didn't actually intend any harm or mean to slight them in any way, these ghosts react to intrusions upon their domains as an affront to their sovereignty. Because of past experience, such individuals when they are incarnated have come to expect to be treated rudely and no matter what the other person does, they assume the individual has been cruel and unfair to them. Although, at the same time, they do often provoke this sort of cruelty by their own behavior.

Such incarnate versions of this ghostly phenomenon are, in a sense, haunted themselves by their own past experience and the ghost, so to speak, of their mother, father or whomever wielded such absolute power over them still taunts them in their memories even when that person is still alive for it is really the energy that is haunting them, not the actual person who was cruel to them (check out Object Relations psychological theory).

And sometimes, when they die they carry this reactionary behavior into the ghostly or spirit realms or really that behavior and the deep and powerful feelings associated with it echoes in some physical location while the spirit of the individual that emitted these feelings has, in fact, moved on. Sort of like a stain, in a sense, that one just can't get out of one's clothing, only in this case it is the fabric of one's experience that has been stained.

On the other hand, in modern reality ghost hunter shows, the ghosts they are usually investigating are the ghosts that are mostly noted for haunting this or that place, which are often abandoned buildings, old mental hospitals, haunted houses and such and these ghosts are usually shards, and generally evidence no sign of consciousness or even mimic consciousness at all, and usually they are not hostile nor vengeance fixated. Saying they are shards is to say that they are not conscious beings, as ghosts/spirits are often thought to be, but rather are clearly echoes of the past and past events. They are most often really a sort of recording of a traumatic occurrence that is broadcast over and over again in the same place through time playing periodically in some sort of energy loop.

In that case, the house, or area, has absorbed the traumatic energy and this energy in its ghostly form just resonates there until some other, greater energy comes to purify it or it fades away naturally in time like sun-bleached paint on the walls of an old house slowly growing pale until it disappears entirely.

These ghostly occurrences, however, are not directly due to the spirits that experienced the actual trauma but rather a sort of energetic memory of the profound feelings that those who suffered the trauma expressed/felt when the event occurred. And it is these feelings, that great emotional outpouring, that imprinted themselves upon the surrounding environment and, we might say, periodically throb outwardly, like a sore that hasn't yet quite healed. And will continue to do so until this suffering is resolved.

It is possible that the person that set such energy in motion in the first place, may unknowingly reinforce or recharge such hauntings, to which they are psychically connected, when they express similar feelings in their current incarnation. And it is possible as well that such individuals are naturally drawn to the places that have deposits of such traumatic energy expression. By altering their lives in the present and no longer reacting in such fashions in their current life, it is possible that they not only will release themselves from their immediate karma but that this will have a karmic resonance that helps clear these past life experiences, which will then diminish in the place of haunting.

In most cases however, the spirit itself, which is to say the person who experienced the traumatic event, has gone on to a new life and left the shard behind. However, in doing so, they have carried with them the karma, good and/or bad, and the experience, which is to say the spiritual lesson of the event, with them, while they have left the resonance: the shouting, yelling, screaming, pain and suffering, which is to say the emotional effluence of the event behind them. These highly emotional feelings were captured or imprisoned or impressed, like a recording, in the material realm and absorbed by a house, building or some other specific location. Still, as we say, development and evolution in their current life can have some resonant cleansing affect upon the shards they left behind them. They are, after all, energetically connected.

Ghost Hunters usually hope for a sort of audible or visual materialization of these shards, as in the poltergeist phenomenon, but usually these sorts of shards and their resonance are perceived mostly in one's feelings and by one's psychic perception rather than in bangs, knocks and transparent forms passing by. Although it is possible that a very feeling oriented and emotional person, again like poltergeist activity, will evoke such shards into more material manifestation.

Now, each of these previous cases or examples of ghostly forms are all slightly different. In the first case, which is to say the *Topper* series, the ghosts are conscious and are spirits that can affect the world around them as well as converse and interact intelligently, if a bit mischievously with living beings. In that case, they seem somewhat like the idea of guardian angels who have taken a liking to Topper, an individual that they then both haunt in a sense but also interact with, help and guide through the various circumstances of his life.

From that perspective, these ghosts, the Kerbys, are really more like lower level Shining Ones, who abide in the nether realms, yet, are very close to the Earth plane, as is often the case in various lore and tales concerning elves, fae and the sidhe. As far as these elves are concerned the Kerbys are actually elves or pixies of a somewhat higher level than we Silver Elves currently have achieved and they have obtained the ability to consciously abide in the realms that most of us only encounter temporarily as we pass through the Between. And they do so while manifesting in a sort of ephemeral form on the material plane.

The ghosts in *Topper* are rather pixie-like in terms of their behaviors and attitudes. They don't mind, in fact they love, having a martini or two and they hardly fit the rather somber and serious idea of higher spiritual beings that most people presume the Shining Ones or angels would be. And it is in this way that they are more like elves or pixies, as we said, rather than being like the sort of starched collar and uptight puritanical librarian image that most people associate with holy people (not to say that librarians are really all uptight and staid individuals, for we have known many who are not).

But then, most people's ideas concerning spiritual beings, or holy people, are often derived from the prejudices and proscriptions of their particular religion and may have little to do with the reality of what being highly spiritual actually connotes and involves. For we Silver Elves, being spiritual or holy, if you will, is mostly about being a decent being to other people. If you treat others well than you are holy enough for us. A sense of connection to Nature and the Divine Magic doesn't hurt either, but only if the part about being decent to other peoples is included in the package.

As to the priests, ministers, rabbis, imans and reverends of the world, it must be hard to live up to the image and the social expectations of being a holy one and to have to keep up appearances all the time. We feel for them. We thank the spirits the only expectations most people have concerning those of us who know ours'elves to be elves manifest in the world is that we are weirdos, crazies and eccentrics. Living up to that expectation is easy and just comes naturally to us.

The case of the *Canterbury Ghost* is a bit different than that of the ghosts in *Topper*. In this case, the ghost is conscious, it would seem, but connected to the castle it is imprisoned in, like a resonant shard, and cannot leave or go on to the heavenly realms, or perhaps another life incarnation, until its cowardice is atoned for. And the purification of its karma can only be done, in this case, by its descendant, rather than by any action it can perform itself since it can no longer deeply affect the material world.

This is not utterly unlike the Christian notion that we all had to atone for Adam and Eve's original sin, at least until Jesus sacrificed hims'elf for us and supposedly washed away that stain from humanity. We elves are thankful that we are not descended from Adam and Eve, but perhaps from Adam and Lillith, and that the original sin doesn't really have anything to do with us. Although perhaps we were affected by the original divorce where Lillith tells Adam to take his macho image and bossy disposition and stuff it.

Also, in the case of the *Canterbury Ghost*, it cannot die, being a ghost already, and thus courage or the facing and overcoming of the fear of death doesn't come into the equation for it. If we knew that we couldn't really die, most of us would be a great deal more courageous about life.

The *Canterbury Ghost* is really more like a manifest latent memory of someone who had been cowardly in the previous life and now is faced with a circumstance, much like that previous incarnation, where they must decide again to be brave or not. We might think that the descendant in this case may actually be the living re-incarnation of the being/past incarnation, which created the ghostly shard in the first place. In that case, he would be, in fact, his own descendant and his own ancestor, and is haunted by his own karma and past cowardice and the neglect of his duty. In encountering the ghostly shard, he is really encountering an echo from his own previous incarnation manifesting as a projection of his own unconscious or deeper inner consciousness secreted in his spirit cast outwardly upon the world aroused or evoked by a similar situation in his current life.

The third case, in which a ghost is seeking revenge or merely being demonic in some way and preying upon other people, is surely a form of a shard, or an energetic memory, only a memory that isn't primarily one of trauma and suffering directly but of the highly emotional reaction to such suffering. Thus, these sorts of shards display less in terms of victim consciousness in a passive way, but much more in terms of hate, violence and a hunger to get even with those who have done them wrong.

The ghosts in such tales seem conscious on the surface but, really, they are unable to go beyond their drive to get back at those who harmed them or to prey upon those who intrude into their domain. They are revenge oriented and very territorial but unable to think beyond those parameters. They appear on the surface to be thinking beings, but really their thoughts are totally restricted and limited by their endless desire for revenge, much, as we say, like some people we elves have encountered in the course of our lives in the material world who are stuck in an emotional loop and ever in conflict, or in unending vendettas, with others. And it doesn't matter where they work or live, they will create this situation where they feel they are disliked and abused over and over again wherever they are. And in a sort of self-fulfilling prophecy, they bring about or invite the very abuse that they anticipate.

In such ghostly cases, the intense hatred of a previous life has impressed itself upon a particular area, which must be purified in order to release it. Perhaps you have been to places that feel particularly malevolent or hostile. It is this we are speaking about here. An ambience of negativity and hostility that a certain location may happen to exude due to events that have occurred there in the past, manifesting in the ghostly form/shard of those who experienced the trauma and who responded with unrelenting hatred and a hunger for vengeance. Such energies are usually more powerful in artificial areas, such as boats or houses, etc. than living nature, but crystals and rock formations can store such energies. And, of course, such hate and hunger for revenge is often passed down culturally from one generation to another for decades even centuries of hate between particular peoples or races. The Middle East seems to be an area particularly afflicted in this way.

This is, in part, why realtors are often legally obligated to inform potential buyers that someone had died or had been killed in the house or property they are trying to sell, or that some violent event took place there for the property may still contain the resonance of that event. However, the spirit that experienced the trauma has moved on, and what is left is really a haunted form of the cruelty that had been imposed upon them. In a certain sense, it is not their karma entirely but really the karmic responsibility of the individual who caused the trauma in the first place. However, like molesters who were themselves molested, these things get passed on from person to person and from incarnation to incarnation, the victim becoming the abuser, so discovering where the energy started or got instilled in a particular area can be difficult sometimes.

Still, magically, we are all responsible for our own actions no matter what we have suffered or endured in the past or we are going through in the present. Blaming other people for our actions merely gives them power over our lives and as magic wielders we seek to master our own lives and energy and in order to do that we have to assume responsibility for all that happens in our lives or, at least, our reactions to all that occurs.

Some people might bring in a priest or minister to exorcise such a place. We'd probably do a good bit smudging in all the rooms, corners and nooks and crannies of such a haunted house. But that is something which we usually do when we move into a new place whether it seems haunted or not. Just a bit of psychic cleansing that we often combine with sweeping the floors and cleaning the windows and so forth. Some folks, of course, would sit around delightedly hoping for the ghostly form to appear with their video cameras ready as they do in ghost hunting shows. But how do you capture a sense of impending doom upon a video? And how do you film a string of bad luck due to being in the vicinity of such a place that hasn't been cleansed? Movies exaggerate such things for it is near impossible to capture the subtle reality of hauntings on film.

The stories of *Topper* and the *Canterbury Ghost*, however, are old ghost stories and probably most of our readers are not familiar with them. On the other hand, Charles Dickens' *A Christmas Carol*, the tale of the haunting of Ebenezer Scrooge by the ghost of his former partner and the spirits of Christmas Past, Present and Yet to Come while older still is surely familiar, to the point of nauseum, to most of our readers.

This story has been retold many times in movies and television and has been abbreviated, as often happens in stories that have been translated from print to modern media, so that it is the ghosts of Christmas Past (Marley being, in this case the ghost of Christmas Past), Present and Future, instead of the ghost of his former partner and various Christmas spirits that appear before the miserly Scrooge who is such a near soulless being he almost might as well be a ghostly shard himself.

And in fact, we just got a notice from our landlords right before Yule that our rent was going to be raised in the New Year, so we're pretty sure Scrooge's own ghostly spirit still haunts the world in a powerful way. And this is not the first time we and others we know received such unwelcome tidings around Yule time, or Christmas as those who give us their *bah humbug* notices at that time of year insist on calling it.

At the same time, this relation and interchangeability of the idea of ghosts and of spirits is a rather common one. The Catholic church in its Holy Trinity of God the Father, the Son, and the Holy Ghost, will also speak of God the Father, the Son and the Holy Spirit. Ghosts, after all, when they are not just energetic memories or echoes or shards, which is to say cast off emotional expressions, are, in fact, spirits and most spirits inevitably move on to new incarnations seeking to fulfill their desires and their destiny. For we as spirits are simply unable to stay in the Between, as we might imagine the Kerbys of the *Topper* stories are able to do, until we earn the magical power and have developed the potency of spirit to do so.

We may think such ideas are purely fiction and yet, we Silver Elves have had numerous individuals even in our own genetic families tell us of their experience of a person appearing before them, often waking them from sleep while they are still in a sort of hypnogogic state and standing at the end of their bed and saying goodbye to them. And they thought at the time that the individual was actually there for they saw them clearly as though they were solid, living beings and not in a see-through ghostly form. However, they awakened again later and found out that the individual, usually someone very close to them, had just died at that precise time or shortly before.

Spirits who have left their bodies are often still very much attached to their previous life, and even more so to the individuals that they love and feel an emotional attachment toward, sometimes hanging around for a while and communicating, as best they can, to the individuals they are forced to leave behind.

And, of course, there is frequently a lot of emotional energy anchoring them to the world as their funeral and burial proceeds. It is not really their body that is holding them there as an anchor, although that is part of it. This is why, in part, Buddhist tend to burn the dead rather than bury them, for it is the intense emotional energy that is given off by people surrounding the person's body that is so attractive that it can bind the spirit to the material plane, at least, temporarily. It is, in a sense, food for the spirit, in the same way that devotion and faith and offerings given with feeling are food for the higher spirits and demi-god forms.

But soon, most spirits, upon getting no response from the world or the people they have departed from, move on deeper into the Between, where what happens to them becomes a bit like a dream where they encounter the visions and experiences of their inner world and the energy of the Universe as expressed by and through their soul and by their deeper, normally unconscious, mind and they soon become rather s'elf absorbed, in sense, or totally focused on the new worlds and experiences arising before and around them. For, as well as being frightening, these worlds can also be dazzlingly attractive and fantastic.

In the case of *A Christmas Carol*, we might think that the ghost of Marley, Scrooge's former partner, might represent Scrooge's conscience (a term that was popular when these elves were very young but isn't used much anymore) or that they are subconscious memories resurfacing from his past, telling him that he had done wrong, or failed to see the true meaning and value of life and more specifically of the Yule tide spirit. Maybe these are echoes of a kinder childhood or at least a time when he was younger when he thought the world might turn out to be a more compassionate place only to discover through cold, hard experience that it was not.

But the Spirits of Christmas Past, Present and Yet to Come, would surely be Shining Ones of some sort seeking to evoke a deeper and repressed aspect of Scrooge's psyche, what some modern Jungians refer to as the 'bright shadow'. The Bright Shadow is a bit of good nature that has been stuffed down into one's unconscious often in the form of stifled feelings because of a need to function in a difficult and often dangerous world where nearly everyone seems to be out for themselves and their selves alone and people feel they must be hard, cold and tough to survive and be a success in the world. It is like men telling their boys to repress their crying. It protects one's better self; and in *A Christmas Carol*, it finally emerges from within Scrooge transforming him and thus his life.

The Spell:

I hear your voice call out to me
By powers great I set you free

Arvyndase:

El lys le'na jålf koar zes va el
La eldroli ralt El pånd le alo

Pronunciation:

Eel liss lee'nah jah-lf co - air zees vah eel
Lah eel - dro - lie rail-t Eel pond lee a - low

☙

Chapter 9:
How Long is the Between Experience?

lice A. Bailey, author of 24 books on theosophical subjects, claims in *A Treatise on Cosmic Fire* that we have 777 incarnations, but we expect that is really more of a symbolic number than a precise or exact indication of possible incarnations needed to learn and develop the abilities and powers that are necessary to expand into the vaster and more powerful dimensions of evolutionary being and manifestation.

Once, over thirty years ago, we Silver Elves went to a movie with some of our elven kindred at a theatre in Santa Cruz, CA. And while we were waiting in line to get into the film, a stranger standing behind us noticed that we were wearing the seven-pointed acute angled elven star as an amulet around our necks, which is something we have been doing since the late 1970's when we first came upon elf stars for sale at a lapidary rock and gem show and bought a number of them. We were so joyous to find them. Those elven stars, however, were made of brass rather than the silver ones we currently wear, but we still have those ancient stars and sometimes attach them to our hats or other items of clothing.

Noticing our elf star, the individual, who apparently was a mathematician, began talking about how the angle for the elf star formed what he called an impossible or infinite angle since it subdivided endlessly mathematically. Just as if you divide 100 by a third, you get 33.333333333+ to infinity. Thus, the seven-pointed elf star represents infinity in its way and having 777 incarnations, symbolically indicates that life is infinite and you have as many lifetimes and incarnations as it takes to get to the place where you live forever in the same bodily form and manifestation or at least into those realms and dimensions of being where you have the power to shape-shift and manifest whatever body you may happen to desire to inhabit and live within. In time, our bodies of light, our imaginal bodies, will become our permanent bodies that we abide in.

And doing that takes time and development and the amount of time or lifetimes it takes surely varies from one spirit to another, as the Buddhists indicate as they note that any spirit passing through the Between is able to achieve instantaneous enlightenment if they are able to grasp the illusory nature of the dreamlike experiences that they mistakenly assume to be real in that world (the Between) and most probably in this material one as well, which most people assume is reality. That is the purpose, in part, of the *Tibetan Book of the Dead* to talk to the spirits of the recently deceased and guide them through their passage in the Between in hopes that they will see the illusionary nature of what they are experiencing, grasp the self-created nature or self-filtered nature of what they encounter and in doing so awaken to the reality of their true being, which is pure sentient energy and awareness.

The Tibetan Buddhists say that the Between states, which they call the Bardos, take about 49 to 50+ days to navigate, at which point one begins to hang around people fornicating in hopes that an opening into another incarnation and thus a body will present itself. Sounds like fun to us elves, sort of otherworldly porno. So, at least, most of us begin life with high hopes and while later, as teenagers we may act appalled to think that our parents ever had sex; before we were encultured by society, our parents having sex was surely something we (as spirits) were truly joyous about and most likely, when we were spirits in the Between seeking rebirth, an act that we eagerly encouraged them to do. Worried about teenage girls getting pregnant? Blame all the spirits hanging around hungry for rebirth egging them on.

This hunger by spirits to be born again is rather like wishing a portal to Elfin or Faerie to open in its way, only here the portal is to and through the material dimension (and your mother's womb). Just as incarnation is the way that Buddhist say we utilize to develop our spirits and our consciousness and thereby achieve enlightenment, so, we Silver Elves see incarnation as our means of manifesting Elfin in reality. Although, it is important to understand that all creation is, in a sense, an illusion. What we call reality is a creation of our combined magics weaving together, sometimes conflicting, in the world. And yet, in time, it all works out, even the sea doesn't rage forever.

But, is it really the case that we tend to find a new womb to inhabit in about 50 days after we pass from our previous life? Does every spirit reincarnate, unless sHe (she/he) obtains instant enlightenment in the Between, in 49 to 50+ days? Honestly, we don't know the answer to this, but we suspect this is not quite the case or not always the case and certainly not for everyone. Nearly everything else about life varies, why shouldn't that?

Things are probably similar for most people as they pass through the Between and the time they spend in the Between may be relatively the same in most cases. However, individuals sleep for different lengths of time so why shouldn't our time in the Between vary? We live for different lengths of time, some dying early and some later, why wouldn't that affect our life in the Between stages as well?

If we use our occult principle of As Above/So Below, one might theorize that we are actually born again after about one half of the time we lived in a particular life. Although, that also may vary from one individual to another. After all, most of us spend about a third of our lives sleeping, 8 to 10 hours approximately in 24. So maybe if we die at forty using that as a standard and if we accept sleep as an analogy for the Between, we may come into a new incarnation after about 14 to 20 years or so. And if we die at 100, we may return after about 33.33333+ to 40 years.

Or we could view it like we do the seasons. There are four seasons, which vary from year to year in actual manifestation and length, but which have been divided more or less equally between the Equinoxes and Solstices and designated as Spring, Summer, Autumn, Winter. If winter represents death and the Between, and spring is an analogy for youth, summer is thus middle age and autumn an indication of old age, then we would spend about a quarter of the time that we lived incarnate (the spring, summer and autumn of our lives) in a body in the Between or the winter state/season of our spirit. So, by that token, if we lived 75 years, we'd spend about 25 years in the Between.

There are other ways we might look at it as well and our point here is that it is not entirely clear how much any one of us spends in the Between. And what makes calculating this more difficult is the fact that the Between is rather like a dream or sleep state. If you fall asleep and wake up five hours or eight to ten hours later, it seems as if almost no time at all has gone by. You could sleep for days and the time would simply have gone by un-experienced by you while you did so. You would fall asleep and then suddenly you would awake again having almost no sense of time having passed or certainly no sense of how much went by, even if you spent some of the time dreaming.

It is, in a sense, a sort of psychological teleportation. First you were here and then, almost instantly, you are elsewhere, only instead of space, we are traveling through time or experiential awareness actually. Although, if you were traveling through space while you were sleeping, say in a car or on a plane, boat or train, you would be in one place where you fell asleep and then elsewhere when you woke up seemingly in an instant and all the long hours of excitement or boredom of travel will have been circumvented.

In reality, since our planet rotates on its axis and travels around the sun at the same time, while that sun star wheels around the galaxy, which itself is in motion in the Universe, even if you fall asleep for only a minute and wake up in what seems to be the same place you still will have journeyed far from the place where you started, although that may not be immediately apparent. We are in constant motion even when it seems that we are sleeping, sitting or standing still.

We are not saying the Tibetan Buddhists are wrong about the time we spend in the Between transitioning from one incarnation to another, just that things are not always as exact as we might assume and in the Between, like in sleep, it is somewhat difficult to know exactly how long you spent there unless you have some way of noting approximately when you left the world, or departed/died in one incarnation, and when you returned again, reborn into your next incarnation and a new body.

And this is especially hard to know because the body that carried the memories of one's former life has passed away and the memories we do carry are mostly stored in our deep consciousness or unconscious, if you will, and manifest, for the most part, as instincts, intuition and feelings embedded in our spirits that sometimes emerge in our lives as a sense of déjà vu or feeling of familiarity with people or things that we've never encountered previously in that life but feel instinctively that we know. And quite often it is not that person that we actually remember but their previous incarnation. It is their spirit we recognize, not their actual body but then sometimes spirits remind us of other spirits we have known in the past and that can stir an echo or remembrance as well.

It is possible that some of our memories and experiences are stored in the Universe itself, and we can only connect to them through our soulful function which is to say our feeling and intuitive connection to the Universe and all that is within it. In a certain sense, our unconscious resides in the Universe around us. Emotional events can evoke these feelings of connection and familiarity, but such interactions can also be clouded by the emotions that provoke them, sometimes casting the spell of the past upon the present in unclear ways or a vague sense of association.

Serenity of feelings and the calm that comes from meditation or other magical and shamanic trance practices, on the other hand, open us up as pure and clear receptors to the soulful energies that are naturally connected to us. Thus, developing a serenity of being can be very helpful in clearly sensing the energies around us and provoking elf sight by doing so and perhaps this is why elves are often seen, particularly in Tolkien's works, or interpretations thereof, as being, for the most part, serene beings.

But calculating time spent in the Between can also be difficult for time passes differently in the Between, and surely our own sense of time differs there in the same way that faerie tales tell us that a person can be in Faerie for what seems to be days or hours and then return to the world and find that twenty or so years has passed, as is the case in Washington Irving's story *Rip Van Winkle* originally published in 1819.

And when you return to the world with a sort of amnesia, as most of us do after passing through the Between, and often born again in a totally different family, it is hard to know how much time has passed if, in fact, we are as yet unaware of precisely who we were previously and when we departed that particular incarnation. There are anecdotal stories, mostly from India, about people who in remembering their past lives have gone to see their former family. But that is a rare occurrence and most people who say they are recalling their past lives are just using a feeling and psychologically associative connection they sense to someone who was once famous, claiming that they were such a person, often to bolster an inadequate self-image and make themselves seem more important in the world than they currently are.

Many otherkin have a sense of former incarnations, but these are usually ancient manifestations in other realms and dimensions where Faerie once flourished. But again, they are using their feelings and imaginal intuition to sense their previous lives, which often occurred during the second or third root race aeons ago, instead of in this current evolutionary time. And most of those who think that they were some famous person in a previous life, are really only sensing that they were in fact someone who isn't famous but who was like that or similar to that famous individual and not necessarily that actual being at all. The famous person, in that sense, has become a sort of archetypal being for them. But the sense of connection is real even if it is not exact. What they are feeling is their spiritual connection to that particular person for the person that they were previously in a past life has faded from history and memory and this is as close as they can get to representing that personage.

The Spell:

As I travel the Between
Time is not quite what it seems
Days pass by without a thought
Until, at last, a new life's brought

Arvyndase:
Tat El onjor tae vyrlan
Mern da kon ven wu ter kacerlu
Leåli gol la enåkon na ponthïn
Murted, zan zas, na fae ela'da casyna

Pronunciation:
Tate Eel ohn - jour tay ver - lane
Mere-n dah cone veen woo tier kay - seer - lou
Lee - ah - lie goal lah e - nah - cone nah pone-th - in
Muir - teed, zane zayce, nah fay e - lah - dah case - sin - nah

෨

Chapter 10:
As We Think

It is possible, but we think unlikely, that the afterlife differs with different people, according to their particular beliefs in this lifetime. By this line of thought, someone who truly believes in the Christian version of the afterlife would wind up in heaven or hell (or perhaps purgatory for a while); another who was sincere in their Islamic faith would end up in their Muslim paradise or the alternative; Hebrews and Jewish would go to their afterworld, perhaps surrounded by diamonds and delicious pastries; Vikings would still be battling forever, killing each other and being endlessly resurrected; Buddhists would reincarnate or ascend the ladder of illumination and free themselves from the need to incarnate on the material plane at all and Atheists, we suppose, would simply evaporate into the void, never to be seen again even by each other. Some people would say good riddance, but then we'd lose a lot of great scientists that way and we can ill afford to do that.

And perhaps the Atheists will leave their mark behind them for the rest of us to see and it will be the number zero, 0, the eternal circle of being that is non-being (see our book *Faerie Unfolding: The Cosmic Expression of the Divine Magic* for our thoughts on the nature of the Universe), the vast void from which we have all sprung into being in the first place. The impersonal Ein Sof of the Kabbalah about which nothing can be grasped because it *is* pure nothing that, none-the-less, *Is* by virtue of its non-being.

But, while there are individuals we have met who insist that success in the world is almost entirely due to positive thinking and believe that whatever they think will come to be and thus say that their thoughts create reality, we've noticed that such ideas don't always apply to their health in general, their teeth in particular nor even their financial success or their relationships in the world. We've also noticed that they are generally trying to sell us something. If not a product then certainly an idea or a religious dogma or spiritual doctrine of some sort. Sometimes it is that *old time religion*, but often as not it is some New Age formulation. But at its essence it is just an attempt to get us to believe in them, whatever they may be selling, and it is just another version of a confidence game. Hale fellow, well met, a broad and hearty smile upon their face, a pat on your back while they reach around to filch your wallet.

Of course, sometimes it is just their way of dealing with the inequalities of life. If they are successful and others aren't, it's because those others weren't thinking positively enough, not because these positive thinkers inherited money and others didn't, or the fact that some folks must endure prejudice and discrimination due to their gender, race, religion or are persecuted for the mere fact that they think or dress differently than others, while our positive thinkers are accepted in mainstream society.

However, when the particular ideas these positive thinkers had so insisted upon finally don't work out after all, these individuals are usually flexible enough to utterly change their notions and, most often, pretend that they never held those particular thoughts or opinions in the first place, often after a short period of depression until they find a new scam or person to believe them. They have convenient memories.

Except that they still hold that whatever they think, combined with the power of positive thinking, will manifest in reality. Only now it is their new reality and line of thinking that they say one should believe in with all their mind and heart and which ideas they now insist they actually always held. They try to convince us, or whoever is involved with them or will listen, that you just have to have faith and believe hard enough and all will be as you wish it to be or as they tell us it will be.

Although, previous to the moment when they finally give in to the practicalities of reality and change their tune, such individuals will still continue to try to talk everyone involved with them into believing as they believe and they will tell their spouse or mate, who is fed up with being told they should believe and think in a particular way and has decided to leave them, that if they just had faith, which is to say to continue to buy into their particular spiel and continue to believe in whatever they are selling, everything would work out just fine. However, by that time it is usually far too late.

Of course, in changing their tune, they don't change their instrument, which is to say in losing one mate or failing at one venture, they do what most of us do and go forth to find or start another. However, they are still proclaiming loudly the power of positive thought and their personal success in using it to obtain all they want and deriding those who have failed or been unsuccessful in the world for not having had enough faith, while ignoring their own failures. It may be a new song but it is the same old dance.

Thus, we Silver Elves are rather disinclined to believe that Christians, Muslims, Buddhists and so forth all have utterly different worlds that they encounter in the afterlife or Between states. And yet, at the same time, we find that there is some truth to these ideas, even though the truth of them may not be exactly as those who hold these beliefs, or one of these beliefs, may suppose them to be. Beneath our differing religious or spiritual exteriors and our various notions and ideas and political views concerning the world, we are all spirits born into the material world and transitioning through it. We are not as different as we seem to think and yet each of us is unique in our own way. We are different, yet similar, and we expect our life in the Between is also similar, yet differing for each of us.

There was a psychological study years ago that found that people who had a positive self-image had greater success in general social relationships than those who didn't. And this was despite the fact that those same folks who did well in the social world most often overestimated how much people really liked them and what people thought of them. While those who had a less positive self-image, while having a more accurate view of how people felt about them, were less successful in their social interactions. Thus, the delusions those individuals held concerning their own popularity actually served to make them more popular than those with an honest appraisal of their interactions with others. Curious, is it not?

Surely, this explains why some individuals, even very successful politicians, can be so delusional and successful at the same time. Some people looking for a leader are eager to buy into their hype and are impressed by their absolute sense of self confidence. That is the upside of a Narcissistic Personality Complex, a deep and abiding belief in one's self and one's importance in the world.

So, we are not saying that positive thinking isn't a power and that it doesn't have any effect upon the world. We are just noting that it is not an absolute power as some seem to preach. And yet, it is precisely the power that we are each seeking, in a sense, as magicians. It is the power to think what we desire or wish into being. The power to fulfill our own idealistic visions and intentional dreams through magic. To declare our Will as magicians and have that Will manifest into reality. Those with Narcissistic Personality Complexes might be delusional, they surely are, but it is a delusion that, like deep religious faith, gives power and meaning to one's life and helps one succeed in the world.

And this is a power that we have, at least in part, as our spirits are freed from our material bodies temporarily and we pass from one material incarnation to another via the Between. And in that realm, the realm of the Between, the worlds that we encounter, much like our dreams, are a product of our own being and consciousness, our inner psychological world cast outwardly upon the movie screen of the Universe.

Our thoughts, fears and wishes manifest almost instantly in those states of being, although they are also affected, to a degree, by our relationship to and our position in the Universe in its spiritual or energetic form, which is to say as pure energy manifest but unformulated. And thus, our thoughts are able to take on any form or seeming that we give them. Rather like a cloud in that sense floating across the sky before we see the form of a dog, dragon, ship or some other image in it, given life by our imaginations. So, in just this way, we give life and form to the Between.

And so it is that in the Between most of us will encounter Hell states, or states where our guilts, fears and paranoias actively manifest themselves. And also, we will experience Heavenly states, where all our wishes and desires and perhaps inner beliefs about the realms of the spirit will manifest around us as well. So, in that way, Heaven and Hell do exist, but not usually as other dimensional realms that we are trapped in eternally in the case of Hell or can abide in luxuriously forever as is the idea concerning Heaven, but as transitory states of being in the Netherworlds of the Between. Theosophist will tell you that these Between realms seem like an eternity to the entity experiencing them, so that is why Heaven and Hell are considered an eternity, even though they are actually transitory states of being.

So, for instance, in the case of Hell, like getting a root canal, it can seem like it will never end. Or like falling in love, those Heavenly realms can feel as though they will never fade away either and that we will be in love, which is to say heaven or paradise, forever. Which is, in fact, the illusion that most people in love tend to fall into. Love is, in a sense, a delusional state of being, but one that most of us are happy, even eager, to participate in. Much like Elfin and Faerie, in that sense, which are also realms of our own creation. And by our own creation, we mean, us together, not just us as individuals but we as interconnected spirits, linked by way of our souls, weaving the world through our magic.

We do manifest our imaginal worlds in the Between, although most of us aren't able to do so consciously. It is that very fact that leads the Buddhists monks to speak to us as we initially begin our passage through the Between urging us to wake up and to lucid dream in a sense, and thus see that we are dreaming and in doing so potentially creating the reality that we truly desire, only consciously rather than instinctually. Or, even better from their point of view, to opt out of the illusion altogether.

The realm of the Between is, for the most part, a very private world. Just like our dreams, what we experience there is mostly our own inner projections of consciousness and our connection to the Universe, where anything we desire may happen, but which has almost no effect upon the material world or the other spirits around us who are also passing through the Between on their individual journey. It is an introverted and private reality. It is in awakening in that realm and weaving our magics together that we eventually will be able to create Elfin as it is usually imagined to be as the etheric otherworldly realms of magic and power.

We, as spirits, are destined to create our own worlds. That is what magic is all about in many ways. As occultists say, *thoughts are things*, however, positive and negative thinking upon the material plane, while they are powerful and do affect this plane, don't usually have the instantaneous effect that they do in the Between, although that effect, as we said, is mostly in our own minds and perceptions. This is due to a protection spell cast upon us by more powerful spirits, which really is to say by our own higher s'elves, in order to keep everything that we think from manifesting immediately and thus turning the material world into chaos, which is how we got here in the first place. And it is a fairly chaotic world as it is anyway even with the limitations of our magics that are upon us.

And, of course, we are ever, nearly every single one of us, seeking to transcend those limitations and gain mastery over the material world and our manifestation here. We are ever seeking to fulfill our desires and to do so we need to master ours'elves and through that the world we create around us. Or, we could, as Buddha tells us, yield our desires altogether and rejoice in whatever the Universe offers to us. If you are happy and satisfied with whatever you get and whatever happens, you will always be happy and satisfied. But achieving that state of being is a great challenge.

The material world is a realm of tangled and knotted magics born of our desires that have come into conflict with each other all working at cross purposes, the big bang so to speak of conflicting magic and longing and the entangled result of spirits seeking to dominate the Universe with their individual wills instead of cooperating for mutual prosperity, fulfillment and success. We are here to learn to harmonize with each other and thus coordinate our magics, to wield our powers cooperatively, so we can all achieve what we wish and desire in union with each other (see *The Book of Elven Magick, vols. 1 & 2*).

However, on this material plane action speaks louder than words. This is to say that while our thoughts do have power and words have power here as well, it is action that is most efficacious for producing results upon the planes of matter. Actions tend to have more immediate effects than our thoughts or words and this is why upon this plane our magics are not just done in our heads or minds and we don't just speak a spell and leave it at that, we combine our spells with acts, ceremonies or rituals to link our thoughts to actions, even if those actions are primarily symbolic when it comes to magic.

This is not entirely unlike the saying that we've heard Christians express that *god helps those who help themselves*. It is not enough upon the material plane, or usually not enough, to simply do the magic. Although, as the bummer sticker proclaims sometimes, perhaps often, *Magic Happens*. It does. It just does. All of one's magic will be fulfilled in time, but that time factor can be lifetimes in some cases. Therefore, it helps if one combines one's magic with practical efforts to achieve what one desires.

This idea can also be found in the introduction to Aleister Crowley's book *Magick in Theory and Practice* where he delineates the connection between Magick, Science and the practical application of magick on the material plane and how taking what seem to be ordinary or quite mundane actions in the world can really be seen as forms of magick when you understand them correctly. Really, when you think about it, all that we do with will and intention is a form of magic. Every action that we take to fulfill our visions, ideas, and desires when combined with will are magic, especially if there is any symbolic aspect attached to our actions.

As we said when we described smudging a new abode to cleanse it of old energies when we first move into it, sometimes those actions are not just or not entirely symbolic, as when we use our witch's brooms to sweep out old unwanted energies (see our book *Elven Hedgewitchery and Found Magic*) but we keep the idea of the magic of purification that we are doing in our hearts and minds, which is to say we are clear about our intention to cleanse the abode on the various planes of being (we may also use our wizard's vacuum cleaners as well. We are modern elves).

We combine our symbolic acts with actions that have real, if in some cases, small impact upon the world around us. Thus, we are acting upon the planes of spirit, the astral planes, and other dimensional realities while taking direct action on the material plane at the same time. We become one in heart, mind and body and create a resonance of magic that vibrates through the Universe and the dimensions about us acting not just on one plane of manifestation but on a number of related planes all at the same time. This, naturally, increases the power and efficacy of our magic.

In the course of time, as we learn to do our magics in harmony with each other, as well as within our own s'elves, rather than each striving to obtain our individual will upon the material and spiritual planes without consideration of any others, our magics will become more powerful and more effective.

At the same time, as we go through the Between and realize the true nature of reality we will also become aware that we can create worlds that we desire to live in as we wish them to be. We will create Elfin together. And what would Elfin be, really, if we individually were the only elf there. We don't know about you, but we Silver Elves need each other and our others overall. It is our kindred that inspire us and without your input, interaction and connection, our world would be a far duller one than it is. You bring wonder to our world, beloved kindred. You help make it all worthwhile.

However, we need to remember that those Between and ephemeral worlds are, as is the entire Universe, created worlds. They are illusions that we are choosing to live within and it behooves us to create worlds in which we and all our others may abide in love forever, in perpetual harmony and wonder. Just as we build a house to live in, just as we create a home within that house born of family, relationship and love, so we create Elfin, our magical realm and abode for our bodies, minds and our spirits in the midst of Faerie. Let us create a realm that is truly wondrous and magical for all of us.

American theologian Reinhold Niebuhr wrote the much repeated spell, or prayer if you will, "Grant me the serenity to accept the things I cannot change, the courage to change the things I can, and the wisdom to know the difference." Magic is about using one's earthly and otherworldly powers to change what we can in our lives and the world around us, and to subtly influence those things that we don't have immediate power to change upon this plane but which we wish to be different. For we know that they can be different, and know that our symbolic acts have power to shift things, although not always, perhaps seldom, immediately upon this shared plane of being.

Life on Earth is a negotiation. Courtesy, diplomacy and kindness are some of the greatest magical powers of the elfin folk. Enchantment is our chief form of magic, and persuasion through personal example one of our most powerful magical techniques (See our book *The Keys to Elfin Enchantment*). As we join and coordinate our magics, our powers will grow and blossom ever more.

On the material plane, we have to negotiate reality with all the other magicians, sorcerers, witches, wizards and every other kind of magic wielder currently incarnated here, as well as deal with the magics of those who came before us, which is to say the magics or karma of our previous incarnations. And nearly everyone here, whether they believe in magic or not, is really a magic wielder of some sort. Knowing that one is a magician/magic worker, however, does give one a slight advantage over those who don't even realize that they are doing or attempting to do magic.

This is especially true of we elfae folk, who not only understand that magic exists in the Universe and that we can use it to shape our lives, but that it gives us an expanded awareness of the possibilities of the Universe and the various dimensions. We are particularly amused by those who claim to believe in an all powerful god based upon their faith but deny that we are elves or that magic is possible at all except, of course, for their particular god and then they call it miracles, not magic. But miracles are just the ancient magic of thaumaturgy (see our book *Creating Miracles in the Modern World*).

To the minds of these sort of folk the magic/miracles their god does is necessarily good, even when it destroys nearly all of humanity and the magic anyone else does is either ineffectual or evil by definition. We elves are unclear why they would wish to be slaves to such a god, other than they have been terrified by a threat of eternal punishment if they don't bow down before him. But we Silver Elves are clear in our own s'elves that we wish nothing to do with gods such as that.

For just as we seem to be evil to their followers for attempting magic at all, their gods act very much like demons, which is to say Unseelie Fae, from our point of view and while we acknowledge their existence and their powers in the world, we wish as little to do with them as we can. However, while we do believe in their existence we are not so foolish as to believe their followers hype about them. They are powerful, surely, but not all powerful. And they are not the only one with power.

Worse, in many ways, to our minds are those individuals who believe in magic and are themselves practicing magicians, but express the opinion that us calling ours'elves elfae folk is simply a bridge too far, at least for their limited minds and imaginations. And even worse than that are those folk who say they believe in elves, faeries and magic but would deny us our right to manifest in our elfae beings or at least our right to declare the reality of our soulful and spirited manifestation.

We are creating worlds here. We are magic wielders and when we come to realize this and coordinate our efforts, all that we desire will manifest on this material plane as it does in the stages of the Between. And in time, as we create Elfin upon the Earth and among the stars we will become essentially immortal in form and the Between realms and this plane of material being will merge and become as one.

But in order to have that sort of magical power here, we must spiritualize ours'elves and our bodies, but we must also have pure or clearly focused minds. By this we mean, until our thoughts are clear, focused and utterly directed toward success for all, it is dangerous for us to live in this world and have our random thoughts create every notion that occurs to us. That again, is, at least in part, how we got here in the first place. We created barriers for ours'elves, Rings Pass Not, that we must master by means of increasing adeptship if we are to abide more permanently in the realms where our wishes find instantaneous fulfillment. That is our dream. That is our vision. And it is also our destiny.

In the meantime, we need to develop our power of directed and intentional thought. Otherwise, we might be angry and think about killing someone and they'd instantly die. Or consider suicide and find our wrists slit open. Or fear that we might fall off a cliff and immediately plunge to our deaths. Some barrier between thought and effect is needed to protect us from continual apocalypse, and that barrier is the material world where our magics are knotted together creating the sticky spider's web of material reality that traps us all and we need symbolic acts of magic whereby we may delineate our considerations of things, our thoughts and our musings and separate them from our directed and willed intentions.

The Spell:

I see my life and make it clear
By all the things that I hold dear

Arvyndase:

El ten el'na ela nar kord ter vyrn

La wyl tae jartli dij El gosp fysa

Pronunciation:

Eel teen eel'nah e - lah cord tier vern

Lah will tay jayr-t - lie dye-j Eel goes-p fiss - sah

ॐ

Chapter 11:
Magical Perspectives on The Five Stages
of Grief and Dealing with Death

In dealing with death and grieving, Elisabeth Kübler-Ross & David Kessler defined five basic stages that they have observed most people experiencing when encountering those realities (see: *On Grief and Grieving*). These stages are denial, anger, bargaining, depression and finally acceptance. People go through these stages both as they are dying and as they deal with the grief of losing someone they love and care for. For even though we all seem to die alone, death for most of us is a participatory activity, as *The Tibetan Book of the Dead* indicates as their monks speak to the newly departed spirits and guide them through the Between and as our funerals and rituals concerning death also demonstrate.

It might seem that we could skip these stages and go right to acceptance (or pass Boardwalk and go straight to jail, do not collect two hundred dollars) but there are reasons for us not doing so. The chief of these is our continuing and instinctual efforts to increase our power and magic and in time manifest in realms where Elfin lives and we begin expressing ours'elves as the immortal elfin beings we already know ours'elves to be in our spirits and which we are becoming ever more so through our magic and dedicated actions (intentional acts) in the material realms. We are learning to express our spirits in their purity and power on the physical plane, which is a bit like walking beneath the sea. That is to say, we are in the process of materializing or making real on the material plane our true elven natures and thus mastering that realm. Once we have accomplished that, it is quite possible we will expand into the fourth dimensional realms and beyond, materializing in ever more powerful and profound ways.

The first way we deal with facing death, either for ours'elves or someone we love, is Denial. That is really to say that the first thing we do is attempt to change what is going on with our 'positive thinking' magic. By refusing to accept that we are dying or that someone we love is dying, we seek to use our magic to alter what seems to be reality and compel it, through magic, to change course or be different than we are told it must be. We are, in fact, seeking to shift from one parallel world to another one that is similar, nearly identical in fact, to the one we currently abide in. However, this parallel world is different in as much as we do not die in this altered reality but continue living in what seems to be the same body, or at least for a while, and eventually, as we master the material plane, forever.

Alas, we are trapped in the realms of consensual reality and most of us don't have the power to overcome it, otherwise it is somewhat unlikely that we'd be here in the first place. For if we elves, for instance, had the power to create and live in Elfin right here and now, wouldn't we already be doing so?

Well, we can create Elfin and we do live within it, at least in our own small realms that we create through our individual and mutual efforts, but still that greater, wider realm of Elfin where we shall all abide together is still to come, and will be born of our cooperative and united magics on a broader scale. And that is the realm, which we are ever seeking to manifest, where we exist as immortal beings. We are in the process of connecting to our true s'elves that exist within us as pure potentiality and as an expression of the Divine Magic that lives in all things and beings. At that point, our entangled magics go beyond being a miscellaneous and confused combat of competitive magics each seeking to fulfill its will while dominating all around them and they become a tapestry of magic, a magic carpet that we will ride to Elfin upon. (If you like novels about magic read Clive Barker's book *Weaveworld*.)

However, the ability to overcome the supposed reality of the consensual world, the greater world that even our small ealds (individual elven homes and demesnes) exist in, is not without precedent. More than one person has defied their physician's prediction concerning the time of their demise or the length of their life expectancy that was supposed to be shortened due to some disease, and more than one person has mastered a disease or gone into spontaneous remission when it seemed like their inevitable end might be near.

Doctors themselves have noted that an individual's will to live, their spirit, has a great deal to do with the speed of their recovery from accidents and diseases that otherwise would have killed them. Depression and stress weaken us and make us more vulnerable to illness. A strong spirit and a will to live increase our odds of doing so. Life in the world is not ruled utterly by statistics concerning material probabilities; those are just estimates after all. Rather life on the material plane of manifestation is influenced and determined by the strength of our soulful spirits as well as by our often clumsily integrated magics.

That some people are able to avoid what seems a certain prognosis of death really means, from a magical and sorcerer's point of view, that some individuals actually succeed in shifting from one parallel world to another and in continuing on in a particular incarnation when otherwise they would have departed for another incarnation in the world they currently abide in. Or failing that, if they do depart this incarnation, they may happen to shift to another parallel world in the Between. For it would surely be easier to do so there than here in the realms of consensual reality, which means the realms where our magics are powerfully interwoven with all the magics of those around us. Still, in reentering the material world, in this or some other parallel world, they would, in fact, be descending again into the realms of entangled magics or, if you will, into the Matrix, the combined energetic web of our magics interwoven. We are here on Earth or the material plane, really, learning how to weave our spells together, instead of ever getting in each other's way as we try to each become Master of the Universe.

The second stage of grief or dealing with death is Anger. If it happens that our attempts at positive thought magic, via denial, don't work, most of us get frustrated about this and some get angry and just fume about things, others get angry and pour more energy into the situation, which really are the same thing when you think about it. They are both ways of expressing anger, one inward really and one outward.

There is the idea, very popular among mankind and some of the unseelie races, that if their magic doesn't immediately work they should push harder and try to force success, *to go with the Force* and pour more power into the situation as though muscle, strength and will power are a cure-all for everything. It is the belief of many men, orcs and trolls that power is the panacea for all things, even facing death. As men, orcs, goblins and trolls like to tell us, no one's going to give you anything, if you want something in life, you have to take it.

And sometimes that does work. But many times, they just break things or make things more entangled than they already are or they beat their heads uselessly against a wall or punch a hole into it to no avail and then, most often, leave it for someone else to repair as though it wasn't their responsibility at all.

We elves have had more than one experience where we were facing a problem and some macho type person we knew insisted that they could fix things only to make the situation worse by attempting to do so, often damaging the broken object even further, much to our chagrin while they usually just shrug and slink off like a naughty dog.

We Silver Elves actually feel somewhat sorry for mankind, for being such buffoons at times with their overweening machismo and their arrogant, boastful and unwarranted confidence in their ability to do things they are actually incapable of achieving. Or, at least, incapable of achieving in the way they go about it.

We've encountered more than one of these types of people who make bold claims about taking action in a particular situation then get things going and recruit others to their cause, only to abandon things as soon as the situation gets really difficult. And, in the end, we elves are the ones who usually wind up having to finish what they so unadvisedly started. For if we get involved, we see things through to their completion. We do not take our commitments lightly. We are magic folk and our word is our bond.

This second stage is also attached to the idea that somehow getting angry, which is putting more energy into a situation, even if one has seemingly given up, will somehow magically change the situation as though pure force will make a difference. This is along the lines of supposing that if we don't immediately get our way, we can always throw a temper tantrum and see if that works. And, let's face it, that does sometimes work for children and for the very rich and powerful but mostly it just puts more tension in the atmosphere. And, let's face it, death thrives on tension and stress.

In television shows and movies, you often see a scene where the person in charge will ask a technician how long it will take them to accomplish something and then when the person who actually knows what they are doing, the expert in the situation, informs their superior of the shortest period it will realistically take to complete the task and tells that individual it can't be accomplished in less than a week, or whatever. And always longer than the authority desires, the boss angrily says something on the order of *you have two days* and then stalks off, as though the mere fact that they said that so authoritatively means it can actually happen in a shorter time period. They apparently think that putting more pressure on individuals, who are already under great strain and in the process of doing their very best, will somehow make them do better, make them work faster and that it will miraculously make things that can only be done at a certain rate magically happen more quickly. This, however, is just another instance where a person mistakes arbitrary authority for power. It is the conceit of martinets.

On the other hand, in time, as they develop their personal magics, it is possible that such individuals will be able to empower those beneath them with great energy so that they can accomplish more and do so more quickly. And perhaps, they will also be able, in the course of time, to master the energy that designates how long things actually take to happen in life thus superseding the normal laws of Nature — just like the scenes in movies like *Princess Mononoke*, where a powerful spiritual being passes by and flowers that would usually take months to grow and blossom will suddenly do so within a few moments affected by the potency and energy of the spirit's aura.

On more than one occasion, we Silver Elves have worked in some factory or other place doing manual labor and had our boss come in dissatisfied about the rate people were working and decide they will demonstrate to everyone how they should work. This usually involved the boss during the same job as the rest of us for five or ten minutes, working very fast and hard for that time and then, when they had exhausted themselves, they'd stop and say something on the order of, "that's how you do the job," and go off to twiddle their thumbs in their office. Just once, we'd like to see them keep up that pace for an entire hour or more, not to mention an entire day of work.

However, even when people do nothing but get angry in these situations expecting others to be able to do what they, themselves, cannot, they are just attempting to use more energy to get their magic flowing and compel the situation to conform to their liking. Alas, in these situations, the reality is that they are most often just putting more energy into old magics that didn't work in the first place, rather on the order of the saying *throwing good money after bad.* For what they are actually doing is putting more stress on a situation that is already breaking down due to stress and expecting that merely giving orders will somehow make things work out the way that they demand. And yet, that is the ideal of ceremonial magick, is it not? To command the Universe and the spirits and have them obey without question empowered by the potency of one's will? It is simply that most of those attempting to enact such magics are not actually developed enough, as yet, to do so.

And yet, to command the Universe, is really to demonstrate mastery over one's own being, over one's own inner world, not the world beyond us where other masterful magicians abide as well. However, in mastering one's s'elf one puts ones'elf in harmony with the Universe and in doing that all things begin to flow to us. When we are in the right place and inwardly attuned, Nature and the Universe respond easily to us and things that would seem to be miracles to others do happen.

On the other hand, not everyone gets stuck for a time in the realms of anger. Some people when faced with the possibility of death will then open themselves to experimental treatments and a variety of possible cures and remedies and this is their way of expressing their anger in a more positive and potentially beneficial way. Although, these experimental treatments don't always, in fact seldom, work either.

However, this opening of their minds does bode well for their next incarnation even if they are unable to escape impending death in their current situation. For life is not just one incarnation. People might say, as we often hear them do in dramas, that we *only have one life to live*, and that is true. But that one life passes from body to body, from one incarnation to another, throughout time and it goes on forever. It is the life of our spirit, the pure sentient energy that our consciousness attracts to its'elf born out of pure possibility that is the essence of the Divine Magic.

It is not that we elves never try harder, or never increase the power of our magic in a situation, but usually we are more apt to attempt to alter and refine our spells. We are not the type to *go with the force*, so much as to *go with the finesse*. Perhaps a symbol of the elfae folk could be a block and tackle pulley system representing the transference of force so one can use less power to achieve a great deal more. If the magic that we elves are doing isn't working, we examine what we are doing and see if there is a way we might do it better. As the saying goes, *work smarter not harder*. We are ever seeking to improve what we do and how we do it, in magic and in every aspect of our lives.

While, as we say, we elves may in some instances try harder, or pour more energy into a situation and thus, in the case we are speaking of here, increase our efforts toward the avoidance of imminent death, we generally find that skill and expertise is a more potent and sophisticated magic than force. In terms of disease or dying, anger usually just hastens what is already in progress. Especially, as it is seldom directed in a way that would actually make any difference in the situation but randomly flayed about like people who are frustrated will rail at everyone around them. This just creates more stress and simply seems to accelerate one's end. Anger is often like a light bulb flashing brightly just before it burns out entirely.

As for the magics involved in the third stage of dealing with death, Bargaining . . . When denial doesn't work, which is to say our positive thinking magic fails, and anger doesn't work either, which is to say pushing things even harder or yelling at one's god or, in the case of the elves, trying a clever new approach or innovation if one can think of one or find one out in the world doesn't work out, most people turn to bargaining. This is a natural thing to do.

According to the Scottish anthropologist Sir James George Frazer in his introduction to his classic work *The Golden Bough: A Study in Magic and Religion* the first ancient magic wielders used magic directly, in coordination with the laws of Nature and it was only later that they turned to religion, which is to say looked about to other spirits or demi-gods who were supposed to be more powerful than they to help them when their positive thought magic, spells, enchantments and direct and forceful action failed.

If at first you don't succeed, try, try again, and if that doesn't work out see if you can find someone with greater knowledge or power to help you. This is the essence, in its way, of the specialization of work and activity in society. If you don't know how to fix your car yours'elf, you take it to a mechanic. If you can't overcome death by your own magic, you seek those spirits who may have the power to do so. This one does most often, we assume, after first having gone to a doctor and having them try everything they know to do and acknowledge their inability to save you. It would be nice if medical science could cure every disease but that is also something that awaits evolution and development.

In most cases, this supposedly more powerful being is conceived of as being a god or some spirit of great potency (as, for instance, when people are said make a deal with the devil or one of his demons usually in exchange for money or power in the world, but sometimes also for an extended life or youth), who is often from another realm or dimension of being. Who else is reputed to have the power of life over death other than gods or, possibly, demons in some cases? Except perhaps death itself, which in a curious way is really to say Life itself? For death is merely a passage, or transition from one form or body to another and life goes ever on. (Still, you may wish to read C. J. Cherryh's novel *Arafel's Saga,* which is also known as the *Ealdwood* stories, for the interesting interchange held between the elf Arafel, the last elf on Earth in these novels, and the personage of Death).

When we can't get what we want directly by pouring as much energy into it as we are able and we consequently fail in our attempts to postpone death, it is only sensible that we might turn to more powerful spirits who might aid us in our efforts to fulfill our wishes in order to continue in a particular body. But often, we are informed, this only happens for a price. As the television shows and movies like to tell us about magic, and which they proclaim religiously like some sort of magical axiom: *there is always a price.* We've heard this so often it's begun to sound like something some crazy old aunt might gibber at a family dinner. Invite Aunt So and So over for dinner, she's always amusing to listen to. Or maybe something your parrot or macaw might repeat over and over, "There's always a price! There's always a price! There's always a price!" Perhaps, it is a cracker?

Well, surely, that there is a price is true concerning most of what happens in the material world anyway; whatever you are dealing with. Even healing and medical assistance has a price in this world. However, it is generally true that religious services are usually free (we wished they'd pay us for attending, then we might go) but they nearly always have their hands out in expectation anyway. They don't have a price so much as a suggested donation. They are like carnival barkers trying to lure you into seeing the mysterious bearded lady, only in this case it is the mysterious and invisible god. Dealing with invisible gods is like having a dog whistle that blows at a pitch too high for you to hear it. How can you even tell if it works? We suppose you could see if your dogs come to you when you blow it. When we blew one, our dogs just ignored it. So people pray and see if their prayers are answered. Or if not, as is often the case?

What the price may be, when it comes to magic, greatly depends upon the particular spirit or demi-god but the usual cost varies from blood sacrifice to devotion and belief. In other words, the price is some form of energy. People, in fact, offer all sorts of things and make a variety of devotional promises when they are faced with death, including the promise not to be such an asshole anymore.

One might get the idea that death was created by gods in order to make sure we pay up, live in fear of them, and render them the devotion they believe they deserve and have come to expect. This is rather in the same way that rich people often look upon those who serve them and look down on them with an expectation that they (the servants) should treat them (the rich) with awed subservience. But if that were the case, that some god or gods created death in order to subjugate us, we might have to consider that those beings that most people think of as gods are really just demons of some sort. Landlords, if you will, of the material plane. But, we thought that was the Devil.

Dealing with gods and more powerful spirits is what ceremonial magick is often about, the summoning of those spirits, or gods, or the elementals, and the effort to command them to do as we will, or more often, and perhaps more wisely when dealing with more powerful beings, bargain with them and make a deal that is acceptable to both parties. Or in the case of religious people be obsequious and subservient, pray and offer to do this or that, or to believe this or that, or make an offering of this or that, in order to obtain the powerful god's or spirit's favor and have them do for us what we cannot directly do for ours'elves or at least hope and have faith that they will, in fact, if it suits their mood, do so. For there is no guarantee they will fulfill one's wishes and most often when they don't do so the person bargaining with them is told that they simply didn't have enough faith and thus didn't fulfill their part of the bargain rather than the other way around.

In the Celtic Fairy Faith, the normal folk who were believers in the Fairy Folk had a practice of making offerings to the Fae so that our cousins, the Sidhe, would look favorably upon them, or, in some cases, just not sour the milk or make the crops fail or otherwise plague their lives, much in the way that various religious folk tell us we must be good and flatter their god or we will be punished for being bad or just failing to be subservient to those more powerful than we, which, in itself, is often considered a form of blasphemy.

And there is surely some wisdom in recognizing greater power when one encounters it. And, from the point of view of we elven, it is always wise to be courteous and polite to everyone whether they are currently more powerful than we are or not. As they say in show business *be good to people on your way up because you will probably encounter them again on your way down*. Rather sagely advice, when you think about it.

The practice of ceremonial magick, which involves standing as the god or goddess of one's magic circle and evoking and directing spirits, as a king/queen or god/goddess might do, is more in keeping with the first stage of positive thinking and sometimes, if the spirit is recalcitrant, one might move to the second stage of anger, using the magical sword, athame or bell, or some other magical tool to compel the spirit's obedience. But that takes us back to the earlier stages of grief and grieving. While praying, on the other hand, is definitely an attempt at bargaining, or perhaps, in some cases, that of pleading, often in a whiny, hopeful way, of getting what we desire. They offer their prayers, belief and devotion with hope that their prayers will be answered, or fulfilled really, for a negative answer isn't really what they are hoping for.

However, this evocation of the spirits or gods often involves a humbling of ours'elves before the god or spirit, or really the Universe, and an acknowledgement that we are not individually all powerful and that there are other and greater powers than we in the Universe that may be able to assist us if they'd only deign to do so, supposedly as we said, for a price. A lot of promises are made at this stage. And people are often given to wonder why after having been faithful and having led a good life by the principles of their particular religion as best they can understand them that their god often doesn't seem to take notice of their plight or their pleas for reprieve at all. They pray but they seem to get no answer. Although, as we said, no answer from a demi-god is in fact an answer, just not the one the person wishes to hear.

Still, as faerie tales often tell us, we must be careful what we wish for, very careful about how we formulate our wish. Bargaining with spirits or gods or even our fae kindred, while it seems less powerful than commanding a spirit, is also less likely to evoke that spirit's attempts to thwart our will and seek any and every loophole available to get around it (read Jonathan Stroud's novels *The Bartimaeus Trilogy*). Although, there is no guarantee that some spirits still won't seek to fulfill our will in ways that are to their advantage and not our own, as the business world around us confirms and as tales of the unseelie fae often caution us. For they have a habit of sticking to the letter of the agreement but not the spirit of it and using whatever technicalities and loopholes are available to get around it, achieving their will while bypassing our own. Be careful of the spirits with whom you do business, even magical and spiritual business, and be sure to read the fine print.

Even so, mutual success and fulfillment is always the preferred way to go as far as we elves are concerned, but even then, you have to be careful of some of the spirits or demi-gods you may be dealing with. Some of them are the used car (or pre-owned car, as they now tell us ... see what we mean?) salesman of the spirit world. Still, a win-win situation is always the best way to go whenever possible. For even if they are tricky and sly, their karma for ill acts is ultimately on them. But in the meantime, it is wise to be careful for there is karma that is due to our deeds and there is also the greater karma of fate, our entangled magics seeking to each fulfill themselves. And those magics ultimately can't manifest as we wish them to do until they come to a harmonious union or compromise, or marriage if you will, with all other magics in motion for that harmony will provide mutual success for us all.

The fourth stage of dealing with death is Depression. As much as we might evoke, pray, bargain, kneel and offer sacrifice, we don't always get, especially from demi-gods, what we hoped to get, which in this case is a reprieve from impending death. And the failure of this effort often leads people into the fourth stage, which is the onset of depression, although it is true that some folks continue with their anger even unto death and possibly into their next life as well; sometimes being born into their next incarnation with a vague sense of being pissed off with everything, although often these folks can't quite figure out why.

Depression, curiously, is still a form of action and effort, although it doesn't always seem that way. In some senses, it is the opposite of anger and is thus related to it. Depression is a sort of anger turned inward. Instead of raging at the world, at the spirits and the gods, and the apparent unfairness of it all, we turn our anger toward our own s'elves and feel the deep sense of frustration at our inability to move and affect the material plane. It is our frustration over the fact that we don't have total control over our own lives and bodies. It is a sort of introverted magic instead of the extroverted forms of magic as the previous stages mostly were. And it is a transitional stage really. One that takes us from the three earlier stages to the final stage of acceptance that prepares and eases our way into the Between.

Rather than depression, we elves often call this stage *The Brooding*, for it is a very inward activity. It is one where one introspectively withdraws from the world and seeks within ones'elf. It is where we explore the depth of our being and while we may feel utterly isolated in doing this, it is by going in, and thus connecting to the deeper aspects of our soul that we, in fact, reach outwardly to the Universe overall. For in some very important ways, the Universe is as vast within us as it is outside of us. For the Universe exists outside of us but, in many ways, it is even vaster or deeper within our beings. It is hard to conceive but the Universe is infinite in all directions, outwardly and inwardly.

And usually, during this stage, those who are in the process of dying no longer wish to interact with others in the world, or as little as possible, just as very elderly people often spend most of their time sleeping and withdrawn from the world. So, it is that these folks are withdrawing their energy from the world around them and going inward and preparing in that way for their journey through the Between and their eventual rebirth into a new body and what seems to be a new life.

One might wonder why one would get depressed about dying at all. If you believe what most religious folk say on the matter, you'd think nearly everyone with any expectation of going to heaven might rejoice to know they would die soon and dance about with glee if they were well enough to do so, but that doesn't seem to be the case at all. Although, the great elf Timothy Leary, the acid guru of the 60's and 70's, declared his own excitement at facing and exploring death when he discovered he had a terminal illness (you might enjoy reading his book *High Priest*, where he expressed the idea that he might be the spiritual and magical successor to Aleister Crowley).

Some people, it seems, are able to master their enculturated training and their instinctual reactions toward death and dying having obtained a wider and more enlightened view of the nature of the Universe and of Life through the use of meditation or psychedelic experience or the trance states of magic and shamanic experience (see Mircea Eliade's book *Shamanism: Archaic Techniques of Ecstasy*).

It is understandable that people who expect to go to hell might wish to delay their sentence, but then you might also think that they would then seek to make amends while they still had a chance to do so, which some do, but many don't even bother. They may confess their sins but only because they think they have been caught, so to speak and have no choice. It is not a true conversion but a social action, like convicts who become reborn to Christianity and suddenly find Jesus because they think it will impress their parole board. It is said that beauty is only skin deep, often that is true of religious beliefs as well. But while men might be deceived by hearing what they wish to hear, the higher spirits, the Shining Ones, cannot be fooled in that way. We can't trick our way through the Between and into a better life for it is our own true s'elves we are encountering there and we instinctually know what we need to learn and develop as soulful spirits and we are destined to become who we truly wish to be.

You'd think the Buddhists and we elfae folk, also, would joyfully embrace death as well, knowing as we do that our powers will be, at least for a while, unleashed in the Between, but the unknown next life circumstances and situation often gives us pause. This includes the period of pooing and pissing on ours'elves when we are newly incarnated, having our diapers changed, thus the helplessness, struggling to learn to walk again, and then going to elementary school and beyond, which often means being bored to abstraction and dealing with all the bullies and harassment that those institutions tend to breed and tolerate, frequently from orcs and trolls disguised as men in the world, all eagerly vying with each other to get to be the King of the Hill or of the trash heap, really.

And perhaps even worse than that, we elfae folk are hesitant about being raised among the normal folk again and suffering their efforts at enculturating us to be normal and us having to slowly struggle to come to realize that the reason they treat us as aliens is because, in fact, we are alien to them. They instinctively sense we are different, just as we do. We are not normal. We are otherworldly folk. We are elfae folk and we trust that in our next incarnation, we will awaken to this fact even sooner than we did in this one. However, whenever we awaken, early or later, it will be to our great joy and satisfaction.

After all, that is one of the purposes of these books we Silver Elves write, not only to help our awakened kin, and help others of our kind as yet unaware of their true natures to awaken, but also so that hopefully these tomes will be awaiting us in our next incarnation to help us realize our elfae natures again as well. We are leaving messages for ours'elves to find in the future written in the mystical language of the elfin that appears like English, or some other language, but is really a whole other way of interacting with and perceiving the world. It is the language of feeling, imagination and intuition more than of letters and script. Just as music is said to be a Universal language, Elfin as it awakens our imaginations is a sort of universal language of the elves and elfae folk.

Although, next time we incarnate, we do so hope we will have a bit more positive attitude about learning than we did this last time. We were rather recalcitrant students in this life, more inclined to play than to study. But that may be our pixie blood. Still, school, as it usually exists in the world, can be deathly dull. Unless, of course, you are educated and homeschooled by elves, as our children were, and that is marvelous fun; but that is another matter, for another time and perhaps if we get to it, for another book.

And, there is a reason that most of us fear and avoid death, as we've explained in others of our books, and that is because we are programmed by Nature to do so. We are meant to try to live as long as possible because we are attempting to develop our capacity to live in the material world in resilient and enduring bodies and the development of these bodily forms takes time and practice. We are here learning to be immortal in the material realms and to evolve the types of bodies that will be able to contain and endure the power of our immortal spirits within them. In a certain sense, our spirits burn our bodies out. We need stronger more enduring containers for our spirits, which are flames of elfin being.

The fifth stage of dealing with death is Acceptance. As we indicated, the stage of depression or brooding is really a transitional stage. It is a movement from effort to Zen acceptance. It is a step from the major arcana tarot card of the Magician to that of the Fool or we might call it the card of the One Who Goes with the Flow. In that case, we might think of the stage of depression as the Hanged Man, where one is temporarily suspended and unable to act. And if the first stage of denial is the Magician, and the fourth the Hanged Man and the last stage, the Fool, then the second stage of anger, which usually ends with things falling further apart, might be the Tower and the third stage of bargaining would, in that case, mostly likely be represented by the Devil or the Art of the Deal.

In this final stage of acceptance, we give up trying. We accept our impending death or the death of another and we cease putting energy out at all, neither positively or negatively. We place ours'elves in the hands of the Universe and the spirits that abide there and we await our time or move on with our lives if it happens that it is another for whom we mourn. We become, in a sense, effortless, accepting the motion and movement of the Universe because, in this particular case, we really have no choice but to do so. Forces greater than we have hold of our lives and we are not as yet powerful enough to guide them as we wish. But we elves relate to those greater powers as the Shining Ones who are sort of parents for us, loving parents that we can trust to do their best to help guide us in the direction we truly need to go.

And curiously, this yielding to the Universe and thus to our fate and destiny, sometimes has miraculous results. In giving up and yielding, we are sometimes unexpectedly uplifted and given a reprieve from death. This, in some ways, is like the process of creation, inspiration and invention. Sometimes, we struggle with ideas and various notions, seeking inspiration, working hard constantly and continually, pouring more and more energy into our chosen project, sometimes seemingly to no avail, faced with a puzzle we can't quite figure out and striving for a breakthrough. And then, when we relax, take a bath, take a break or go do something that takes our mind off things for a brief period, having given up, at least for a while, inspiration comes to us. The Voice of the Universe speaks within us and suddenly we awaken to new realizations, sometimes on new levels of awareness. We have that Eureka! moment, that peak experience and revelation dawns on us and suddenly we comprehend in whole new ways, having experienced a quantum leap of consciousness.

Of course, giving up and accepting death does not always, or even often, save us from death. However, in accepting death, we are also accepting, often unknowingly, the release of the limitations of our incarnate form and the unleashing of our powers in the Between. We become who we truly are and the Universe unfolds before us. What we embrace in accepting death, really is our own destiny and power and while we might still have things that we need to work out in the Between as we are confronted by the mirror of our own psyches and inner beings. And while this nearly always also means karma that we need to face in future incarnations, we may get a glimpse in terms of a Vision of our true being and our destiny in the Universe that carries us, often with profound optimism, into our next life.

The Spell:

Though we grieve for what we've lost
And know full well the sacred cost
We know as well that life goes on
And we'll awake to a bright new dawn

Arvyndase:
Nåt eli selthyn fro wu eli'tir wusïn
Nar ken fel darl tae elfro dos
Eli ken tat darl dij ela tasïn gos
Nar eli'yon vasa va na ilu fae lan

Pronunciation:

Knot e - lie seal - thin fro woo e - lie'tire wooce - in

Nair keen feel dare-l tay eel - fro dose

E - lie keen tate dare-l dye-j e - lah tace - in go-ss

Nair e - lie'yone vay - sah na eye - lou fay lane

આ

Chapter 12:
Genetics or the Land?

There is a basic question and debate in science, especially in the social sciences, about whether Nature or Nurture (or lack thereof) has the greatest effect upon the character of an individual being. This is to say whether our bloodline or genetic heritage influences us as much or more so than the circumstances we are born within and the environment and individuals that surround us and influence our development as we grow up. Although, for many people their genetic heritage does, in fact, determine the environment in which they are reared so it is often hard to separate the two. They are definitely intermingled and many people are raised in cultures that have been in the same area and had the same genetic and social influences for decades, even centuries.

There is no question that certain people raised in harsh and abusive circumstances sometimes become cruel individuals. Those who are abused as children sometimes become abusers themselves. Others are just traumatized for that particular life. And yet, not everyone becomes a pervert because they've been abused and not everyone spends their entire life suffering from the trauma they've experienced earlier in life.

Nor, on the other hand, do all those who are born to brilliant parents turn out to be brilliant individuals. Great and famous actors, singers, world leaders don't always produce children who have the same degree of talent and ability. And many great artists come from parents that don't seem to have had any talent at all in their chosen field. Both genetics and our environment appear to have an effect in the shaping of our character. But what exactly is it that they are actually shaping? An empty form, like sculpting clay that they fashion into a particular structure, or is it something else more essential to the individual? Something that is deeply and truly our own s'elves?

At the same time, in studying the lives of truly unique and exceptional individuals, James Hillman in his book *The Soul's Code* did indicate that nearly every one of them had encountered another unique or exceptional individual that had a primary influence in their upbringing. So it is that we elves are most deeply effected in our spiritual development of our true s'elves by encountering other manifest and awakened elven kindred. We learn from them through a sort of vibrational sharing and osmosis.

Still, we Silver Elves know from the nurturing of our own littles that they have aspects of being that are all their own, due neither to their environment entirely nor their genetics. It is something they have carried from one lifetime to another. It is an essential essence of inner character that makes them who they truly are wherever they are born and whomever they encounter there. Death and the loss of our current body strips away our ego, our opinions about ours'elves and others, and all the memories (for the most part) stored in that body, but we retain our inner natures, our drives, desires and deepest aspirations to be the most successful and powerful beings we can become.

Anyone who has had multiple children with the same person that are all raised under the same circumstances will know how very different their children can be from each other. Even dogs have their own personalities. And you will note that children will often have their own preferences and aversions, frequently to particular foods that they like or dislike, no matter how much we might tell them that eating vegetables or whatever is good for them, or that they should have variety in their diets and not to just eat spaghetti or peanut butter and jelly sandwiches or some other favorite food almost exclusively.

This is not to say that children are not influenced by their environment, nor that there aren't things that they inherit, such as hair, skin and eye color and so on at the very least. Clearly, there are. But there is also something within them, as individual spirits, carried from one life to another, that helps to make them who they are. And these things seem to manifest mostly as aspects of personality, personal interests and one's preferences and aversions. Thus, elfae folk have a natural attraction to things Elfin and Faerie and this is not necessarily due to parental or ancestral influence nor our surroundings and environment.

Although, one might make the case that their attraction to things Faerie is genetic, although it must be, in many cases, a very sub-dominate genetic stream if that is so. Or it might be argued that even though no one in their immediate environment loves elfin and faerie things the way that they do, that Faerie Tales and the *Lord of the Rings* and so on are part of their environment and clearly available to them. But the question is why does the notion of elves or faeries attract them (and us) so strongly when others are barely affected or not interested at all? What is it in them that draws them to things others pass by hardly noting their existence?

How is it that some individuals are born with artistic talent or musical gifts or other abilities from a very young age? Why are there child prodigies? We could say that they inherited these things, but there is not always anyone we can directly point to in their familial line from whom they would have inherited such abilities. And the idea that they have great artistic ability from an early age due to the environment doesn't seem viable even if they are surrounded by great artists for if that were so why wouldn't every child raised in that environment be so gifted?

We Silver Elves are more inclined to suspect that their genetic inheritance is not something that is placed upon them from the outside, but springs from their own evolutionary history and their individual decision to be born into a particular genetic line. They do inherit their talents and abilities but mostly from their own previous lives. Lifetimes of effort are what create talents and abilities that we seem to be born with.

We Silver Elves once knew two sisters who were identical twins. You couldn't tell them apart. Even their parents were fooled sometimes. They were both beautiful, lovely people. We adored them. Of course, they also adored us, which is part of the reason surely that we adored them. We were part of an elven mutual admiration society. Yet, one of these sisters had leukemia and the other didn't. How is that possible? They had the exact same genetic makeup. They had the exact same parents, upbringing and surrounding environment, and yet... Surely fate was involved, was there some karma, as well?

But there is another possible factor here that helps determine our character. And this is not genetics precisely nor, from this point of view, is it our social environment. And that is the idea that we are, at least in part, shaped by the land in which we are born and live. Here we don't mean the culture in which we are brought up, so much as by the living, breathing land that we live and develop upon. Just in the way that food grown in different soils will taste differently, so the idea is that individuals growing up in different areas will be affected by the varying material and spiritual properties of that region. Our environment is not merely the people and culture around us, but the Living Earth and its vibrations and energies.

This sort of idea, that our land, our Earth, the Nature that surrounds us, affects us deeply, to our very core, can be seen in the story of *Dracula* by Bram Stoker in which Dracula must carry his own soil to sleep in as he travels by boat to England from Transylvania. Being born at a particular place upon the Earth, according to this notion, affects our very being. It is our homeland and not simply in a political sense. People who travel afar and settle in new places, still feel a connection to their homeland and culture, but if their children are born in the new land, those children become connected to that new place more than the former. As the saying goes, *be it ever so humble, there's no place like home.* Of course, it is not just about being born in a particular region on the Earth, but about being raised in a particular area. Our relationship to the Earth is ongoing. Even extending, for most of us, from one incarnation to another for thousands of years.

Of course, since food comes to us from all over the globe in the modern world, we might think that this affects our beings as well. *We are what we eat.* And we are becoming international beings not simply due to travel and trade but due to sampling the foods of other cultures and particularly eating foods grown in the soils of other regions.

We Silver Elves, for our own part, have experienced that in the various migrations we have made in our lives that it takes about a decade before a particular region fully accepts us as its own. We, for our part, however, pay homage to the spiritus loci, the spirits of the area, from the very beginning and this serves to help us settle in. We honor the spirits of Nature wherever we go, requesting their assistance and favor as we pass through or make a new home among them. They open the vibrational energies of the land making it easier and every decade they open the way even more and things are revealed to us. We discover places and connections that help us that we did not know existed prior to that moment.

This same idea can be found in a way in the ancient practice of the sacrificial king, of which Jesus was one and Pythagoras another. Yes, that Pythagoras, the great mathematician and perhaps the first person in the world to designate himself as a philosopher, who was also in his time said to be seen as a son of god, whose coming was prophesized, who was born by immaculate conception due to the intercourse between a god and a human woman, and who was also betrayed and murdered/sacrificed by those who envied and feared him for being different (see Manly P. Hall, *The Secret Teachings of All Ages*).

In that ancient practice, the god king, who had mystically and magically and often ceremonially married and mated with the Earth, who was considered a goddess, would be killed as he grew old and/or feeble and his blood was shed upon the land to renew it once he was too aged to be a viable king anymore (see the old movie *The Eye of the Devil* starring David Niven that has this practice as its theme. Note, the movie *The Wicker Man* for another instance of this practice). Kingship in those days was not so much god given as goddess given. The king was anointed by the Goddess Earth who was mother to us all and the source of success, abundance and prosperity.

This is the notion that Nature renews itself through death, just as the autumn comes and everything seems to die and then spring arrives and all is resurrected. This is the theme of the British folk song *John Barleycorn*. And it is also the theme of the faerie tales that tell of the conflict between the Holly King and the Oak King or the Winter and Summer Courts of Faerie, as they struggle for dominance throughout the cycle of the year, one reigning through spring and summer and the other ascending in autumn and winter.

Note, however, that most modern faerie tales and novels, even if they seem to be about the conflict between the Winter and Summer Courts are really about the discrepancy and disagreement between the Seelie and Unseelie Courts of the Fae, which is to say between those who wish to help and enlighten Mankind and those who see Man as their natural prey and quite often wish to enact revenge upon Mankind for the persecution we elfae and others have suffered at their hands over the ages.

One might also consider the attachment so many people have to a particular land, especially the land of their ancestors or a land that they deem to be holy (often the same thing). For thousands of years, yes, thousands of years, people have fought and died and killed each other in the Middle East and continue to do so to this day and, we expect far into the future, over who may live in and control the "Holy Land", which as it turns out is mostly a desert. They're killing each other over a desert and they were doing that for thousands of years before petroleum, and the energy and wealth it represents, was discovered there.

From an elven point of view, this conflict of religions and cultures in the Middle East is really a war that is being waged between competitive djinn who have lived there nearly forever (see Tim Powers great and brilliant spy novel *Declare* that speaks to this idea) each seeking to raise up their own followers who pay homage to them under the guise of their particular one true demi-god.

One might say that various religious and ethnic groups squabble over this region of the Earth for the most part because of politics and a conflict of cultures and religions, but from where do those politics and religions arise but from particular regions upon the Earth. There is a certain argument to be made that they arise from the soil itself, or from the sand in this particular and perhaps peculiar case. For there doesn't seem any other place on Earth that we know of where people are so determined to kill each other over soil that can hardly grow anything. But value, like beauty, is in the eye, or mind really, of the beholder.

We elves, for the most part, however, are star people. We know that we are composed of energy, of stardust and there often isn't one particular place that attracts us on the Earth but rather we feel connected to the whole of the Earth and from that outward among the stars. We embrace the Earth and the Universe in entirety and look upon each and every place upon the Earth as potentially holy just as every individual bears the Divine Magic within them in potential and this potentiality is something they are destined to realize and express through their unique and individual manifestation.

Although, one might say that as far as particular places go upon the Earth, we elfae folk are most attracted to wherever our kindred might be gathered. We tend to seek each other and no matter where it is that we start out in life upon the planet we ever hunger to be with our very own. We gravitate toward each other like magnets. It is not land exactly that we seek but our elfin family, not a house so much as a home. And while there is surely some purpose in us being scattered upon the Earth when are a reborn here, we ever feel alienated from those around us until we find our kindred.

However, we elves are also attracted to the forests and the wild places of Nature and most often, when we have yet to find our kindred, we seek solace there, for those are ever holy and sacred places to us. Yet, we are just as comfortable with the idea of living in outer space as we are upon the Earth (although we usually imagine carrying forests into space with us) and you will find many elfae folk are avid devotees of science fiction and science fantasy (as well as just plain science). This starry nature of ours frees us from being born upon a particular place on the Earth and opens the possibility of rebirth for us in other star systems and other dimensions as well or wherever our spirits deem best for our evolutionary development. For we do not calculate our lives by individual manifestations but by the trend of our life through the various lifetimes and incarnations.

Some people never travel very far from the place that they were born but we elfae folk, for the most part, love to wander. We are nearly all, in a manner of speaking, natural trooping faeries. The famous Faerie Rade (ride, parade), after all, is a peregrination through the realms of Faerie, Elfin and the world.

And yet, we are homebodies as well, ever delighted to be at home among our very own.

You might say that the Earth is like a magnet. In fact, the Earth is a magnet with a north and south pole and we are spirits born upon it, and many people, due to their particular karma, are drawn like metal filings to the Earth plane over and over again, often in the same particular locale or to the same ethnic people, just as we elves are ever attracted to our own fae race wherever on Earth we may find them. We are not the only ones who gravitate toward our own. In fact, this seems a behavior that one can find among all sort of peoples, human, humanoid and even animal and insect.

And we elfae folk are continually drawn to those lives where we might discover our true natures, most often by encountering our own kindred for we learn primarily through a sort of osmosis from being near each other. And while much of elvish lore comes from Western European cultures, there are various faerie-like beliefs to be found among nearly every people and culture upon the Earth, particularly the ancient and aboriginal cultures of the globe who valued their link and connection to Nature and understand that the spirit/spirits live within it (see the scholarly work *American Elves: An Encyclopedia of Little People from the Lore of 380 Ethnic Groups of the Western Hemisphere* by John E. Roth). Our relationship, as manifest elfin folk, to the more ethereal beings of our race is familial in nature. We do not view them as separate from us but as our fair cousins, different in form, seemingly more ethereal than us and yet, being fourth dimensional beings actually more manifest in a wider form. They are advanced in evolution but clearly and deeply related to us.

However, the idea that there is a specific Earth connection to our individual beings can be found in Astrocartography or Astrogeography, where a person may use their astrological chart, either natal (born) or progressed (developing over time) to find the place best suited to them upon the Earth (a progressed chart takes each day after one's natal or birth chart as being indicative of a year in one's advancing life; thus if you wish to see an astrological chart for your thirtieth year, you do a chart for the configuration of the stars, luminaries [the moon] and planets 30 days after your birth and so on).

The whole idea of astrology is that we are, at least in part, shaped by the forces of the Universe that surrounded us when we were born. But, we might also think that we are born at that particular time, during that particular configuration of the stars and planets precisely because of who we are as developing spirits and because of what we seek to accomplish in the world to enhance the evolution of our beings. And thus, as we said, born into a particular genetic lineage for the same purpose. We choose or gravitate to a particular place upon the Earth because of our connection to its energies or ambience, you might say, and sometimes to the people who live there. Although, some people, perhaps many, are karmically bound to a particular area. Still, if you view astrology not as a force that compels us to be a particular way, or determines our lives absolutely, but rather as a configuration of forces into which we choose as spirits to be born, the idea that we are each conceived 49 to 50 days after we leave our current body is again somewhat questionable.

There is also the related esoteric idea of ley lines or energy lines, which are like veins or mystic roads upon the Earth, or the Earth's body so to speak, (the Australian aboriginal peoples call these Song lines, which we think is very elven, indeed), and surely these ley lines create different energies at different regions and spots upon the planet, just as there are chakras at various points on the body that exude and channel different energies. And much in the way, different parts of a town or city will have individual energies or vibrations due to industry, or commerce or restaurants, housing, governance or whatever. In most cities, there are areas where some of us would be unwise to go or would feel less than comfortable entering but to which others are naturally drawn. Usually it is those who grew up there. Although, there are nearly always some of those who wish nothing more in their lives than to move and get away from that place. Perhaps these are elfae folk.

The point is that many of us are drawn to the Earth over and over again from one incarnation to another working out the various aspects of our spiritual development because there is a karmic link connecting or binding us here and because this is also the best place for us to evolve as individual soulful spirits. The Universe is a connected whole and we live within the web of its being. But like cells that are drawn to different areas of the body, we are attracted to different areas of the Universe and most specifically the Earth itself due to our own unique and individual natures and destinies.

The Spell:

I will find the place for me
The perfect place for me to be
Born again among my kin
In eald or nest or in a den

Arvyndase:

El yon låc tae al fro el

Tae nucha al fro el va te

Daend sasnana arae el'na eldi

Ver ald sa pyn sa ver na farv

Pronunciation:

Eel yone lock tay ale fro eel

Tay new - cha ale fro eel vah tea

Day - eend sayce - nay - nah a - ray eel'nah eel - dye

Veer ale-d sah pen sah veer nah fair-v

࿇

Chapter 13:
Death in the Tarot

The Death card is one of the major arcana cards of the Tarot. It is perhaps the most famous of the tarot cards. It is the card that even those who know nothing else about the tarot, couldn't possibly name another card in the deck, know exists.

The Major Arcana, or the major secrets or mysteries, usually denotes those things in life that are both universal in a sense, occurring to nearly everyone in their lives, and deeply life affecting, the major developments, influences or events of one's life. In that way, the Major Arcana of the tarot is much like our natal chart, which itself indicates a sort of synopsis of a particular incarnation overall, a general outline of our life, energies, powers, talents, abilities and obstacles in our current life, while a progressed chart is a synopsis of the various individual chapters of our life.

You'll note that in a previous chapter, we associated the five stages of grieving and of dealing with death with various major arcana tarot cards, but the entire process of death, dying and grieving would come, of course, under the auspices of the major arcana card of Death, the great transformer. All things associated with a major change or transformation in one's life are linked to this card. It could be called the Life Changes card. It can represent changing jobs, moving to a new place, getting married or divorced or any other change that makes an important difference in one's life. The major arcana, overall, refers to life transforming events.

The tarot is a small symbolic language with 78 basic ideas attached to it and as tarot readers often tell their clients, the Death card doesn't necessarily or just indicate physical death. It can't. Because the language base of the tarot is so small, the Death card has to represent death and transformation in all of its forms, permutations and stages if the tarot is to be an effective representation of life and all that goes on in the course of life.

We Silver Elves, who have done somewhere over 75,000 readings for other people in our lives, many of them repeat customers, know that getting the Death card simply doesn't mean the person will die soon or even that someone they know will die or that they will have a near death experience in the foreseeable future, although it is surely possible and we have seen that happen. But most of the time in a reading the Death card indicates other changes in one's life, but still events that will be important to one.

We once had a customer come to us for a reading who was pregnant at the time who got the Death card as the outcome of her reading. We did our best to frame the card in the most optimistic way possible, speaking of how much a child would transform her life, while reminding her to get good prenatal care, but she returned about a year later and informed us that she had miscarried. She said she had known instinctively on seeing the Death card that this would be the case, despite our attempts to reframe its meaning in the best possible light. And she thought that we had really known the truth of the situation, in spite of what we said about the card, but while we knew that Death was a possibility, we did not know that it would become an actuality in this case.

And as we say, in most cases, the appearance of the Death card in a reading doesn't indicate the Death of a person. But she was right, whatever sense we had that something could go wrong with her pregnancy, we were not going to tell her that she or her baby were about to die. As much as we seek to tell people the truth in our readings, as best we can, sometimes it would be just irresponsible to do so.

If it was the case that someone died every time the Death card appeared in a reading, we Silver Elves would have died decades ago and so would have nearly all of our regular customers. And yet, the Death card does include the notion of material death, the death of one's physical body and the end of a particular incarnation among its many possible meanings. However, the actual number of times a person dies shortly after receiving the Death card in a reading has to be somewhere far less than 1%.

Notice, that in television shows and movies that have a tarot reading in them, the Death card nearly always comes up, and they always act shocked and surprised like that was the first show it ever appeared in. This is, in part, why people getting an actual tarot reading are often a bit shocked when the Death card does appear. Although sometimes in these shows the reader looks horrified, gathers up their cards and declares that they (the reader) simply can't go on with the reading. Can you imagine going to your doctor for medical tests, and when the results are in your doctor hides the lab data and tells you it is just too terrible to tell you about their findings?

Unlike doctors who sometimes can't do anything to prevent your demise for all their knowledge, training and efforts, the tarot has the power to warn you of impending dangers so that you might act in such a way as to avoid them or minimize their influence on your life. That, after all, is the cards' true purpose. Although, not everything can be avoided and despite all our efforts fate, karma and destiny will have their way, as the doctors well know.

If you are familiar with the tarot and the Major Arcana, then you will also know that Death is card number 13 of the group that comprises the twenty-two major arcana cards. Thirteen is also associated with idea that Friday the 13th is an unlucky day (although why Thursday the 13th isn't, we don't know. Or perhaps it should be Saturday the 13th, since Saturday is Loki's day), although we elfae folk nearly always look upon Friday the 13th as being lucky for us. For we feel that if normal folk think upon the number 13 as unlucky it surely must be good luck for the elven. We like black cats as well and encourage them to cross our path, for we know that magic will be forthcoming.

In our experience, the normal folk are nearly always wrong about nearly everything, especially spiritual and esoteric things, although they are not all that good at understanding Nature and the world either. For instance, 13 is also the floor some buildings, and hotels in particular, skip in numbering and call 14 instead because they think people superstitiously believe—and some do—that being on the 13th floor would be unlucky and would draw death, ill luck and misfortune to them. This is done as though changing the number of the floor somehow tricks the spirits, who they apparently think aren't smart enough to realize it is really the 13th floor. Of course, it is not the spirits they are considering, actually, but the superstitious nature of some of their customers and many of them probably don't realize they are actually on the 13th floor.

Note, however, that in Chinese culture it is the number four that is considered unlucky because the number 4 is nearly homophonous to the word "death". Which is to say it is a word that is pronounced nearly the same but has a different meaning, such as the word 'file' in English that means both a line (of say people) a box or container for documents and a tool for wearing down one's fingernails or wood, etc. Or perhaps it is even more like the words depth, death and deaf that sound so very similar in English.

The Chinese also, due to the association to death and ill luck, sometimes rename the fourth floor and call it the fifth floor, and further sometimes skip a room number 4 in their hotels. Interestingly in Hong Kong, which was occupied by the British for over a hundred years and thus has a mixed Chinese and western culture, sometimes rename both the fourth and thirteenth floors.

No matter how much the normal folk may know logically that their superstitions are without foundation, there is still something deep within them that believes. This is probably why they cling to their ideas concerning their various all-powerful gods as well. They are afraid to do otherwise. And, in fact, they are often threatened with eternal torture if they don't believe. And most likely, the fact is that their superstitions draw those energies to them creating self-fulfilling prophecies that merely reinforce these superstitious notions. This is part of the power of thought and the power of magic that focuses and directs that thought with will power and intention, sometimes with an intensity of feeling.

Although, most of the superstitions the normal folk hold are apotropaic in nature, which is to say they are designed to ward off ill luck and misfortune, such as the prohibition against breaking mirrors (since that will bring you seven years bad luck), knocking on wood (to ensure against one's bold or possibly arrogant statement being taken askance by the spirits) or not walking under ladders (general bad luck), opening umbrellas in one's house (since that will invite the roof to leak) and so forth. These are old magic formulas of folk magic or Hoodoo as it is popularly called today, ancient magic formulas passed down from one generation to another over hundreds of years, and despite the normal folk's belief in science or religion, they still cling to them. And we elves, for our part, still knock on wood, for we try to be humble folk and know that the trees are ancient and wise spirits and some of the best and deepest meditators in the Universe and thus often great sages.

Take note that the number 13 is also sometimes associated with Judas as Jesus's betrayer (Jesus and the twelve disciples, thus a coven really). Why Judas is number 13 we don't know but we expect that this is a retrospective association based upon the notion that 13 is associated with Death and is thus unlucky. Thirteen is also linked with Loki as the trickster/devil god of Norse lore because of a banquet where Loki showed up as the 13th and uninvited guest and this resulted in the death of the god Balder (a god much like Jesus in aspect) due to a trick of Loki's. It was similar in its way to the tricking of the Egyptian god Osiris by Set and to the Last Supper of Christian lore, although Judas is not usually portrayed as clever, like Loki, but rather as a low and cowardly being who failed to have enough faith.

On a more positive note, there are also thirteen moon (mystic/magic) cycles in the year, thus the influence of the netherworlds upon our lives, and we Silver Elves believe there should be thirteen instead of 12 astrological signs as we Silver Elves imagine elven astrology to be. But, while our sisters of the Elf Queen's Daughters taught us basic Western astrology, we are not experts in that esoteric field. Perhaps in another lifetime we'll study astrology more deeply. There is so much to learn; fortunately, we have forever to do so.

Notice, however, that while the Death card is the 13th card in the Major Arcana of the tarot, it is not the final card in that sequence of twenty-two cards. Death, in that sense, as in life itself, is not the end. It is followed by Temperance, the fourteenth card, the card of Art and Alchemy and thus the card signifying the art of learning to live forever, to refine ours'elves by turning the base materials of our beings into the gold of enlightened and illuminated spirit and by doing so learning how to achieve the true powers that are our ultimate destiny through the balancing of our energies. Those magical powers live within us in potential in the form of the Divine Magic that abides within the Prima Materia of our energetic soulful spirits that is transformed into the Philosopher's Stone of exulted being. It is the alchemy of becoming immortal elven mages, which is to say wise and sagely elfin magicians, wizards and enchanters. Surely, this was the goal of the ancient Taoist alchemists and sages, to obtain immortality and the wisdom that leads to life eternal.

As we said, we might, as we have done, assign individual major arcana cards to the various stages of grieving and dealing with death and therefore the Death card would denote the process overall. If we accept that this is indeed the case, then the Moon card, number 18, with its otherworldly, psychic and mystic connotations, might represent the experience or process of the Between that most of us encounter, unless we are able to awaken and lucid dream during the Between stages in which case the Star card, number 17 of the major arcana, might symbolize that more conscious passage through the Between as well as the down pouring of light and energy into our lives by the Shining Ones.

As we have indicated, each card out of necessity has a variety of related meanings along a certain symbolic theme. It is the skill and adeptship of the individual reader that enables hir (him/her) to distinguish which meaning applies in a particular reading and thus to the person inquiring of the oracle, intuitively selecting the meaning that best fits the individual and their circumstances as presented by the cards.

Following this idea of the association of the major arcana cards with the processes of reincarnation we might, therefore, extend our thought to propose that the Sun card, number 19 of the major arcana, would be the card representing our rebirth into new body, born anew under the Sun.

Although the Fool card, which represented our acquiescence to the inevitability of death in the grieving process could also indicate our early, baby stages of a new incarnation. It seems to be no accident that it is part of the cycle of Nature that very old people, before they die, often become like little children and babies, wearing diapers, and needing to be changed and taken care of. Usually when you get to the point where you are so elderly that you do almost nothing but sleep, as newborns tend to do, it is time to wake up into a new life after passing through the stages (or the instinctual selection process) of the Between. But what is death really but a time of sleeping, resting and dreaming until one awakens again.

And once again, it is important to remember that there are various meanings to each particular tarot card and, out of necessity, variations on each of these symbolic ideas. So you need not take these particular musings of ours regarding the cards and their associations as any more than thoughts concerning the tarot and death and their symbolic connections and not as absolutes in any way. Still, think about it. Formulate your own understanding of life, the tarot (if you do it) and the processes of life.

The Spell:

The Death card falls and speaks to me
It mentions powers soon to be
Unleashed, empowered and set free
Across the ancient cosmic sea

Arvyndase:
Tae Fanth maka lotlu nar norlu va el
Ter bylthelu eldroli qun va te
Marhagïn, taeldro nar pånd alo
Wylyal tae elan ripatu oto

Pronunciation:

Tay Fay-n-th may - kay lote - lou nair nor - lou vah eel

Tier bill - thee - lou eel - drow - lie q-un vah tea

Mare - hag - in, tay - eel - drow nair pond a - low

Will - yale tay e - lane rye - pay - two oh - toe

༄

Chapter 14:
Tarot and The Last Judgment, Zombies, Revenants and Ghouls

istorically, the first tarot decks, as far as we can tell, originated in northern Italy during the late 14th or early 15th century and, due to the Christianity of that time and region, were deeply influenced by Christian ideas concerning the world and the Universe. Although, we might point out that the cards are often associated with Romani fortune tellers (or the slang word "Gypsy," so called because they were originally and wrongfully thought to have come to Britain from Egypt).

The Romani seem to have been an early Kali cult (that later devolved into the Thugees or stranglers of India, from which we get the word thug, meaning a potentially violent miscreant) that migrated from India into western Europe. Thus, the Romani often honor the Virgin Mary as Sara-la-Kali, the black virgin, who is the patron saint of the Romani. But whether the Romani brought some form of the tarot cards with them from India (which apparently got merged with a deck of playing cards) and started using them to read fortunes in Europe or merely picked up the tarot once they migrated into European continent, we don't know.

By the way, this practice of associating oneself and one's magic with the Ancient Egyptians is not simply something that the Romani did. For instance, in the book *Trolldom: Spells and Methods of the Norse Folk Magic Tradition* by Johannes Bjorn Gardback, the author speaks of Scandinavian folk hoodoo magic practitioners of a hundred or so years ago also making claim in their books to a connection to Egyptian magic. These days, however, with the resurgence of interest in Norse lore, people are more likely to associate their works with the Scandinavian Viking Culture of olde. But there was a time when if one wanted to add credence to their work and make it seem like a book with some esoteric authority, then one linked it to the ancient magic of the Egyptians.

For our own part, we Silver Elves started reading fortunes with a variation of a playing deck when we were as young as eight years old. We have on occasion used playing decks to do readings at social gatherings and parties, when a regular tarot deck wasn't available, but then we've even used *Magic the Gatherings* cards to do a reading for a young lad (who was getting the reading at the insistence of his parents) who collected those cards and for whom tarot cards where too strange and foreign seeming but the *Magic the Gathering* cards were perfect. We've often said that we could, in fact, use any deck for reading as long as we have some understanding of the symbology of the particular cards. For instance, while we can read a *Magic the Gathering* deck, we would be no good at reading baseball cards since we know near to nothing about baseball and its players, but if we did we could use those cards as well.

As is the case in Haiti and elsewhere, the practitioners of Voudon, variously named Vodou, Vodun or Voodoo, and other similar practices merged their African aboriginal magics with the Catholicism they encountered in the *New World* in the same way that the Romani integrated their beliefs with the dominant religion (Catholicism and then, after the Reformation, various Protestant sects) of Europe. Thus, the 20th card of the major arcana of the tarot is called the Last Judgment and this denotes the end of the world as prophesized in the New Testament, which according to Christian scripture has the Dead resurrecting, rising from their graves and walking the Earth again, where the rest of us apparently will be waiting with various sharp objects to stab them in their brains.

Of course, the idea of a last judgment in terms of an individual's life goes back at least as far as the ancient Egyptians, from whom Jewish folk got some of their religion, which, of course, the Christians then got from the Jewish by way of their favorite Jewish prophet, Jesus (sometimes the only Jewish person that they actually like, while they pretend he wasn't actually Jewish at all, or do their best to ignore this fact), whom they worship as the son of and, at the same time, as being God. Thus, the Christians say Amen at the end of their prayers, which is, of course, taken from Amen Ra (sometimes Amun, Amon, Ammun), the ancient Egyptian god of the sun, air and sky. And they say a prayer that goes *gives us this day our daily bread*, which is a variation of an Egyptian prayer that went *give us this day our daily onion.*

Ammon Ra is similar in that way, and perhaps a variation of Anu the divine personification of the sky, ruling as a supreme god, and thought to have been the ancestor of all the deities in the ancient Mesopotamian religion of the Babylonians,

Beyond Death.... 155

Sumerians and Akkadians, the lord of the Anunnaki and progenitor of the Tuatha De Danaan, one of the ancient tribes of the faerie folk of Ireland (see *Realm of the Ring Lords* by Laurence Gardner and *The Dragon Legacy* by Nicholas De Vere. Also, see these two authors for the connection between Jesus, Egypt and the ancient bloodline of the elves as popularized in *The Da Vinci Code* by Dan Brown).

The notion that Jesus is the son of God and is God the father at the same time seems a somewhat crazy idea on the surface, unless you consider that their god may be an amoeba that reproduced through binary fission and created a duplicate of itself. Are we all born of the Divine Magic replicating itself and individuating through experience? It seems so. Thus, we are all children of the gods.

The Egyptians believed, or at least their mythology proclaimed, that one's soul was weighed in what was called the rite of the heart, where one's heart after death is balanced on a scale against the feather of the goddess Maat, who symbolized order, truth, and fairness or justice and thus, in that sense, represents karma or the idea that everyone ultimately gets their just desserts, whatever that may be. And, therefore, through the balancing one's deeds in life against one's eternal ideals (which is to say one's internal destiny), one's place in the afterlife is revealed or if you believe in reincarnation, one's place in one's next life is delineated. We are ever moving toward the realization of our true s'elves. Note however, it was their heart that was weighed, symbolizing their true inner s'elf and intentions, not their brain, which would symbolize their minds and opinions, or their hands that would symbolize their actions.

But the Christian idea of the Last Judgment at the End of the World is not individual in nature as the Egyptian one is, so much as the Judgment for all people at the End of Time. Apparently, when the end times come (which the Norse called Ragnarök), according to the Christians the dead rise again, somewhat in the manner of the zombie apocalypse and they wander the Earth once more. This is more on the nature of assembly line final judgment with everyone alive being judged, more or less, at once or in quick succession. Whereas, all those who have previously died have apparently already met Saint Peter and God (in one of his three Christian forms—father, son or holy spirit ghost) and been judged prior to this time and so don't need to be judged again. But they believe that they will still rise from their graves (which is why Christians are often against cremation and like to seal their bodies in boxes so the worms don't eat them).

But perhaps, like the idea some fundamentalist Christians have that there will be a Rapture in which all faithful Christians who are currently living will be beamed up into heaven, leaving the rest of us (and their clothes apparently, which makes it sound like they are going to Elfin) to fight it out over everything (except their clothes, which are atrocious to our elven fashion sense), maybe, all the fanatical people, past and present, will become zombies suddenly, and all the rest of us will have to go around bonking them on the head to try to get them to use their brains again. After all, zombies are nearly always said to be seeking brains to consume, probably because their own don't work so well anymore. And in zombie shows, humanity is ever seeking the cure for the zombie apocalypse through scientific experimentation. Perhaps, therefore, reason, logic, data, facts and science are the cure for the zombie infection. Use your brain, don't believe things on faith without any facts or proof or reasoning at all or you might turn into a zombie. However, all teasing of the normal folk aside, the idea of the good folk rising from their graves and living in material bodies at the end of the world, is not all that different really than the idea of Elfin coming into material realization.

Why people don't go on living in heaven, in their heavenly bodies, or bodies of light, at this point, we don't know, but this notion, which can be found in various places in the Bible, surely points to the idea of reincarnation, if only, in this case, in one particular rebirth or reanimation, a final reincarnation, into an earthly paradise, at the end of the world. Or at least the end of the probationary period of the world, because after that everyone, by which we mean every spirit who has not been consigned to Hell, is thought by the fundamentalist Christians to return to live on Earth as a paradisiacal state. So, it seems that Christians do have a belief in reincarnation into physical bodies, only in a more limited fashion than we elves or the Buddhists and Hindus do. It is just one rebirth and into their same body revived and made whole, but it is a reincarnation in its way.

Yet, there is another idea that is attached to zombies and that is that the body has a sort of consciousness of its own that exists without the higher functions of the brain. This is often seen as the automatic reflex system that enables us to breathe or react to certain things, such as blinking our eyes when something comes near them without having to think about doing so. This is the sort of lifeforce and body consciousness that keeps our bodies going when we are in a coma and have no surface consciousness or awareness at all or when we are otherwise brain dead but still have a beating heart and are still breathing. This deeper body consciousness is also an extension of the basic animistic idea that all things have a life, a spirit and an energetic consciousness of their own. Every atom has its own life, and every electron, proton and neutron has a life within that life, just as we have our lives within the greater being of the Universe and are part of the life of the Earth itself.

Zombies, in a certain way, are like chickens' bodies that may run around after their heads have been chopped off, except, of course, if you chop off a zombie's head that is usually, but not always, the end of it. Sometimes, however, they just lay by the roadside opening and closing their mouths and blinking their eyes. You have to kill the brain, but apparently it is a brain run exclusively by the brainstem and a sort of damaged cerebellum, since the cerebellum regulates muscles, balance and coordination and while most zombies can stand and amble around, let's face it, zombies, for the most part, at not usually that good at walking. They often are presented as being like drunks toward the end of a night of binging as they stumble home. Or inebriated frat boys shambling back to their house from a sorority fling. Frat boys are also, apparently, often in need of some brains.

We might point out that the whole idea of zombies comes from a Caribbean Vodun notion concerning people who have been drugged, rendered somewhat brain dead, like people who have had a lobotomy, but can still carry out minor tasks (see the movie and the book *The Serpent and the Rainbow*. The movie is a highly fantasized extrapolation of the more anthropological and scholarly work of the Wade Davis book). Of course, in modern times, numerous people seem to quite willingly self-medicate themselves into various zombie-like states of being and if many politicians had their way, we'd all be brainless beings anyway, totally subservient to their wills and whims.

Still, this whole idea of zombies calls to mind that we are not our bodies. We inhabit our bodies and they do in some sense, through our particular genetic inheritance, give us certain powers, while also limiting us in various ways. But our bodies are composed of energies that are not us, merely that are under our control somewhat, for a brief period of time, like when we are in charge of a car that we are driving.

This should be clear to us since the cells in our bodies are replaced about every seven to ten years. You might say that our spirits are to our bodies what the Shining Ones are to us. These energies that compose our bodies are, in a sense, studying with us. They are citizens of the world of our energetic being. In time, they will each find their own realization of illuminated being. Are we then the cells in the bodies of the Shining Ones? And do we die in the course of time as their cells are replaced?

Revenants are said to be like ghostly corpses that have returned to life to haunt the living only in physical bodies rather than ethereal ones. The word revenant comes from the French and merely means 'returned'. It is possible that in the past people who were in a coma for a short time and thought to be dead would revive again and be thought of as revenants. In that sense, those beings whose bodies are reanimated at the end of the world in Christian myth, would technically be revenants and not zombies, for revenants are pretty much as they once were only alive again after death. It is rather like reincarnation only into the same, rather than a different, body and with one's mind and memories intact. (See the French movie and tv series *Les Revenants*, or *The Returned* in English, and the American version *Resurrection*, which, as often happens, is not as good, in our opinion, as the original that it is copying. Also see the Australian show *Glitch*, which are all about Revenants or the dead returning to their old bodies, rising from their graves but in a renewed form, vibrant and alive again without showing any signs or effects of the injuries or disease that killed them.)

We elves surely understand why people don't wish to die and why nearly everyone would desire to keep their bodies and the lives that they have currently, but having already moved into the nether worlds, why would one wish to return into one's old body when one can through reincarnation have a perfectly new and surely better one to inhabit rather than the refurbished old one? That's like getting retread tires, which we have done many times, but only because we couldn't afford new ones at that time.

At the same time, getting one's old body back renewed does bypass all the trials and tribulations of having to be a baby again and to grow up, go to school and deal with all that crap, including for many people, having their parents lord their authority over them until they're old enough to take care of themselves or old enough to get kicked out to manage and struggle on their own as soon as the parents can legally discard them.

However, if you have some mystical and magical control over the body, as a shape shifter does, you can reshape your body at will. So, it's not an entirely bad idea being born back into the same body if it is revived and vibrant again. Still, as we develop as spirits, we will certainly be able to create whatever bodies that we wish to live in, that look like the one we currently have or one that is better, one that is more resilient, better looking, so that is not all that different really. In time, we will be able to look like whatever we choose.

And this is what various otherkin understand and what *transkinder* (a word we Silver Elves coined to mean those otherkin who shape-shift kin type from lifetime-to -lifetime or in a particular lifetime) and also transgender people (who are also quite often elfae or otherkin folk) experience in their lives. Which is that our inner sense and feeling of ours'elves is more important in the long run than our outer appearance, that our soulful spirits are our true beings, and that we should strive to be whom we inwardly know ours'elves to be, not seek to conform to what those in the world outside us insist we should be due to their particular prejudices, religious notions and cultural and fashion based opinions.

And elfae folk understand further that in the course of time, as we seek to transform ours'elves, our outer form will accommodate itself to our will, magic and the power of our spirit. Currently, the means people have of transforming their bodies, such as elves having their ears made more pointed, is technological in nature (prosthetic ears) or surgical in nature (having plastic surgery on one's ears) for the most part, or simply putting on a pair of faerie wings as one would put on a hat or coat or wig. But as we develop as spirits, the technology we use to alter our bodies will be more esoteric than exoteric as currently is the case. We will wish our bodies to change and they shall.

Ghouls, on the other hand, are much more like zombies. The ghoul is seen as a demonic being of humanoid form. This tradition originates in pre-Islamic Arabian folklore. Such spirits are associated with graveyards and are said to consume human flesh, particularly the flesh of the dead. Although the idea of ghouls has been extended to anyone who has an abnormal fascination with death and dying. Are vultures then ghouls? Are ravens and crows, ghouls? Are the foxes and other creatures that eat the body of the dead after a battle, ghouls? Or are ghouls ghostly cannibals that eat the dead flesh of their own kind? And then, if certain ancients sacrificed other human beings to their gods, which we know some of them did, does that mean their gods were actually ghouls? And if we kill people in religious wars are we really sacrificing people to ghoulish gods?

Of course, one might say that since the gods are higher beings that they are not ghouls (if you think that ghouls have to be a form of cannibal) but then, if we are made in the image and likeness of god, as the Christians tell us, they would surely be ghouls according to the traditional definition. However, this idea of the food chain that Men suppose thems'elves to be on the top of, would seem to indicate that it is all right (as meat eaters would have us believe) to eat lower animals. This is also the idea that vampires are shown as holding, looking upon normal folk in the same way most people consider cattle. But that is also the attitude that the Nazis had toward the Jewish folk, the Romani people and others that they killed in their concentration camps and elsewhere. It is merely an extension of the notion that *might makes right* and it is okay to prey upon people or beings that are weaker than we currently are. It is the philosophy of dictators everywhere and throughout time and space.

In a sense, nearly all meat eaters are a form of ghouls. Most grocery (gross-ery?) stores have aisles filled with chopped up, dead and bloody meat wrapped in cellophane with various names that avoid reminding one that a steak is really just a part of a dead cow, or a pork chop comes from a murdered pig. Zombies, on the other hand, seem to crave living flesh and often stop eating as soon as the person dies. Perhaps Zombies are the connoisseurs of cannibals. They certainly like their meat rare and bloody.

On the other hand, in Christian tradition, Jesus is said to have told his disciplines to eat his body and drink his blood. That would seem to make his followers either vampires/blood drinkers, or ghouls, who are flesh eaters, or somehow both, perhaps zombies or cannibals. And when Christians go to their church services, the wine (for Catholics) or grape juice (for more puritan Protestants) are said by them to be mystically (or symbolically) transubstantiated into Jesus' actual blood; and the bread or wafers are transformed into his living body and then offered to the true devotees. Christianity, with its icons of Jesus hanging nailed to the cross and with the eating of his body and blood seems a rather ghoulish faith to us elves, at least in the more expansive definition of that term as having a morbid fixation with death.

Still, we should point out that some yogis make a practice of meditating in graveyards or cremation grounds, not only because it is usually quite quiet there but also because it brings to mind the transitory nature of the human body. And the sorcerers of the Carlos Castaneda/Don Juan tradition are told to keep Death ever near as an advisor so one judges one's actions and intentions in light of the inevitable death of one's body.

However, we should point out that at the Last Supper, Jesus didn't actually cut open his veins and pour his blood into his disciples' chalices, nor did he cut off pieces of his flesh and ask them to eat them. Rather, in the purity of the Christian myth it seems to be the inverse of the vampire and ghoul myths. Jesus isn't asking his followers to eat his actual physical body and drink his blood (as the fundamentalist Churches seem to tell us) but to consume his spiritual, mystical or energetic body, the essence of his being, not its material construction. What Jesus seems to suggest is that we imbibe the light of the spirit, the light of the Shining Ones, and become like them by doing so. What we would be consuming in that case would be Divinity made manifest through etheric light and thus we, ours'elves, would theoretically become more divine by doing so. And we might point out that Jesus is not a vampire or a ghoul (we saw a post recently on Facebook that indicated he was a Lich after he died). He doesn't prey upon those weaker than he but rather is said to sacrifice his own advanced being to uplift us all.

Just as the *I Ching* suggests we should study the words, wisdom and example of the sages and make them our own through our lives and behaviors. So to draw in the blood and body of beings of light is to consume and digest light and therefore, by doing so, increase the power of our own bodies of light. We are what we eat and when we consume light, we become illuminated; we become enlightened.

However, notice Robert A. Heinlein's novel *Stranger in a Strange Land* (a phrase that comes from the Wilhelm/Baynes translation of the *I Ching*) in which it is a custom of the inhabitants of the planet Mars for loved ones and friends to eat the actual bodies of those who have recently died. They were said to do this in a ritual that bears remarkable similarity to the rite of the Holy Communion of the Christian religious mythos.

The Spell:

I take it in
Make it my own
And thus my future
I do hone

Arvyndase:

El rud ter ver

Kord ter el'na os

Nar hern el'na lasel

El ba sherm

Pronunciation:

Eel rude tier veer

Cor tier eel'nah ohss

Nair hear-n eel'nah lay - seal

Eel bah sheer-m

꙳

Chapter 15:
Killing to Live, Vegetarianism

𝖀nless you are a vegetarian, you kill to live. As we said, we who aren't entirely vegetarian or vegan, are metaphorically a variety of vampire or ghoul, eating dead flesh and sometimes, if you like your steak rare, consuming blood. It is true that most of us don't drink the blood or eat the flesh of other human beings, which is an evolutionary step up from cannibalism to be sure, but cannibalism does still exist in the modern times. And while most folks would baulk at eating others of their kind, except in direst emergency (such as the 1972 plane crash in the Andes where the survivors ate those who had died in order to survive in the snowy mountains) and even then with great reluctance, many people somehow don't perceive that animals are also related to us and are living beings worthy of our respect and care, and are also on the evolutionary ladder of development, and have just as much right to live as we do. Some would deny that animals have souls (or spirits) at all and only have inferior intelligence and no real feeling but that is not an opinion we elves share. For based upon our observation of animals, they can be very clever and quite genuinely feeling beings.

Of course, some folks would say that we are doing the lower animals a favor by killing them and eating them, because they then have an opportunity to move up the scale of evolution, but if that is the case why are we not joyous when someone comes along and tries to kill us. Under such a philosophy you'd think such people would be happy to be murdered. Someone points a gun at them and they exclaim, "Thank the spirits, at last a chance to be promoted."

Killing creates karma, whether we do it ours'elves or we have others do it for us as when people buy their pork chops or chicken or beef at the store. It creates violence in the world for which we are responsible and accountable due to the fact that we are actively, even if second-handedly, participating in it.

This is part of the reason why so many of us are drawn back into this world over and over again, incarnation after incarnation, unable to ascend to the higher realms of manifestation because our karma weights us down. In taking part in the killing of this world, we become linked to the spirits here that we have killed and/or consumed, and become entangled in their lives and magic.

After all, we are what we eat. In killing beings and eating them, we become karmically attached to them. We owe them life energy. We become, in a sense, responsible for them and these connections extend from one life to another. And while some might theorize that they are raised up by being part of our lives we, in that case, must surely be lowered in some way in consuming them.

The sorcerers of the Don Juan/Carlos Castaneda tradition in Castaneda's various sorcery books and some of the books of those of his warriors' party (such as Florinda Donner) and others who follow that tradition say that having sex with someone creates an energy bond between the people involved, no matter how fleeting the relationship may have been, even if it was a one-night stand. Well, killing creates an even greater and more powerful bond between those involved and its connections last long beyond a particular lifetime.

Those sorcerers would say that we should be very careful of whom we make love with, yet we elves would say more importantly, be very careful of the violence you participate in. All interactions between people create energetic connections between them. This is similar in its way to Locard's Exchange Principle that holds that every time we come into contact with another person, place, or thing, we naturally engage in an exchange of physical materials. This principle is primarily used in crime scene investigation.

Here, we and the sorcerers of the Don Juan tradition have merely extended this concept of material contact and exchange to karmic and esoteric transactions. Every time we psychically and spiritually interact with people, an energetic exchange takes place. The wise know this and use it for inspiration, learning from every interaction and are thus uplifted thereby.

Some people, of course, are okay with living in a world where violence is taken for granted. Most people would simply ignore the notion that we become karmically responsible for those whose deaths we participate in and go on eating meat while creating a variety of excuses for doing so while at the same time pretending there is no karma attached to their actions at all. But some, as we say, have the courage to embrace the violence of the world and revel in it (as some of the Vikings and Celtic tribal folk did) and don't mind living in a world where war is a fact of life and we kill each other over and over again. Of course, even they are not always all that pleased by being killed, and surely even less fond, we expect, of dying of this or that disease. For, alas, sickness and disease are also part of the energy of living in this world in a violent way, especially when one is a meat eater.

Understand, we are not judging you for eating meat, if you are, in fact, a carnivore. We are in this world as well as everyone else, so we have our own karma that binds us here as well. We are all in this together. Our magics are tangled up with all the others that create the tapestry of this world. It is just that we are somewhat tired of all the violence in the world and thus we have, through the course of our elven lives, severely limited the amount of meat, fowl and fish that we eat, participating in the killing as little as possible and hopefully loosening the bonds of karma, at least a little bit for ours'elves.

Still, we Silver Elves are far from free of our responsibilities for the violence that exists in our spirits and that took place in our previous incarnations and even if we became vegans (and while we are primarily vegetarian, we are not vegans nor are we likely to be) in this life, we'd still have lifetimes yet to come when we will be making up for our karma of the past. As we say, killing creates karma that follows us from one life to another. All our actions are a magic that shapes our beings and our lives. All we do creates our future lives.

Of course, some folks, as we said, will make up this or that reason about why they can't be vegetarian, and that's okay as well and we do not dispute any true medical reasons one has for such a decision. However, some we've encountered in discussions about meat eating and vegetarianism on elfae forums were quite arrogant about their meat consumption, as though there is no price to pay for doing so at all and yet they would be the very ones who would insist with intense fervor that *there is always a price to pay* when it comes to magic; and life, at its very core and in its essence, is magic. No matter how dull and mundane this world may seem at times, this world is a product of magic. It is a spell cast by all of us, only botched together for the most part like a bunch of people all throwing paint on a canvas with a different vision of how the art will turn out and all hoping somehow that their vision will emerge and dominate all the others.

Again, we're not judging. We have our own karma to overcome and don't have time to spend worrying about what others will have to deal with through the course of their lives. But those individuals who embrace meat eating in their lives should realize that what they are saying by doing so is that they are okay with dying by violence, because that is the world they have bought into and contribute to through their own behavior. And if that's the world that they wish to live in, then fine, but we Silver Elves are endeavoring, through our lives and actions, to migrate to some parallel dimension that is somewhat less predatory. We are okay with using our bows and arrows only for target practice.

If we are ever to become truly immortal, like our elven kin of myth and legend who are the Shining Ones, we will have to stop consuming other creatures and refrain from violence except in s'elf defense. Deny this if you will, pretending otherwise, but that won't alter the violent nature of the world we live in nor free us from our responsibilities when we choose to take part in it.

If you are advanced enough as a spirit, certainly you can ascend to higher realms of manifestation, where the crude violence of this world does not exist but you can't do that if you actively participate in the killing that is so common and accepted in this world.

And even those who don't like the violence of this world often assume that war is inevitable. We've observed many of them declare that it is a part of Man's nature. We've even heard quite educated individuals with PhDs express this opinion and we suggested to them, quite politely, that they should think a bit more deeply.

Still, we have known vegans and vegetarians to be determined in their ideals to the point of incredible anger, fanaticism and potential violence. And in this case while they may not eat meat, they are also buying into and reinforcing the violent and aggressive and often intolerant nature of so many people in this world.

Fanaticism is the inclination of grimlins in the observation of the elven. Although, sometimes we call them grim-leans for it is not their ancestry or race we are wary of but their inclination to be so intolerant of anyone who disagrees with them. But, we are not judging them either, who are we to judge? We are merely observing and making note of what we've observed as good scientists should do. We note this reality without accepting it as inevitable.

In some ways, the whole story about Cain and Abel in the Old Testament or Hebrew Bible is about this very issue. Cain was a vegetarian (having descended from the trees as most evolved ape people did and inclined to eat fruits and vegetables) but Abel killed an animal and sacrificed it to his 'god', which his blood drinking, flesh eating, vampire ghoul djinn 'lord' found pleasing. So, Cain killed Abel for killing animals and then was banished and given the Mark of Cain, which protected him from being killed himself.

In other words, their djinn demi-god was saying that it is okay to kill and sacrifice (and we assume consume) animals, rather than just offering (or consuming) fruits and vegetables, but it was still not permitted to kill other human beings for sacrifice, or even to kill humans for killing other humans (as Cain did) and it is certainly not okay to be cannibals. This puts a curious twist to the fact that so many of those who say they are Christians in the modern world are so incredibly supportive to the point of fanaticism of Capital Punishment. They tell us one of the Commandments of their God is Thou Shall Not Kill but that doesn't seem to apply to people that they deem unworthy or especially sinful and curiously the death sentence is mostly given to those who have murdered others, which is exactly what their religion and the Bible story of Cain and Abel prohibits.

Of course, this Bible story is just a metaphor for living in the world, and thus what it tells us is that it is okay for people to kill animals and eat them but not to kill other human beings (or eat them). We elves, however, are still mostly inclined to be vegetarians since our Shining Ones live upon light or even more subtle energy and we seek to evolve to be more like them.

Again, we're not judging anyone. We're incarnated right here, too, because of our own karma. But we all should know that if we actively participate in the violence of the world by consuming the lives of other beings, even if we deem them lower beings, we should have no complaint to make when some being that is even higher up the food chain, such as the viruses are, comes along and consumes us. This is a fact of the life we have created through our own actions. If we wish to evolve beyond a world of disease, and the pecking order and the food chain, we also have to go beyond killing to live. And curiously, or perhaps logically, most of the viruses and pandemics that threaten the world seem to arise from our farming and consumption of various animals, often chickens, but others as well.

The curious thing about killing to live, that is to say consuming other creatures in order to survive in the world, is that it means we are also dying to live. Our actions, which in this case involve killing, make death inevitable. But that is a lesson we are still learning and in time we will surely master the art of living in this world without the violence and killing and then we will truly be on the path to immortality.

As we said in the previous chapters, the Shining Ones, and in Christian lore, Jesus (one of the Shining Ones in elven lore), pour light down upon us that uplifts and sustains us. In time, we will be able to live upon breath and water alone, like Airitarians or Breatharians, as some Christians saints were said to be able to do.

And as we proceed further on in evolution, we will not consume anything outwardly at all. Instead, we will consume the Divine Nectar, which some yogic meditation practices teach how to do. They say that it can be drawn down from the activated pineal gland through the practice of meditation and captured by turning one's tongue back and upward toward one's upper palate and tonsils, which in itself helps encourage the pineal gland to awaken and vibrate.

When we achieve that, which is the ability to draw down and live upon inner nectar, we will be totally s'elf sufficient in our physical form and will become, in a sense, like perpetual motion machines that live forever on our own energy without needing to take any in, while, at the same time, dispensing light unto the world without exhausting ours'elves thereby.

The Spell:

Dying to live
Living to die
Take just a moment
And ask yours'elf why?

Arvyndase:
Flidas va alsar
Alsardas va fli
Rud oda na onst
Nar qel le'naeln vas?

Pronunciation:
Fly - dace vah ale - sair
Ale - sair - dace vah fli
Rude oh - dah nah oh-n-st
Nair kweel lee'nah - eln vace?

❧

Chapter 16:
Amnesia, a New Beginning

One of the reasons people die, among the various other reasons previously mentioned, is that so many people are stuck on the idea that there is one truth and they, being the fortunate beings that they are, who are beloved by their particular demi-god and perhaps political party or people, are privy to what is really true and if everyone else would just agree with them (and do or act as they tell them to), the world would be a better place overall, except for those of different sexual orientation, religion, race or some other element that renders them undesirable, subhuman in their eyes and good only for serving as slaves in their opinion.

When we die and are reborn into new bodies, most of the surface memories we held previously are erased along with all our prejudices, opinions and various other temporary features of our ego and our cultural and ethnic beings. In being reborn, we have a new opportunity to begin again and perhaps do what we did previously a bit better in our new life (for as we said life recapitulates itself especially in one's first 28 or so years), otherwise, almost nothing would ever change in the world at all.

If we weren't reborn with a sort of amnesia, people would be born back into the world with the same hates, grievances and prejudices that they had in their previous incarnation and their individual petty vendettas and racial and religious prejudices would probably be carried on forever. Although, it is not impossible for people to change their views in a particular incarnation and to give up their prejudices, even if it is somewhat and unfortunately rare. We grip our opinions with fervor in part because we formed them in the first place, or accepted them from others, because we thought them to be right.

Still, as we said in another chapter, we tend to be attracted back to the people and places that we know and thus we sometimes become re-enculturated into notions we held before in our previous incarnation because of our karmic link to certain peoples, places on the Earth and perhaps ideas that we held so fervently in our previous incarnation. We might not remember them exactly in our minds but we are still attracted to them in our spirits. There is still something we have to work out in regards to those notions and those people.

However, it is also the case that our prejudices, while they seem specific, are not always so. White people who hate Black people, or fascists who hate Jewish people are sometimes returned with their tendency to hate, but not always returned to the same group or family they were in previously. This is to say that their inclination or habituation to hate is carried over into the next life but the specifics of the hate are not. So, it is that White people who hate Black people are sometimes reborn into Black genetic bodies and vice versa and people who hate gays are born into bodies that are attracted to the same gender. This is because hate, like violence and sex, creates a bond between people that has to be worked out through the series of one's incarnations. And, let's face it, a lot of people who proclaim their hate for gay people have latent gay inner desires they are covering up for fear of being social outcasts if they should come out and live as freely as they might desire. In a certain sense, we are all learning to love ours'elves, only the definition of ours'elves is much vaster than we usually imagine it to be.

Momondo – The DNA Journey — was a genetic study done some years ago shown on a video where people's DNA was tested to see from what peoples and areas of the globe they were descended. Before their inner cheeks were swabbed and tested for its DNA, the researchers asked the individuals if there was any particular group of people that they especially hated or disliked. One person, who was British hated Germans, another who was of Turkish descent hated the Armenians (or maybe vice versa, we don't entirely remember), however, in nearly every case where a person declared a noted dislike for another racial or ethnic group, it turned out after their lineage was discovered through the DNA testing that they were, in part, descended from those very people. In a certain sense, they were hating a part of themselves. And when we consider that all humans are genetically connected, all hate really is self-hate, or maybe s'elf hate, because those they hate are nearly always pictured as the unworthy outsiders, the strange ones and as those who are not really normal, and we elves are always the eccentric, strange, weird ones and we are never really normal. Nor do we wish to be.

Most squabbles in the world are really among family members or people who are actually very much alike as much as they may think themselves completely different, even opposite, from each other. After all, the Hebrews and the Arabs are both Semitic peoples (as are the ancient Akkadians, Canaanites, some Ethiopians [perhaps because of the connection between King Solomon and the Queen of Sheba], and Aramaeans). The conflict between Arabs, the Jewish and Palestinians is essentially a family dispute. In fact, since human beings for the most part are all genetically related, all our wars are actually family conflicts. But then there is seldom anything quite so bitter and hateful as lovers who have broken up or parents who are in the process of getting a divorce and fighting over who gets the children and the house.

We elves, therefore, seek in each life to rid ours'elves of prejudice. Prejudice is prejudgment, and without facts and accurate data such notions are merely obscurations of reason, logic and clear and independent thinking. While we are surely a magical and mystical folk, we are also very scientifically minded. Our magic is based upon what we know and have discovered about Nature, our own and the world around us, through observation and experimentation. We seek to experience the world and the Universe purely, without assumptions, so we may discover what is actually true within ours'elves and the world. After all, as they say in the military *Assume makes an Ass out of You and Me.*

The Spell:

I start again
With open mind
Embrace the truth
That I do find

Arvyndase:
El altu sasnana
Ena caro car
Byrha tae lodver
Dij El ba låc

Pronunciation:
Eel ale - two sayce - nay - nah
E - nah car - row car
Ber - hah tay load - veer
Dye-j Eel bah lock

Chapter 17: Faerie and the Nether-realms

The Faerie realms are often imagined to be much like the nether-realms of the Between, also known as Death or the Deadlands. After all, our powers in the Between are very similar to those said to be possessed by the elfae in various tales and stories in the same way that they can be similar to our dreams where we are able to fly or do things we couldn't normally do. And fae bodies in faerie stories are often viewed as being ethereal and ghost-like.

Of course, one of the things that makes Tolkien's works so popular among we elfae folk existing in this world in modern times is that Tolkien's elves are imagined to be in more material bodies, as ours are, and thus take us a step deeper into the material realm than the tales of those more ephemeral elves usually do. It is somewhat difficult to embrace one's elven s'elf, if the dominant belief is that elves can only be ethereal beings (or non-existent entirely), and yet, at the same time, the spiritualization of our beings (and the increase in the power of our spirits) is precisely why we are here upon the material planes. We might look at the various realms as being separate but they are all connected.

And Tolkien's elves are experienced by other characters in his books as physical beings, as we elves in the modern world are materialized and physically manifesting elfin spirits, not as ethereal beings who can only be seen by those with *The Sight* as is the case in much elvish lore. Tolkien's elves, however, are accepted unquestioningly as being elves by the various other characters in his stories, while our elven identity is often regarded with scorn and skepticism by the general public around us.

This lack of acceptance for our chosen identity is also the case for many transgender people in the world but then many of them are fae folk as well. We may not be accepted by many others as being elves in this world but Tolkien's description of us as material beings is quite helpful in our own understanding of ours'elves in this way and our sense of s'elf validation and acceptance of our elfin nature. And in the long run, this s'elf acceptance is the key to other acceptance, although that is not to say that everyone will accept us for who we are, but some will and do and that is enough to go forward. For a more modern version of elves living as materialized beings in the world see Freda Warrington's novel *Elfland*, although in that book, she refers to us as Aetherials, which makes an interesting link between these forms.

As we say, the physicalized elves of Tolkien stand in contrast to most stories where the fae are etheric beings that a person can only see with their otherworldly or psychic sight and where, according to some of the lore, a normal person will be rendered blind by we fae in the eye that the seer uses to view us (see *Fairy Faith in the Celtic Countries* by Evan-Wentz.). Like the idea concerning some ghosts, these etheric elves can affect the world and those in it while not being entirely of this world.

Tolkien's image of elves on the other hand supports the idea of the manifestation of we elven here upon Earth (or Middle-earth, according to the ancient Norse) as being more genuinely possible in a physical way. Laurence Gardner in *The Realm of the Ring Lords* and Nicholas De Vere in *The Dragon Legacy* do the same thing in their non-fiction works, giving historic credence to our culture extending back at least as far as the Scythians, as does Lady Gregory's book *Irish Myths and Legends*. Tolkien makes elves, real in the sense that most people in the world define reality. We can be seen by everyone, but then only those with The Sight, (or an open mind) will actually realize that we are elves.

And we Silver Elves, and others of our elfae kindred, make this manifestation of elfin being actual in our own lives through our enchantments, actions and lifestyle. We live *The Elven Way* (see our book of that title for the magical and spiritual philosophy of the elven). We are not merely cosplaying elves or engaging in pretend scenarios about our elven s'elves, as children might do, but making our elven lives and beings actual through our lives and lifestyle. And yet, we are not opposed to cosplaying elves or pretending we are pretending to be elves at times in circumstances when to do otherwise might endanger us. Sometimes, it's easier to just pretend, as we do when we pretend to be normal, more or less, as is the case when we have to deal with the various bureaucracies in the world. As the olde saying goes, it is best to let sleeping dogs lie.

However, in the Between, after we have abandoned (or been kicked out of, usually) a particular body, we return to our more ethereal natures and to the purity of our spirits. Here we are not using purity in the sense of being clean or spiritually pure in a rather puritanical way, as most people might use that term, but in the sense of being genuinely ours'elves, shorn of enculturation.

The difference, however, between most people travelling through the Between and the more ethereal elfae folk who might be imagined to reside there, is that most of us pass through those planes in a sort of dreamlike and only partially conscious fashion, whereas the elfae that are thought to exist there, like the Shining Ones on their plane of being, would be more fully conscious in the way we are in this world only more so, conscious in the way that most yogis would use this concept. Or as the elfae hippie folk of the sixties indicated when they urged people to *Expand Their Consciousness*, and thereby awaken to a greater realization of the nature of the Universe and of Life.

And while dying might thus be supposed to open the portal to Faerie for most of us, the vast majority of individuals passing through the Between realms can only glimpse those realms briefly and then return to the Earth plane having no choice but to do so, drawn here by our own karma and desires, and into a new incarnation with little in the way of memory of those realms and only a vague sense of ever having been there in the first place.

Like waking up from a dream into the rush of a busy morning, in our new incarnation we quickly forget most of the dreams we had in the Between as we are overwhelmed by the immensity of all that confronts us in this world and its demands and as the chitta, or mind stuff, the constant yammering of our thoughts, compete for our attention drawing us back into the web of illusion, into the glamourye of the world and the magics we have cast upon ours'elves and each other.

So, it is that the dreams and experiences of the Between quickly fade from our memories for most of us, becoming but vague impressions of another world, except sometimes for a sense of déjà vu for particular events or people that seem familiar to us because we've been through it all before, or something similar, or we were involved with them in a previous incarnation or they remind us of someone we knew in our previous lives.

In some faerie lore, especially ancient Irish tales, the Sidhe, Tuatha de Danaan or fae folk were said to have been driven underground in accordance with an agreement after a war between them and the Sons of Mil, who were a Celtic tribal folk who migrated from Europe at a later date than the Sidhe folk. In this truce settlement, Ireland was divided in two between the Fae and Mankind, as represented by the Milesians, but the Sons of Mil got first choice and used a loophole and chose the surface of the island so that the fae folk were then forced to live underground. (Note in Lady Gregory's *Irish Myths and Legends* the Sidhe/fae retreated into secret valleys and hidden realms much like the elves in Tolkien's stories.)

Curiously, in most faerie tales, it is generally the fae who are said to be tricky in their agreements and negotiations (as is the case in Susanna Clarke's novel *Jonathan Strange and Mr. Norrell*), but that may just be the projection of Men casting their nefarious and untrustworthy natures onto others (we elfae in this case), as so often happens in the world. We are currently observing politicians do this sort of projection of their faults and misdeeds on to others upon a daily basis.

Now, when it is said that the Fae folk were forced to live underground, this is usually taken in a literal sense, as the fair folk living in mounds or barrows beneath the earth. You can still find mounds in Ireland where the faerie folk are said to reside. Although, as we pointed out in another of our books (*Liber Aelf*), this could also be taken in the sense that underground is used to mean things that are hidden from the general public or unknown to them, often because of a lack of interest or a reaction to their prejudices and judgments, such as underground music and so forth and we modern elfae people are, for the most part, even when we are fairly open about our true elfae natures, an underground phenomenon. We are, in that way, rather like the *Rocky Horror Picture Show*. We are a sort of cult favorite (at least among ours'elves) without actually being a cult. Rather like the goth or emo folk in that way, whom we, for our part, see as being mostly pixie folk anyway.

However, note that the early Christians in Rome, due to persecution, often held their meetings in underground catacombs, which were manmade caverns used as cemeteries composed of a subterranean gallery where the bones of the dead were kept. Thus, the Christians were an underground folk at that time, meeting in secret in graveyards beneath the earth. Note further the association between the underworld, or the world of the dead with caverns, caves and other underground realms, including mounds and barrows, where the ancients often buried their dead, and with the realms of the dead of the Greeks and other ancient peoples.

Therefore, it is possible that in compelling the fae to accept the underground half of Ireland, the Sons of Mil were in fact saying they would hound them unto death and out of material existence and we elfae have certainly felt persecuted in the world and our worldly culture diminished (as well as our physical size in much lore till we are seen as but tiny little fairies [see *Cornish Fairies* by Robert Hunt]. Again, thank you, Tolkien for making us authentically sized, again. Our forests and homelands were taken from us by conquest and our ethnic culture is ridiculed even today but you helped us understand who we truly are.)

From that connection between the Fae, the underworld and death, we might surmise that the association between Fae folk and the Between worlds is no mere accident. And there is a sense we modern elfae have that, given the chance, many of the normal folk would gladly persecute us out of existence as they seek to do to others who are different from them due to race, religion, sexual orientation or some other arbitrary feature of their lives. Many aboriginal peoples have faced attempts at genocide upon them through history, and in modern times the Romany, Jewish people, and the First Nations Peoples of the Americas have faced near extinction due to persecution, and we elves are no exception in that way. Our ancient peoples and culture were hounded to the point that few people believe we ever even existed not to mention their disbelief in the fact that we still exist to this day.

And yet, like it or not, we elfae folk have a relationship with Mankind, the Sons of Mil and other clans of Men, and with this planet Earth we share and we cannot help but return here again and again. And if we can't do that in elfin bodies with pointed ears or in faerie bodies with wings or as otherkin with horns or antlers or whatever, we will do it as elfin spirits born among them as their own children appearing to be physically like them but actually being, within ours'elves, spiritually, dispositionally and psychically quite different.

Beyond Death.... 185

Because of that, we often find our own kindred hidden among them, enculturated to think that they are of Mankind when, in fact, they are really our very own folk as yet unawakened. Thus, we Silver Elves do not judge who is elfin or not, we let each individual tell us what they truly are, based upon their own inner feelings, whether they be elves, faeries or whatever they may be. For being elfin is ultimately a choice, a choice of magic. Although, some fae individuals would say they have no choice but to be elfin, which is to say really that ultimately we have no choice but to be who we truly are. And that is also true.

There is karma that attaches us or binds us to material existence, and thus makes it impossible for us to permanently abide in the nether realms of the Between, but there is also destiny for us here, as well as a duty. Whatever our karma might be, ultimately it is really only the challenges we face in fulfilling our destiny. Our purpose here is to manifest Elfin; and karma is merely the knots in a tangled weave of magic that we need to unravel so our magic will flow freely and unobstructed again.

Some people think that entry into Elfin is some gift that is bestowed upon us as though we could pray to some Deity (perhaps one of the Valar of Tolkien's lore) and they would grant us the power to enter Elfin. But in reality, the ability to venture into and stay in Elfin is something we must earn, that we must develop within our own s'elves and beings. It is a skill, like painting or playing an instrument or even lifting weights, and it is a power that we develop within ours'elves that becomes better and stronger with practice. Crowley advised us to invoke often, we elves say exercise your powers regularly, ever seeking to improve them.

There are those that when talking about talented individuals say that they have a *god given gift*. But from the point of view of the elves, the Divine Magic exists in potential in all things, and god given gifts are but skill, powers and abilities we have developed through the lifetimes. If a person doesn't believe in reincarnation, such powers would have to be explained somehow, and so they are seen as a gift from their particular god (why that god didn't give gifts that are just as good to everyone, we don't know) but when one considers evolutionary development of both a physical and spiritual variety, it becomes clear that all these things are progressive accomplishments from our previous incarnations.

This power is not something we can develop in the Between because at first, at least, we are just floating down the river Styx, often laid back with one of our hands dangling in the waters of that dark stream while otherworldly music washes away our cares and memories. In the same way that we can't really learn to drive a car by riding in the backseat all our lives (although some folks seem to think they can drive perfectly that way, and spirit know they have caused more than one accident thereby), we can't develop our magical powers and abilities to ascend to the more subtle but expansive realms, to spread out into the greater Universe you might say, without the challenges that confront us in this material world.

That is the meaning and purpose of the obstacles and problems we face here. The Between is the place of transition, not a realm of individual development. That is where our spirits choose instinctively where our next incarnation will take place, in this world or another, based upon the reality of our individual being.

Of course, those who awaken in the Between and lucid dream in that realm may be able to ascend from the Between to higher realms, realizing that the Between is merely a projection of their minds and inner beings, but they will find in doing so that they have merely entered a new plane of being that has its own challenges.

It is like graduating from high school and going to college or leaving school altogether and entering the working world. Every realm has its obstacles and challenges to overcome and abilities and powers to learn, develop and each offers us an opportunity to obtain even greater mastery. And the idea that someday we will go to heaven or paradise and that everything will be wonderful forever after is such a lovely thought, but life and learning go on forever, even in Elfin.

And perhaps the time will come when we are all powerful and knowing and can live forever in the realms of our own creation but most likely we'd get bored in time, which is, perhaps, what led us here in the first place where we cast a spell of forgetfulness upon ours'elves so we no longer remember who we truly are and can experience this realm fully. In a certain way, it is like being drawn into a great book or movie, only much better for this is a virtual reality movie and it all seems so real.

However, if we relate the Faerie realms to the Between and look upon Fae folk as being ephemeral beings then we would have to face the fact that Elfae folk of that sort are essentially a classier and probably better dressed sort of ghost, and that all ghosts, ghouls, and other such creatures are denizens of Faerie and are therefore a form of faerie folk. However, that would also mean that men and the normal folk, after they died and passed into the states of the Between, would be, at least for a while, traveling through Faerie and would be somewhat Fae touched when they returned to the world in a new incarnation. This might help explain why very young children are the way most of them tend to be, which is to say, simply enchanting, magical and marvelous before they have the wonder droned out of them. Perhaps, this also explains the appeal of kittens and puppies, they still have the magic of Faerie in them.

No one stays in the Between permanently. It would be like living on a staircase. It is a state of transition. It is not really a state of permanent being. There we glimpse the possibilities of our spirit but soon we either graduate to higher or more subtle realms of being or return to the Earth to try again. But, whether we ascend, descend or return to where we were (or maybe shift sideways to a parallel dimension), it is all part of one eternal journey. At the end of that journey, which truly has no end, is the continual fulfillment of our destiny in motion, which is to say the unceasing evolution of our spirits. This really is the Never-Ending Story.

However, it is in returning to the Earth that we are afforded an opportunity to develop and improve ours'elves. We can't really do that in the Between as there is no friction there. The Earth plane provides us with the traction, you might say, to move and particularly to act with intention. In a world like the Between where we seem all powerful, as we can be in our own minds and imaginations, there is nothing more to achieve save to move higher where we will face new obstacles and learn even more. Or move sideways, as we said, which is to develop skills that we haven't mastered already on the same plane of being (sort of spiritual cross training or like musicians who master more than one instrument).

It is true that in certain senses the subtler planes of being have some similarity to the Earth, but only because they are even more prone to the power of our minds and fantasies; and whatever we think, and often what we are habituated to think and expect, manifests. However, in realizing this we understand the illusionary nature of all existence and thus we learn to *Be Conscious* in a sentient way while realizing the world we live in is one that we have created. In doing that, we will eventually create Elfin in its immortal form, which already exists due to the minds of our beloved elven Shining Ones, who evolved before us and left a trail of light for us to follow and gifted us with tales based upon their lives and being. Illuminated bread crumbs leading us to Elfin.

As much as it seems that this material world is dominated by technology, it is actually our inner powers that we will ultimately learn to develop here and which are required for entry into the more ethereal (yet still physical, as fire and air are physical) dimensions. Our psychic powers, our magical abilities, our ability to reason, to use logic and our skills at expressing ours'elves masterfully and becoming adepts in our own powers of feeling expression are all to be developed here. Here is where we increase our powers of enchantment.

True mastery and adeptship in these magical arts may still be far off for most of us; however, the rudiments of such powers exist for many folks already. It is just a matter of practicing them, improving them through practice and letting them develop and increase by doing so. Exercise your powers so they will grow stronger.

The whole idea of AI, artificial intelligence, and all the movies that are made about the dangers of robots and computers learning to think for themselves and taking over the world, is in its way, just a reminder that we need to develop ours'elves and our inner beings and powers and not just rely upon technology to make our lives better. The greatest danger, however, doesn't seem to be that technology will take over but that it will all collapse around us leaving us to fend for ours'elves as we did in more primitive times. But, then, we have those movies, too.

In a certain sense, this divide between technologically dependent and naturally empowered people, which is to say the difference being powers that we might have that are ours due to technology and those that are inherent within us, can also be seen on a more esoteric level concerning magic. All magical powers that are derived from the outside, from some enchanted object, are a sort of technological magic. Lamps that have genies in them, seven league boots, enchanted swords, magical keys, wardrobes to other worlds, magical rings, all lend power to the possessor, but the individual doesn't have these powers without having the object. The object is a piece of technology, like a car or telephone, that the magician (or a quite ordinary person) can use to accomplish certain things. It grants them power temporarily.

On the other hand, natural powers, such as the ability to play the piano or being a genius at math, come from within us and when our magical powers also stem from our inner being, such as psychic and intuitive perception, without assistance from a magical object, then that is truly our own and it is what we ultimately seek to achieve as spirits. For unlike technological magic, these powers cannot be taken from us and we carry them from incarnation to incarnation.

Of course, you might say that some magical objects merely enhance our natural abilities. In the same way that we have the power to walk or run but a bicycle enables us to travel more quickly. So, we might say a crystal ball or scrying mirror helps a seer to envision and that is surely true as well.

We are not against technological magic, understand, simply pointing out the difference and noting that in time our spirits will be able to do, without the aid of enchanted objects, what we now may need assistance in achieving. The development of these powers, however, may take numerous incarnations, and a great deal of practice to achieve. But that's what we are here for, isn't it?

The Spell:

Faerie calls beyond the grave
And says that all is well
Secrets yet will be revealed
That whispered we will tell

Arvyndase:
Farri koarlu hyrlon tae barod
Nar deslu dij wyl da darl
Marynli nov yon te sotosïn
Dij sushïn eli yon fram

Pronunciation:
Fair - rye co - air - lu her - lone tay bay road
Nair deesce - lou dye-j will dah dare-l
May - ren - lie no-v yone tea so - toas [like toast without the 't']
- in
Dye-j sue-sh - in e - lie yone frame

Chapter 18:
Fae Descent into Matter

To learn to fly, a young bird is pushed (or falls) out of its nest and hurtles toward the ground. All of us on Earth, on this material plane, are learning to fly. Like the little bird, we need to go down first (into the material plane) in order to learn we have the power to go up. We need the air from our wings to push against for us to obtain lift. In accepting this magical dream as reality, we are able to weave our way through the world and develop our powers of mind, our feelings and our various psychic abilities that are the basis of our magical powers. The magicians speak of Will, the sorcerers talk about Intent, we elven enchanters speak of the magical Wish but all of these indicate the inner power of our spirits to manifest through our souls (our link to all things beyond us) into the world and obtain what it is that we truly desire, which is to create our own lives in accordance and harmony with our individual and collective Vision and to manifest Elfin, Faerie or Paradise, if you will, upon the Earth.

In merging their Fairy Faith with Christianity, the ancient Irish often said that we Fae Folk were fallen angels that weren't really bad enough for hell but not quite good enough for heaven either (again, see *Fairy Faith in the Celtic Countries* by Evan-Wentz), which rather suits the feelings of most elfae folk in the modern world, anyway. And again, this makes those sort of fae seem rather ghost-like, not quite like the more materialized denizens of Earth, as we are, but not quite of the land of the spectral dead, either, more like smoke or mist or clouds formed into images.

However, the heaven of most religions doesn't really appeal to most of us who are elfae and we'd rather not abide in the torturous realms of hell, surely (which is not entirely unlike the Unseelie realms as far as we are concerned, nor utterly different from living in a world dominated by Men [except that the Unseelie often dress much better] with their penchant for bullying, dominating each other and their assumption that war is inevitable and part of Man's inherent nature and we must be cruel to our children in order to toughen them up for the hard, cold world [a basic grimlean philosophy]).

Rather, we would prefer to live in a world where we may exercise our magical powers to create a better world for everyone while fully developing within our own elfae beings. That seems like the right place for us to be. It is surely in harmony with our own soulful spirits for we have embraced the notion of evolutionary development and seek to foster our own advancement as best we may in every aspect of our lives and individual beings, while endeavoring in as much as we can and in as much as others will allow us to do so, to assist them to do the same.

As it is, we are sharing this world with Mankind, although many of us elfae and otherkin folk wish that we weren't, which we expect is something we have in common with most of Mankind as well. For most would rather not have us in their world either and like to pretend that we don't even exist and never did except in fantasy stories and ancient faerie lore, which they see as the superstitious beliefs of their ancestors prior to the discovery of science or the acceptance and revelation of their particular religious cult.

We elves, for the most part, would like to pretend Mankind doesn't exist either but their presence on the Earth and their devastating effect upon Nature are impossible for us to ignore or deny. Those who ignore the facts are doomed to suffer from them. Although, alas, those who accept the facts of our current reality may suffer as well for ours are not the only powers, nor the only magic, that affects this world, and we elves have primarily enchantment, persuasion, logic, facts and reason, as our only real means of affecting Mankind and they have, for the most part, vaccinated themselves with cruelty and prejudice against us.

Sometimes when we seek to tell some Men of the true nature of the Universe, they stick their fingers in their ears and make gibbering noises to drown out the truth they do not wish to hear. Honestly, we are just glad that they don't usually throw their feces at us, although they have been known to leave it on the doorstep of those they hate, do not like or those of whom they disapprove.

And yet, we are here with Mankind, in humanoid bodies similar to their own. However, we are quite different in many ways from many of them. Not so much physically different, but different in mind, attitude, feeling and expression and different in our inner sense of ours'elves. And we know within ours'elves that we are Other (and they sense it also) and we come to embrace that reality with joyous abandon and to revel in the fact that we are not normal folk.

You could say that we are old souls, and they are, for the most part, much younger, although we elves would say we are old spirits, for our souls are ever young. We are like elder brothers and sisters to Mankind, and like so many folk who are quite a bit younger than their siblings, they haven't experienced enough yet to heed our warnings or advice and are determined, as the young so often are, to learn it all for themselves the hard way.

Surely some, perhaps many of us elfae, tried to fit into normal society for a while, usually when we were younger, but we never were able to quite do it to the normal folk's satisfaction. We are never quite good enough for them, but then almost no one is. They spend most of their time trying to one-up each other and are ever critical of those around them, even their closest friends, relatives, neighbors and acquaintances. They may not be great musicians, athletes, writers, dancers or actors, but they will surely become great critics someday if the amount of effort they put into that is any indication.

And we are continually aware that there is something unique about us, something alien, that they find strange and off-putting but that we, for our own s'elves, revel in. We Silver Elves have long since given up trying to be like Men, although we are surely willing to get along with them, to live and let live, if they would afford us the same courtesy. But our eldritch natures make them feel a bit uncomfortable when we are near them and when they get a sense of us and who we truly are. Of course, part of that is merely a function of their own paranoia. They tend to be xenophobic. Everything different makes them feel uneasy, especially if they can't fit it conveniently into this or that category, and we are a mystery to them and in many ways to our own s'elves. Still, we do our best to soothe the normal folk when we are able to do so, or avoid them for their own comfort and our safety, when we can't.

Man's own preternatural instincts, which they do their best to ignore and deny, tell them that there is something truly strange and otherworldly about us, something just not quite normal, and it can make the small hairs stand up on the back of their necks. Although, for the most part, the only thing our presence actually threatens to do to them in reality, besides arousing their paranoias, is open their minds. And if that should happen, then possibly their hearts would flower as well. But we will have to develop our own powers of enchantment to a much greater degree before we will be able to affect the most fanatical among them. And quite often those fanatical men are not Men at all, really, but grimlins who have long since given up their own cultural identity to make their way through the world of Man and seek to dominate it and Mankind by pretending they are of them.

This is a physical world, to be sure, where technology often rules, but it is not really technology that we are here to achieve, except as it manifests as a reflection of our minds and inner beings and as a preview of the powers we will naturally obtain. We are not here merely to build up our muscles and create healthy bodies, although that is important as well, but here to develop our maturity of feeling, our powers of enchantment in expressing ours'elves, our will power, our intellect and our capacity and power to reason and in many ways, our ability to cooperate with each other willingly to create a more elfin world together. And, of course, the powers of our personalities, which are the charms and spells of enchantment.

That is perhaps the most important aspect of creating Elfin. What our sisters of the Elf Queen's Daughters would call being On the Wing and Flying Together, like a flock of birds, or faeries, or perhaps elves in our vortexes (or vortices, take your pick) soaring on the astral planes and united in our devotion to creating our Visions of Faerie and Elfin within the manifest reality of the material world.

And although we have descended into the material plane, we are not simply physical beings. Our inner world is as important as our corporeal world, if not more so. And it is by mastering our inner beings that we ultimately come to master the world around us or at least our reactions to that world. How we feel about the world and about our lives and how we choose to react to it determines our inner world. It is the realm where happiness is truly created and from which success ultimately springs.

The normal folk would lead us to believe that happiness is a result of success in the world, but how many rich and successful people are really happy? They might feel successful in a worldly way. They may feel important and privileged due to their wealth. They may feel superior to others because of their arbitrary social positions that wealth lends them. But are they actually happy? That is truly questionable. Not that poverty makes people leap for joy, either, or makes them necessarily better or more evolved spirits. So, we are not saying that material success is utterly unimportant, simply that it is not, in and of itself, the key to happiness.

Our ability to create happiness within ours'elves enhances our ability to interact with others successfully and from that master the material world through the powers of enchantment. It is the key to true success in the world, which is to say through our lifetimes in the Universe. Stress wears our bodies down, happiness fills our bodies with energy. Let your spirit rejoice, beloved kindred, we are creating Elfin together and it is and will be wondrous.

The psychologist Howard Gardner proposed that intelligence comes in many types not just as mental or intellectual acuity. He proposed eight styles or aspects of intelligence that centered on 1.) **musical-rhythmic intelligence**, which obviously most musicians have, some being geniuses in this regard; 2.) **visual-spatial intelligence**, which women in general seem to be better at than men; 3.) verbal-linguistic intelligence, our ability to communicate effectively with each other; 4.) **logical-mathematical intelligence**, which might need to be split into logical intelligence and mathematical intelligence because one of us Silver Elves is very strong on logic but not so much math oriented, while another is good at math but could use a bit of development in the area of logic; 5.) **bodily-kinesthetic intelligence**, generally shown by athletes, such as Legolas and the elven character Peter Jackson created for the *Hobbit* movies, Tauriel, or in the materially manifest world Bruce Lee, who could have been said to have had genius level bodily-kinesthetic intelligence; 6.) **interpersonal intelligence**, rather like verbal linguistic intelligence, really, but perhaps with the expression of feelings added, thus again something women tend to have mastered better than most men, and added to that the ability and the power to truly understand others (what we Silver Elves call knowing the person's True Name); 7.) **intrapersonal intelligence**, knowing ours'elves and the inner world from whence our great magical powers of spirit emerge (see the book *Increasing Intuitional Intelligence* by Martha Char Love and Robert W. Sterling); and 8.) **naturalistic intelligence**, an awareness and attunement to Nature, which is a very elven sort of intelligence and is really the intelligence that most animals have in abundance and would probably be an intelligence, among others, accorded to Robin Hood and his Merry (elfin) Men (elves?). We are here to master all these aspects of our being, although not necessarily in the same degree and surely not all in one particular incarnation.

We Silver Elves might add **psychic and magical intelligence** to these eight types, although that may come under intrapersonal intelligence and interpersonal intelligence expressed on a more esoteric level of functioning. We are in these incarnations to develop ours'elves as fully and completely as we can, on all levels of our being as best we are able at any particular time or in any particular incarnation. And these skills are carried with us from one incarnation to another. They say you can't take it with you, meaning mostly money and material goods, but you can take the ability to obtain money, or artistic, musical or other skills, for it becomes a part of your being. And we do this by making these powers natural for us, making them an essential part of our soulful spirit.

Someday, as we advance as a people, most of us will be on the level of geniuses as delineated currently on the Earth as having an IQ of 160 or above. Of course, at that time of future evolution, an IQ of 160 to 200 will merely indicate people with average intelligence. The genius level at that point will be having an IQ of 200 or beyond. And, at the same time, average life expectancy in an incarnate body will go from about 70 to 90 years or so to 120 to 150+ years of age, with a 90 year old person being rather like a 40 or 50 year old currently in terms of their physical shape and health. 90 will be the new 40 as they might say. And certainly, we will evolve even further.

This is the purpose of having heroes both real and fictional that we can use as ideals for developing our own s'elves. James Bond, who is basically a character with great bodily-kinesthetic intelligence but also a good deal of logical-mathematical intelligence and a charismatic personality, which probably denote interpersonal intelligence that enhances his ability to charm women, is one sort of hero. He stands in contrast to Sherlock Holmes who has genius level logical-mathematical intelligence, has some mastery of bodily-kinesthetic intelligence but would most likely score lower on the scale when it comes to interpersonal intelligence, since he looks down on people and tends to avoid most personal contact and would also score low as far as intrapersonal intelligence, since he is a drug addict who apparently suffers from PTSD due to his childhood. Although, this is the case with nearly every fictional hero and superhero, almost all of them suffered a tragic loss, often of the family, usually when they were very young. It is a common feature of the hero archetype.

And although Sherlock Holmes, as a character, evidences a decided distaste for being in Nature, he does seem to have rather high Natural intelligence in his understanding of how things work. His is a scientific appreciation of Nature. Legolas, in that way, would be more like James Bond, while still having high Natural intelligence. And we expect Elrond might be more on the order of Sherlock Holmes in a way, without the drug addiction, although each character is different in their own way, which is what makes them special. Gandalf, for his part, is another form of Merlin (as archetypal magician/wizard), but still unique in his way, not merely a copy of the Merlin archetype but a unique variation upon it or a riff upon that theme. Gandalf shows us that the passage through the Between is a trip (or adventure, you might say) in more ways than one. When Gandalf invited Bilbo and then Frodo to go on an adventure, he was, in fact, inviting them to risk death. Both the possibility of physical death but also the inevitability of great change in their lives and consciousness. Although, as it turned out, it was Gandalf the Grey who in the mines of Moria fell to his death while engaged in a battle with the Balrog and then reincarnated again as Gandalf the White.

Each of our heroes demonstrates advanced abilities that it would behoove us to develop, each of us according to our own feeling of connection and association with those characters and our own aspirations in our current life. We choose heroes who speak to our spirits and who represent ideals toward which we may aspire, even if, as often happens, they are also characters who evidence abilities of which we are individually rather deficit. They frequently represent what we aren't but would like to be. Chosen for the very reason that they help us imagine what it would be like if we shared their particular abilities.

The various bullies and critics that the world of Man seems to produce in abundance may tell us we are not good enough and never will be but if we ignore them and listen to our own spirit we will realize we can develop any power that we have if we only wish to do so and put in the time and energy required. Which is to say, practice, practice, practice, ever striving to improve our technique.

Of course, one might say that Sherlock Holmes was born a genius and this would be true, that his genius is a genetic development. Although, from our point of view, we Silver Elves would say it is a genetic development that is due to lifetimes of effort both by his ancestors and, more importantly, his previous incarnations, where he may well have been one of his ancestors. Otherwise, he could have been born into the same family and evidenced no genius at all or born into another family. In that same way, children of great people don't always turn out to be distinguished individuals themselves. Each individual has the genes they have because of their previous efforts in past incarnations. We gravitate to the body and incarnation that is best suited to our progress and karma in a particular life and which most closely vibrates with our spirit, although sometimes (again due to karma usually) there are adjustments to make. We elves, for instance, would rather have bodies with pointed ears, but there are not many of them available presently.

But, even if one isn't born with genius level logical-mathematical intelligence, one can still increase one's ability to use logic, to learn and use math, and even if one isn't born with an athletic body, one can train and develop one's bodily-kinesthetic intelligence. Every power can be increased if we choose to do so. It is not enough to have heroes or heroines, we must aspire through action to be like them, to make their skills and powers our own in our own unique way, just in the way that Legolas, James Bond and Bruce Lee are all similar but different.

And it doesn't matter entirely where we start with a particular skill, we all started at the beginning or bottom at some point (just as we all begin as babies in the womb), we merely need to develop whatever skills we might have, however little or weak they may currently seem, and make them better.

It may appear that we will not improve enough to be really great, like someone taking up the piano when they are forty or so who will probably never be good enough to be a concert pianist, and that is probably the case. But don't let that discourage you for that is only the case in this incarnation. Whatever we develop now, we carry with us into our next incarnation and start again from our new, now improved, position and ability. We start again, essentially where we left off in our previous incarnation, with whatever karmic developments and handicaps we've accrued added.

The Spell:

We touch the Earth
To rise again
Hand in hand
With friend and kin

Arvyndase:
Eli fost tae Eldanil
Va luft sasnana
Aro ver aro
Ena edar nar eldi

Pronunciation:
E - lie foe-st tay Eel - day - nile
Vah lou-ft sayce - nay - nah
Air - row veer air - row
E - nah e - dare nair eel - dry

&

Chapter 19:
La Petit Mort

The French expression *la petit mort* is often used in relationship to orgasm and translates as *the little death*. This is most surely due to the fact that orgasm sometimes puts us into a state of blissful but basically unthinking awareness. We become pure experience and the chattering thinking mind is, at least for a short while, quiescent. In many ways, it is just this sort of open minded but empty minded bliss, free from intruding thoughts, that is the object of meditation, especially Zen meditation.

Through meditation we seek to obtain awareness unobstructed by any obscuring thought. We see reality without filters or judgment. We become the pure observer, the total feeling individual in a bliss-filled and ecstatic but serene way. This is also, in its way, the process of shamanic trance where one opens ones'elf to the Universe and to the influences and spirits of Nature through drumming, chanting and persistent and continual evocation and focused concentration to awaken the ecstatic sense of connection within (*Shamanism: Archaic Techniques of Ecstasy* by Mircea Eliade). Some shamans also use psychedelic substances to aid in this endeavor. The Shamanic process is, we might say, the process of Touching the Universe in the form of the spirits of Nature and being Touched in return by its magical being.

This sort of ecstatic realization is, in a sense, what one might expect from being in heaven or being in love when that love is mutual and reciprocated, pure happiness of feeling. The fact that such ecstatic sensory awareness is associated with death speaks somewhat to the realms of the Between (also seen as the etheric realms, the astral realms and the shamanic realms), at least as they present us visions (illusions some would say) of happiness and the expression of our true powers. (Of course, there are those who also say that love itself, especially being in love, is an illusion and merely the function of biochemicals in our brains. And this may be true, but those folks are usually very dull individuals having divorced themselves from what is truly magical in life.) The world is an illusion but we are destined to realize that it is one that we are creating through our own magic, or are, at least, sub-creators within.

However, this term *la petit mort* isn't just associated with sex and orgasm and has also been used to denote the loss of our soulful feeling for life or for others in incremental stages. Thus, it can be used to denote the hell worlds, as well. For what is hell, really, but a loss of one's soul or one's empathy, compassion and feeling connection to others and the world around one? Just as tales of bargains with demons so often tell us what happens when one trades one's soul to the devil. And in time, certainly, that lack of feeling and compassion for others deadens one's own inner capacity to feel at all.

And yet, those who engage in such bargains, exchanging their soulful feeling for power, might say that in losing the one thing they gain something better in their eyes, just as a person who is blind might develop their sense of hearing to a greater degree than others around them. But what intelligent being would willingly give up their eyesight in order to enhance their hearing ability, or gain some other power. Well, Odin, of course, but only in one eye.

The Between realms have experiences of hell as well as heavenly possibilities, mostly depending upon the level of our individual evolutionary development and the inner world of our spirit. Just as we may have wonderful dreams as we sleep, perhaps great sexual dreams or dreams of flying, so might some of us also have nightmares in the Between (in fact, nearly all of us do). And these all form a part of, come from and express our inner world of being. And just as our dreams arise from our individual natures, minds and experience so are our experiences in the Between perfectly suited to the level of development of our own spirits. They spring from our relationship to the

Universe and express our own being in that way. We are where we are because of who we are.

In that same way, psychedelic or mind manifesting drugs tend to evoke what is within our own psychés. But then, as we said, our inner world is connected through our souls to the entirety of the Universe and to all of Nature and in taking psychedelic drugs one is not only letting one's own psyché manifest but also opening the door through the unconscious to the vast beyond, which is, in fact, the true reality unfiltered by the rings-pass-not that protect us while we are incarnate from the vaster realization of the reality of life because most of us would be overwhelmed by our contact with the immensity of the Universe, much in the way that it is said that one cannot look directly at the face of god or one will go blind (rather like staring at the sun and thus a connection and reference to the ancient sun gods and the gods of light such as Amun Ra of the Egyptians, Áine, a Celtic sun goddess, Amaterasu of the Japanese, Sol of the Romans, Mithra of the Persians and many, many others including Lugh of the Tuatha De Danaan our own faerie peoples).

Still, we tend to attract those things to us that vibrate with our own resonance and our own nature as it expresses our inner being and reflects our level of evolutionary development either through similarity or opposition (potentially complementary), or filling in those aspects we tend to lack but none-the-less desire. We are like magnets that attract to ours'elves things that resonate, positively or negatively, with our inner beings. This comes under the laws of Sympathetic magic. Like attracts like, but also opposites attract, and if you have a hole somewhere, something is going to come along and fill it.

In the human (or humanoid) body, the filtering of data and input by our awareness is carried out by the Reticular formation, which extends into different areas of the brain and, among other things, controls the processing of what is called Habituation through which our brains learn to ignore repetitive, meaningless stimuli while remaining sensitive to other things that may interest us or pose a danger to us (and things that endanger us as sentient beings usually draw our keen interest).

Otherwise, if we didn't filter the sensory data constantly coming into us, we'd be overwhelmed by incoming stimuli, as is shown as being the case in otherworldly or superpower dramas where a person can read other people's thoughts but has not as yet developed control over their ability to do so and are thus bombarded incessantly by the musings and mind chatter of everyone around them. It is bad enough that we have to listen to our own mind constantly, listening to other people's gibber incessantly would surely drive one crazy. But again, the reticular formation would prevent that from happening and may be the reason more of us aren't more directly psychic and tend to pick things up more from our feelings than our minds.

One time, we Silver Elves took a trip to the big island of Hawaii and went to the volcano park in the southern part of the island. Just about a mile up the road from the active volcano, we got out and walked around in the wilds and discovered it was totally silent there. There were no planes going overhead. No cars going by at that point. No birds singing. No sounds at all. It was quite eerie in a way, but at the same time a genuine relief. It had been many decades since we'd truly heard and experienced absolute silence.

This is, of course, what occurs in sensory deprivation tanks, only more so because all stimuli is shut off and, in time, the individual will begin to hallucinate, the mind and body filling in the empty space. This is similar to the Between experience where our spirits roam the void, and perhaps may be the origin of our manifest beings. Originally, our spirits were in the vast void of space and began to hallucinate/dream/fantasize that which we usually consider reality, which is actually to say, we gave form to pure energetic being.

In the course of evolution, we will surely extend the functioning of the reticular formation to the input of psychic data being able at that point to open or close our awareness at will and thus be able to listen in to the minds of others and to the Universe when we desire to do so or when they allow us to do so, for people will, of necessity, learn to screen their thoughts and to filter out all this psychic data when they desire solitude and quiet, so we won't be overwhelmed by unwanted stimuli. Rather like turning off one's cell phone.

Mankind, for the most part, filters out not only what is habitual and repetitive from outside stimuli but also whatever seems to violate the norms of their consciousness so that mystical and psychic events, while astounding at first, are soon deleted and forgotten as though they never happened at all. If they don't do that, they open the door to the esoteric worlds and begin to wander into the planes of the unknown, questioning what they've come to accept as reality, or have the unknown wander randomly at times into their lives, which tends to arouse their paranoia. And their paranoia is usually never very far from the surface of their consciousness for the reality they have created can be a dangerous one and can make nearly anyone paranoid. Even we elves are very cautious in their worlds.

The expression *la petit mort* has also been used to indicate a sort of weakness one might feel after orgasm, the same sort of weakness one often encounters in very old age presaging the failure of our current vehicle of incarnation. In that sense, we might see life itself as the great orgasm, especially when we are in our peak period of life, although few of us actually obtain the sort of orgasmic happiness that is our ultimate destiny in life. But that really is what Elfin is about, isn't it? Being able to experience each incarnation as a fabulous orgasm and eventually as a never-ending one, or at least a series of orgasms. What if Death is actually an orgasm and our spirits are the ejaculate?

At the same time, this French colloquial expression of the orgasm points to the idea and belief that some people hold that each orgasm takes a little bit of life out of the individual, that each orgasm reduces the life force in a person as opposed to reinvigorating their energy. This notion can be found in Taoist and Tantric practices where one is advised to arouse ones'elf and one's partner sexually without proceeding to orgasm or where males, at least, may use techniques that channel the ejaculate back into and through their body rather than being released directly outwards. Although it should be pointed out in this case that the sperm is still eventually expelled from the body so how much good that technique really does is somewhat questionable. Still, the essential idea is to use sexual arousal as a technique for increasing our life energy and therefore leading us closer toward immortality of the body.

Stephan Mace in one of his books (either *Taking Power*, *Shaping Formless Fire*, or *Stealing the Fire from Heaven*, honestly, we don't remember which one it was in, although they are all interesting) suggests that the magician, rather than using a technique to channel their ejaculate into and through their body, goes ahead and has an orgasm and then consumes their own ejaculate, but we expect that many of our readers would find this notion hard to swallow. But then many may also find that arousing ones'elf without ever coming to orgasm can be a difficult and, for men anyway, painful technique to master.

We elves, for the most part, are great believers in sex and its rejuvenating and healing powers, as long as it is consensual and is safe sex, and we are of the opinion that having lots of sex is good for a person, and most of the legends and lore concerning the fae would seem to confirm our devoted appreciation and our habit celebrating life in every joyous way we can. And yet, the tantric notions of prolonging sexual arousal also seem quite good ones to us for prolonging ecstasy and happiness is exactly what we seek to achieve as elven spirits. For is that not, in fact, kindred to eternal happiness, which is one of the primary goals of the spirit?

But our main point here is that life, sex, ecstasy and death are all intertwined and are not separate from each other, not opposites really, but part of one great evolutionary process that leads us to the fulfillment of our inner beings manifested outwardly, eventuating in the realization of our Visions and the perfection (or perfecting really for we are never finished developing) of our s'elves. Many people separate sexuality from spirituality, but in the experience of these elves it is highly developed spiritual people who are the most sexually oriented and free beings we've ever encountered.

The Spell:

Coming together we are one
United till the spell is done

Ever greater it will become
The parts when joined increase the sum

Arvyndase:
Kosodas eldan eli da ata
Åtåråïn ted tae moja da båïn
Vari raltfa ter yon casae
Tae sunli nas lylïn memarn tae daj

Pronunciation:
Co - so - dace eel - dane e - lie dah a - tah
Ah - tah - rah - in teed tay moe - jah dah bah – in
Vay - rye rail-t - fah tier yone cah - say
Tay soon - lie nace lil [as in lily] - in me - mare-n tay day-j

ॐ

Chapter 20:
The Crown of Creation

It is said in the Bible that Man is *The Crown of Creation* (check out the Jefferson Airplane song and album/CD of that title), indicating thus that Mankind is the highest form of creation and is subsequently given mastery over everything upon the Earth and therefore dominance over all animals, plants and growing things upon the Earth. And we expect they will declare dominance out in space as well if they don't destroy us all before getting there.

Of course, they would say that about themselves, wouldn't they? It excuses nearly every vile thing they do to every other species, while they pretend this notion comes from their particular god in order to lend it credence, while blaming all the evil they do on some devil. It is also the notion they use (the Nazis used the idea of the Super-Man, which is essentially the same thing) to excuse their killing of other Men, although they relegate those others to being sub-human, or inferior beings, in order to excuse doing so (Remember the Mark of Cain? Don't kill other human beings, unless, according to Mankind, they are not really good enough to be human). This is the same excuse Mankind uses for enslaving others and holding them in bondage. In fact, when slavery was legal in the United States, the slaves were listed as 'livestock,' along with the horses and cattle and so forth, by their owners/oppressors.

We sometimes find this same sort of prejudice among those who claim to be of genetic elven blood and feel thems'elves to be somehow superior to those who are not bodily descendants of the Scythian folk and the Elven Bloodline (see Nicolas De Vere *The Dragon Legacy*). We not only find their claims and proof of being genetically elven to be rather dubious in most cases, but we Silver Elves do not discriminate against those who are elven spirits and who are born, of necessity, as the genetic descendants of Man.

We Silver Elves have no notion of people being half elven or half fae, or whatever. It doesn't matter how much elf or fae or other you have in you, if you embrace your elfiness, however little you may feel it to be, that is elfae enough for us. To us you are elven or other or whatever, and we embrace all our elven kindred and if Men would accept and embrace us and our identity, we'd embrace them as well. For in becoming more open to the notion that we are actually elves, they are, de facto, becoming more open minded and thus more elven, at least in spirit, and spirit is the foundation of reality from an elven point of view.

Some people, perhaps most at this juncture, hold the opinion that the material world is the foundation of everything and all else stems from it. But the material world is just form and substance. It is like Jell-O that has no flavor and no nutritional value. Without flavor it is just gel. Spirit is the flavor and the vitamins within the Jell-O and the Jell-O is the human body.

This idea of being the Crown of Creation goes along with the notion that Man (Mankind) is the alpha predator (although this is more of an evolutionary point of view), and that Man is at the top of the food chain and so forth, which from an elven point of view is pure nonsense. Clearly, the viruses are at the top of the food chain. They eat Man and he, and we for that matter, can hardly do a thing about it, except to do our best to avoid them (viruses and Men, for they both have a tendency to be predatory).

Although, we elves are of the opinion that we may have to negotiate with the viruses at some point and attempt to reach some sort of conciliatory truce with them as we did with the common cold while increasing our resistance and natural immunities through exercise, a positive spiritual attitude, dedicated hygienic practices and a good diet. Ceasing to prey on other species (which men excuse doing by seeing them as less important than them and calling themselves alpha predators) would certainly help.

Still, viruses are not simply one tribe but many (as are we elfae folk) and we will need to negotiate with each of them in turn. And, so it is with Man as well. We talk about them as though they were one group, for this is often how they think of themselves (although they frequently claim their particular group or tribe are the true Men and all others inferior species).

The idea that one's particular country and nationality, one's religion or ethnic group is the best in the world is quite common among men. Although, that is rather like preferring one's mother's cooking or the ethnic foods that one grew up with over any other available in the world. It is simply a form of provincialism and something that Mankind, especially as they move out into space, will need to overcome. Although, we expect they will simply adopt a new provincialism based upon space station ethnic values.

We Silver Elves know various individuals from different countries and ethnic groups and most of them prefer the food of their upbringing and home country and often dislike foods from other peoples. Except for most Americans who will eat nearly anything. Americans don't really have a cuisine that is especially our own, except perhaps for peanut butter and jelly sandwiches.

On the other hand, when it comes to the consumption of pizza, nearly everyone in the world loves to eat and delights in pizza. Pizza is a unifier, transcending nearly all cultural boundaries. We might say the same thing about sports, particularly international football, except that football most often promotes conflict and rivalries among different teams, their regions and countries and their supporters, whereas the only conflict that pizza usually arouses is over who will get the last piece.

But the truth is that Men are as varied as we elfae folk, only not quite as willing to admit it or embrace it, and many of them demand that others be like them. Or that these others are so inferior to their particular tribe that they will never be good enough to be like them. Many of them claim to be the elect or the chosen ones, the only ones deemed worthy by their particular god, and often the only ones willing and wise enough to believe in Him (once again, it is nearly always a him).

Whereas, we elfae folk urge people to strive to be their own s'elves in harmony with all others, however they may imagine that to be. Men tend to view the world in terms of dichotomies of good vs. bad, white vs. black, god vs. the devil and so forth, while we elves are rainbow people. We see the world as being varied, wondrous, ever changing and filled with surprises and we know that there are colors we have yet to discover, vast worlds we have still to encounter, and knowledge unending, but we have not, thus far, developed eyes able to see those colors or those worlds, or developed our minds to the point that they can understand and encompass all that knowledge. But this certainly will come in time.

The tales of elfin folk would generally contradict this notion that Men are alpha predators or at least that they are a superior species to us, for the stories of elfae folk lead one to believe that we are far advanced to Men in nearly every way, although we are much less inclined to be predators at all. This might mislead one into believing that most faerie tales and lore are written by ours'elves about ours'elves, in the same way that Men like to put themselves on pedestals in their own histories, but curiously it is usually Men who write tales about us. Or perhaps, elfae who have come to think of thems'elves as Men but carry deep in their unconsciousness and inner beings memories of their true natures.

Elfin folk, for the most part, tend to be far more modest when speaking of ours'elves as a people and as individuals. One might think that as Men evolve they may become elfae folk, but really, while they will surely become more like us in certain ways, they will still be their own Mankind selves, only better at being so. We are not trying to turn Mankind into elves, we just wish to encourage them to be better and freer at being their own true selves, to fulfill their own higher and heroic visions of themselves, and to loosen the grip, at least a bit, on their need to compete with every other species and with each other.

We elves, overall, at least we who are Seelie folk, seek harmonious association with others, not dominance. After all, according to most tales about us, we elves are immortal or nearly so. Something which Mankind has been trying to get their hands on forever, although they seem to think it will come to them through technology, whereas, we think it will be primarily a development of an increasingly powerful spirit that transforms our DNA, although we are not against some combination of the two. We are not opposed to technology or science, but rather we embrace mysticism and magic as well, finding the truth to be found in the whole rather than in the separated parts.

And we elves are, for the most part, according to legend, lore and fiction, better looking than Mankind. We are the fairest of all peoples, it is said, in the eyes of each other if not in anyone else's but then what do they say ... beauty is in the eye of the beholder? And we elven see beauty nearly everywhere and perceive it in almost all things and beings, surely in mankind as well, goblins and trolls and various and sundry Unseelie fae.

We observe Mankind's drive to be heroic and just. Why else would they continually write their histories to reflect this idea? Even when, in fact, they have done great wrong, they cannot help but frame their behavior as being heroic and justified. And we elves cannot help but appreciate the beauty of that great spiritual endeavor of creating fairness in the world. Although, far too frequently, Man falls back upon the idea that *might makes right*, rather than that might and power merely make the rules and force them upon everyone else.

We elves acknowledge that it is important to be strong and powerful, certainly, but it is also vital to be fair. Power without fairness strays inevitably toward oppression and the tendency to do evil, whereas fairness without power cannot attain the justice it righteously seeks to bring about. And it is only through fairness that the world will come to peace and fulfill its destiny to be a paradisiacal realm shared by everyone in harmony.

Mankind clearly aspires toward greatness, which is a good thing, but usually they simply won't admit that they haven't actually achieved it as yet, except in their own minds and their own accounts of their history or fantasies, which are often the same thing. Rewriting history to make yourself seem heroic may fool your descendants but it doesn't actually change the facts nor alter who you truly are and thus will not affect the circumstances of your next incarnation. Karma cannot be fooled.

Mankind urges their kind to fake it till they make it, but they often forget that they are actually faking it and consequently they then accept their own hype as reality assuming they have made it when they are far from having done so. It's somewhat similar to the sort of drug dealers who get high on their own supply. Men are high on their own hype. They have drunk the Kool Aid, as they say, only it is Kool Aid they have concocted for themselves leading them to believe they are an exceptional folk for having done so. It is the supportive echo of sycophants and yeah-sayers assuring them that they are indeed whatever they proclaim about themselves.

And, according to Tolkien, we elves are also the wisest of all peoples. If they are so less wise than we are, then it is no wonder Mankind continually votes to put idiots in public office and often scorn those with educations greater than their own. We can hardly blame them, can we? Really, if the lore is true, which it isn't always, they can be clever in cunning ways, but so much less wise than we. So how can we criticize them, really, for doing such idiotic things?

According to the lore, Men are inferior to the elven in terms of evolutionary development overall (or as it is with angels in their lore, we were just made better than they from the get go) but they can never actually admit that this is so. And yet, if they would but hold out their hands in friendship, we would gladly uplift them. We are not the ones who are holding them down. They simply refuse to rise up without attempting to step upon those around them or drag down those above them or pull those ahead of them back into an idealized past that never actually existed except in their own imaginations. They spend nearly all their resources preparing for wars that are not really necessary and which then come about due to their unreasoning paranoia and inability to resist trying to dominate each other and their unfortunate dedication to greed. We might think that the practice of going Viking and robbing and stealing from others less powerful has been altered by the imposition of Christianity, Islam and other 'peace-loving' religions in the world, but it is not so. Mankind still starts wars to steal other people's oil and natural resources. And they still engage in economic, if not always direct, enslavement of the others.

And yet, does it really seem that Mankind is the Crown of Creation? Really? They just don't seem that advanced to we elven, for we look at our own s'elves and know how very far we have to go before we become fully whom we strive to be. We examine our own beings realistically and see how very much there is to learn and develop in ours'elves; and as soulful elfin spirits, we gaze into a future that blurs into the horizon so we have no idea of how far we have yet to go. For evolution continues on beyond our ability to envision it, only that it seems, and we suspect that it is true, that it goes on forever. We will be learning, evolving and developing ever after. Life is eternal and perfection, it turns out, is just another landing on the stairway to heaven, or to Faerie, or Elfin in our way of seeing it. Yet if we are so far advanced to Men, as legends about us proclaim, can they really be the top of the line, the end point of all evolution? Surely Man, like us and the all of life, has ages yet to go to fulfill their true potential.

Does it really make sense that Mankind is the pinnacle of perfection and development and that they will have only one life and no others, other than one in paradise or heaven? And that they need never develop themselves or evolve any further? And why is it that some men (and women, obviously, but then men insist on subsuming women under the title of Man, whereas elves are just elves, female or male, equal and united) are born with great intelligence and abilities and others are born with far less intelligence? Which doesn't seem to prevent them from rising to high office, however, in our experience and as history will confirm. The Crown of Creation? Really? More like a stop on a long adventure down the road, a necessary but temporary resting point in our great Quest to become who we are truly meant to be.

And what about the angels in Christian lore, who are said to be so much greater than Mankind in power but have no free will at all, or have abnegated their free will because, if they decided to do anything contrary to what their god dictates, they will be cast into Hell forever? Aren't they the Crown of Creation, being so much higher and more powerful as spirits than Mankind and Elves? And, are they willing servants, or living in terror forever, doing what they must to get by or face the possibility of being tortured forever for making a free choice? Or are they like robots, simply doing as they are programmed to do with no real choice to do otherwise? But, if that were the case, how did the fallen angels choose to rebel? Was it just a programming glitch? Or are the fallen angels the first instance of AI?

Which reminds us of when Zardoa was a young elf at a military school run by nuns. Each year, near the end of the semester, always on a Saturday, every boy (or pixie, as we like to think of them) would be given a large bag of candy and set free to spend the day outdoors on the rather extensive playground, composed of about a half dozen or so acres. However, a nun who gave out the candy would also ask one or two boys to stay with her afterwards and spend the day helping to clean up the candy closet. Zardoa had done so on previous years, but on his second to last year, the nun asked if he'd like to help and he told her that he had already made plans with friends and thus, that year, chose not to assist her. He mistakenly thought it was a free choice and the nun acted as though it was, but the next morning, for she was also the one who was in charge of his dormitory (one of five currently in use), she came in ranting and raving that he had dared to refuse her, that she had informed the principal of the school (also a nun) about his refusal and that the next year, when, according to tradition, he might expect that he would be promoted to be an officer of the school, he surely would not.

This, actually, turned out not to be the case. A new principal was unexpectedly appointed the next year, brought in from elsewhere and she told the students they were all getting a fresh start and a clean slate. Zardoa became the Captain of Company A and stayed in that position throughout the year, receiving high praise on a number of occasions from the army Coronel, a veteran of D-Day, who would come each Saturday from his job at the Pentagon to drill them. However, this false choice the nun had given him seems similar to the choice that is said to have been given to angels and men. Bow down, obey absolutely or be punished. How is free choice real when it is really only a choice between being submissive or suffering for one's failure to do so? That's not a choice, that's a dilemma.

Although, in fact, this is the very choice we have in life. Not to obey authoritarian figures and their arbitrary rules, as they would make it seem, but to choose what is good in life, choose to do what is harmonious for ours'elves and others or suffer the consequences of violating Nature in its material and higher esoteric forms and accruing karma thereby. It is a subtle and complex Universe and things are not always so simple, but the essential choice is. Obeying the Divine isn't about praising some god, or believing in particular doctrines or dogmas, or accepting so and so as your master, lord and savior, but about doing what is right as best we understand it in every situation. For to do otherwise is to choose suffering, like a child ignoring its parent's warnings and placing its hand in a fire and getting burnt for doing so. The parent doesn't do the burning. The burn isn't punishment for disobeying, although it may seem like it. It is a natural consequence of violating the laws of Nature.

Mankind, on the other hand, while not as powerful as angels, supposedly has free will but, like angels, can only use it to obey his god or not and failing to do so will also be cast into Hell to be tortured forever. He is offered the same false choice. If the whole idea of creation is about absolute obedience to god, then why make Man at all? Why not just make angels from the get go? Why create lesser beings at all unless you just enjoy watching people fumble around like in some old silent slapstick comedy film?

Or if, as some people think, you become an angel after you die (or a demon, if you failed to obey) why bother to create angels in the first place? Why not let everyone go through life as a human being and then ascend to be angelic in form or descend the other way if you fail to meet up with their standards of behavior?

For the gradual evolution of spirit through form starting at its lowliest and simplest place and advancing to more complicated manifestations is exactly what esoteric theory says, that we begin as the most primitive of beings (even the angels or Shining Ones, as we call them, did so). We are essence taking form in the physical plane and eventually evolving into greater and more complex forms, mineral, vegetable, animal and upwards. Just in the same way that the Universe is said to have started with the simpler elements of the Periodic Table, and increased in complexity as the Universe evolved. Thus, in that way, incarnation after incarnation, we ascend gradually toward the realms of the Shining Ones, those spirits who went before us and have illuminated the path for us to follow, deeper and deeper into the realms of Elfin, incarnation after incarnation, increasing our capacity for knowledge, skill and power.

The Spell:

Ever higher, we ascend
To heights beyond our view
Clearer we do see the way
And come to know what's true

Arvyndase:
Vari altfa, eli rystar
Va altarli hyrlon eli'na sant
Vyrnfa eli ba ten tae yer
Nar koso va ken wu'da lod

Pronunciation:
Vay - rye ale-t - fah, e - lie riss - stair
Vah ale-tair - lie her - lone e - lie'nah saint
Vern - fah e - lie bah teen tay year
Nair co - so vah keen woo'dah load

❧

Chapter 21:
Wild Hunt

The Wild Hunt is a European folklore theme (that can also be found in *The Witcher* books and video game). The Wild Hunt is usually represented as a group of spectral and supernatural hunters riding across the sky chasing after someone. While this myth is usually associated with ancient European lore and with the fae folk, notice the song *Ghost Riders in the Sky* and the country western group *Riders in the Sky* as somewhat associated themes.

As an aside, while people typically separate different genres, such as fantasy and science fiction, westerns, modern crime and so forth, the notion of Faerie and fae folk and magic existed in the early American colonial times (note again the story of *Rip Van Winkle* and the story of the *Headless Horseman* by Nathaniel Hawthorne and the otherworldly and horror oriented stories of his contemporary Edgar Allen Poe, who none-the-less generally set his stories after the Colonial Period and many of them in Europe). But this theme of the occult and otherworldly has also been associated with western themes as exampled by the short stories of Ambrose Bierce (among his many works note *The Devil's Dictionary*), which take part in the west and have vampires, werewolves and many other otherworldly beings and supernatural occurrences in them. Our point is that our tendency to view faerie stories as only happening in the fantasy worlds or, in some cases, in science fiction is too limiting for a culture and a people that have existed, and continue to live, in every time period both in reality and in the continuation of legends, lore and fiction concerning our culture.

The riders of the Wild Hunt are sometimes said to be elves or fae or the dead (notice again the link between elfin folk and ghostly beings), and in ancient times the Wild Hunt was thought to be led by a god figure of one of the early pagan beliefs such as Odin or whatever god was deemed the chief god of a particular people or region at that time. However, with the advent of Christianity and what was often the forced conversion of pagan folk (see Bernard Cornwell's *Saxon Tales* series upon which the television show *The Last Kingdom* is based), but with the preservation or absorption of many of their folkloric beliefs, such as Yule that became Christmas, the leader of the Wild Hunt came to be seen as Satan leading his demonic horde or sometimes they use the more generalized term of The Devil.

Christians, quite naturally, seek to view the world from the perspective of their Christian beliefs and mythology. We elves do the same thing when we view the world and all that goes on in it and every being of it, as being part of or related in some way to our own elven point of view and the realms of Elfin and Faerie. Thus, we see that those who call themselves Men are often, from our point of view, actually orcs, trolls, goblins, grimlins or pixies, fae or elfin folk or some sort of otherkin. Mankind is a rather catchall phrase and it might be better if they used the term human or humanoid.

It is said that the presence of the Wild Hunt in the world often forecasts some catastrophic event such as a world war or plague. The nuns at our military school used to tell us elf, fae and pixie (and some goblin and orc) boys, that the Northern Lights would appear all over the world to presage the apocalypse. This is, in that way, a similar mythological motif, filed under the general category of signs of the End Times. The so-called Rapture, where Christians are supposedly going to be beamed up to "heaven" is really just another end of the world myth that, as it turns out, has other associations to the Wild Hunt theme as well.

However, the Wild Hunt is not always associated with apocalyptic times, sometimes it was said that seeing the Wild Hunt was an indication that the individual that saw it passing would die soon (like hearing the cry of the Banshee). It is also said that anyone who encountered the Wild Hunt might be abducted to the underworld or the fairy kingdom (we wish). This is another Rapture like situation, although Christians tend to associate Faerie with Hell, as some tales, both old and new, say that the Faerie realms are obligated to pay a tithe to Hell (we believe you can find this bit of lore repeated in some of Holly Black's Faerie novels as well as other places), so this would be a Rapture for wicked folk from that point of view.

But, as we've indicated earlier, the Underworld, the Between, the Faerie realms and the realms of Death and sometimes the Demonic realms of Hell are often seen as being the same or as very similar places or are accorded similar atmospheres or inhabitants. Since most Christians don't believe in Faerie then, for them, seeing it as being Hell (or paradise in some cases) is an understandable association.

We might wonder why, in fact, the Rapture that takes good Christians out of the world involves decent people at all when it would seem so much easier and more efficient to our elven minds to just beam all the evil folk to hell and leave the good people on Earth since that is where they will eventually return anyway according to this Christian myth. It seems to us it would be much better if the whole process was simpler, as the theory of Occam's Razor hints.

As you can see, the introduction of Christianity into ancient Europe blended many of these ancient myths, as they took on a Christian persona in order to survive. Just as elfae folk through the ages have pretended to be Men in order to continue on in the world and gays often have to pretend to be straight in societies in which they are persecuted and often killed for engaging in same sex activities or sometimes for just dressing differently, as is the case with cross-dressers who must hide their yearning for and practice of wearing outfits that are, for some reason we elves don't really understand, arbitrarily deemed and designated to be worn exclusively by a particular gender.

Being kidnapped and taken off to Faerie is the same in a certain sense as dying and going to the Between and then returning to the world again years later reincarnated in a new rather than one's old body (as is the case in the stories of Rip Van Winkle, Thomas the Rhymer, Tam Lin and other tales where individuals are carried off to Faerie but come back again to their world years later but in the same bodily form). However, this old lore of Faerie abduction is also, let's face it, the same general idea as alien abduction in more modern times (see *Fairies: Real Encounters with the Little People* by Janet Bord that speaks of this idea) where the aliens take a person for a while, return them, but they often experience that time is missing, a memory lapse has occurred, or time has moved differently in the individual's perception while they were away.

It is also said that in some cases a person's spirit (their true being) would be drawn to join the Wild Hunt as it passed, but this may merely be reference to dying in one's sleep or, perhaps, experiencing a wild sort of dream, although it could also be an indication of mob mentality when people get fiercely aroused together, often losing their sense of social boundaries. Or this could even be making reference to the idea of evolving to the point where one joins the Shining Ones, which is the goal of spiritual evolution.

In this same sort of way, the Elf Queen's Daughters passed by these elves one day as we were going about our lives and we soon followed after, filled with both caution and expectation in the beginning. On meeting each other and spending time together, they said, 'you are surely one of us', and we said, 'yes, we know.' For our spirits hummed together and recognized each other almost immediately. We surely weren't abducted to Faerie but we were definitely enchanted and went quite willingly and never wished to return.

In some ways, the Wild Hunt could be like wandering into a bad neighborhood, the wrong side of town, the other side of the tracks, a rival gang's territory, and so forth, being noticed, and then having to flee for one's life. This is not unlike the experience of one of the members of the Louis and Clark expedition who was captured by a tribe of 1st Nations people in Missouri who released him and gave him a head start so that they could chase after him and hunt him down with the intention of capturing him, torturing and killing him, except he evaded them, made it to the Missouri river, plunged in and spent a cold, wet night hiding from them and then escaped to rejoin his people the next day.

This is also reminiscent of a scene in the wonderful movie *The Emerald Forest*, where one of the main characters is captured by a tribe of cannibals, but let go because they already have his guide to eat (raw) for dinner that night and they tell him they will stalk him through the forest the next day when they get hungry. Sort of an ancient form of ensuring that one's meat is fresh when one doesn't have a refrigerator.

One evening, back when Zardoa was in his first year in High School, he went to a school dance, taking the city bus to the event since the school was some distance from his home, although the bus route didn't go all the way to the school and would let him off a few blocks away which, as it happened, was just on the edge of Unseelie territory and he'd have to walk to the dance from there. This was usually not a problem in the daylight, but with night fast approaching...

When Zardoa got off the bus that evening, with the light of the day fading, he heard and then saw a crowd of approximately 40+ unseelie fae about a block away who were gradually coming his way, knocking on doors and calling out to their friends in the surrounding houses as they passed by. From these houses, by ones and twos, others of their kind would excitedly come to join them, swelling their ranks so that this fae crowd was fast growing and clearly feeling powerful in their increasing numbers.

There is almost nothing so empowering in its way than being surrounded by one's own pack or tribe. This is, of course, the basis of gang mentality, but also the sense people get when they are united by patriotism or a shared religious fervor. It is the sort of energy that predominates most cults. One of the Fox River Elves, a vortex of the Elf Queen's Daughters, once commented to us that in the modern world (as well as the ancient, surely) it was good and much safer for an elf to have one's own band to go around with.

However, as it happened on that particular night, the unseelie crowd hadn't as yet spotted Zardoa. They were too busy gathering their friends at that point and rejoicing in each other's company. So, he calmly walked around the corner until the unseelie fae wouldn't be able to see him at all and when he was out of their view, he ran as fast as he was able up to the next block, turned the corner again, ran to the next corner, and so on, zig-zagging his way to the school and to eventual safety.

Would he have become the subject of the Wild Hunt? A lone Seelie elf on the edge of the territory of the Unseelie? We cannot know for sure, they may have simply ignored him, but he wasn't interested in taking the chance, either. Better safe than sorry, as they say.

In ancient Hawaii, there were kapu (taboos) or laws that were enforced by individuals known as the ʻilamuku. A person violating these kapus would be sentenced to death without trial or even an opportunity to explain themselves. However, if the individual fled and could make it to Puʻuhonua, a sanctuary area, before the ʻilamuku and his Wild Hunt, so to speak, caught him, he would be safe and taken care of, even forgiven his trespasses, rather in the way of confessing to a Catholic priest, only with Catholics you did not have to run for your life first, usually.

This idea of churches or sacred spots as sanctuaries was also the case in Catholic Europe at one time and as long as an individual could get to a church and stay within its doors, they would be safe from the police and prosecution for their crimes. It may be, in part, this notion that leads the current Catholic Church to wish to deal with pedophile priests directly rather than simply turning them over to the police and civil authorities, although that seems a rather misguided idea to us for it doesn't appear to stop the pedophilia from occurring and while such priests may find their god's forgiveness, they still need to be held responsible for their actions, at least in our opinion.

Actually, if you want our elven point of view concerning an issue that is really none of our business, they should let priests and nuns (priestesses) marry, assign a priest and priestess to every church and the priestess could, among other things, make sure the priest isn't fiddling with the kids.

The Spell:

The Wild Hunt streaks across the sky
It sees us not as they pass by
We are safe, secure and free
In Elfin's grace, we'll ever be

Arvyndase:
Tae Zet Sålk lec wylyal tae faln
Ter tenlu eli kon tat tam gol la
Eli da del, yader nar alo
Ver Êldat felsh, eli'yon vari te

Pronunciation:
Tay Zeet Sulk leek will - yale tae fail-n
Tier teen - lou e - lie cone tate tame goal lah
E - lie dah deal, yeah - deer nair a - low
Veer L - date feel-sh, e - lie'yone vair - rye tea

❧

Chapter 22:
Banshees and Black Dogs

The Banshee or Bean Sidhe, literally meaning woman of the sidhe or fairy woman, was said to wail outside a house when someone was soon to die in that household, thus giving a sort of warning or providing a premonition of what was to come. The Bean Sidhe is often said to be a ghostly or spectral spirit, but clearly, as the name indicates, one of the faerie folk. And it was said that they would provide this warning or announcement of impending death, especially if the person to die was related to the fae. This gives the idea that elfae and normal humans could intermarry, or as we Silver Elves look at it, that elfin folk are able to reincarnate into humanoid bodies similar to Mankind and be born again among them yet still retain our essential elfin spirit and soulfulness, which is to say our intuitive and feeling connection to all things elfin.

And, in time, due to the inheritance of legends and lore about us, thanks in great part to the wonderful contribution of authors such as Lord Dunsany (see *The King of Elfland's Daughter* by that author) and Tolkien, as well as the fae works of Marie Brennen (*The Onyx Court* series), Freda Warrington (*Elfland*), the *Elf Quest* comics by the Pinis, and other modern fae works, such as things like *Dungeons and Dragons*, *Forgotten Realms* and *Magic the Gathering* and other such games, we have the continuation of our ancient culture and the possibility of encountering it in the modern world and of awakening to our true otherkin natures.

For we still have our elven culture, somewhat filtered and sometimes distorted to be sure, but existing for us still, as well as having each other to help awaken us. It is true that, in our opinion, modern authors often rely too heavily upon the ancient legends (which themselves were so deeply affected and distorted by Christian beliefs) rather than trying to understand these tales from a truly elven point of view, but still, it is wonderful that they exist for us at all.

And we Silver Elves are truly thankful. And we use our own inner sense and intuitional memories to sort out what is really accurate concerning us and our culture and what is not, and what was once true or close to the truth but is no longer applicable for modern elfin folk. For while we honor the past and our ancestors, we are not obligated to live or be exactly like them and if our culture is to grow and continue it must, like every other culture in the world, evolve and be a living culture. And we make it a living culture, mostly, by living the life elfin (see our book *The Elven Way*). A living culture is a culture that is lived.

Similar to the Bean Sidhe of Irish lore is the Bean-nighe, which means washerwoman, of Scottish legend. This being can be observed by a lake or river, washing the bloodstained clothes of the person who is predicted thereby to soon die. There are tales about those who come upon this faerie woman by accident and see her washing bloody garments only to recognize that the clothes she is cleaning are their own and the individual thus realizes that this encounter is a premonition or forecast of their own impending death.

The legend of the Bean Sidhe seems to be about mourning the death of some person before that death occurs. However, the warning or prediction of impending death does us little good if, in fact, we have no way to avoid dying, unless it is merely to give us time to prepare ours'elves, like a prisoner about to be executed being given their last meal, or asked if they have any last words to say before they are executed, or perhaps writing a final letter, seeing a minister or priest or evoking the Divine Magic in the case of we elfin folk, and putting one's affairs in order as the expression goes. We may not always be able to avoid Death, but such premonitions and signs may help to give us an opportunity to prepare for it.

For death is not always unexpected and many of us have to wait in deep sadness for one we love to cease suffering and move on into the Between realms. The question becomes whether we are destined to die at a particular time or whether we can alter the course of our lives by heeding the warning that comes to us. Is life absolutely predetermined, as some people believe or is our life dependent upon our choices, which is to say our magic and our actions? We Silver Elves are of the opinion that we can, sometimes at least, avoid what seemed to be inevitable death and we see this move from potential death to an extension of life in our current incarnation as being connected to a movement from one parallel world to another in a Universe where there are near infinite worlds and dimensions.

For from our elven point of view, every significant decision that causes a change in one's life is, in fact, the process of stepping from one world to another—one that is similar but not exactly the same. We sometimes call this shift from one parallel world to another the Dance of Life. It is rather like the fact that in order to avoid being eaten by the sand worms in the *Dune* novels, an individual must walk across the desert sands with a varied rather than a rhythmic step that would attract the worms. Thus, we elves hop, skip, jump, twirl and dance through life zig-zagging in an irregular fashion like someone running away and trying to evade someone shooting at them (or evading the Wild Hunt).

In the case of the Bean-nighe, this vision of clothes being washed (usually to get blood out but let's face it not all death involves bloodshed, although most of us do release our bowels when we die and leave behind our parting gift and comment upon the world, so maybe that is what is being cleaned up) speaks of the washing away of our worldly concerns, our memories from our just abandoned body and incarnation. The cleaning of our clothes, which is to say our facades or personas, also indicates the relinquishing of the selfish aspects of our ego as well as denoting the purification of our spirits as we move deeply into the Between, taking only what is essential to our beings as we do so.

Which is to say we carry with us the powers and abilities that our spirits have earned through continued practice and the effort to improve these skills during our accumulated incarnations, so that we might be born into another incarnation appearing as though we have been born with a special gift or inherited ability or talent. Which, in fact, we do inherit, only from our own efforts in our previous incarnations instilled in our spirits. Life may seem random, unfair and accidental, but beneath that there is an order to the Universe and all things in it.

This, surely, is the point of view of Chaos Magic, which acknowledges an underlying connection between the random aspects of the world. And this is also the theory behind the efficacy of fortune telling and the seemingly random appearance of certain tarot cards when a reading is conducted for ones'elf or others. The apparent random fall of the tarot cards are said to reveal a deeper order than would be immediately apparent.

A black dog is another bit of faerie lore and it is generally seen as a ghostly, sometimes demonic being. It is found in the folklore of the British Isles but in other lands as well. It is sometimes said to have shape-shifting abilities, and also deemed, in some instances, to be a hellhound that collects the souls of those who've made a deal with the devil (or some demonic representative of Satan, like a door-to-door salesman) when their contract comes to full term and they refuse to surrender willingly (you can find this bit of lore in some of the episodes of the television series *Supernatural* as well as other places).

As far as modern lore goes, take note of the *Damien* movies about the son of Satan being born upon the Earth and eventually being raised among diplomats who are from a high society family who groom him to become the Anti-Christ as he ascends to the Presidency of the United States. In these films, Damien is protected throughout his life by sinister looking black dogs, usually Rottweilers, although in reality these dogs can be quite sweet, and we think Dobermans might have been a better choice in this case but Rottweilers look large and stocky and potentially menacing, which may have influenced the movie maker's choice. Here again we have a transformed interpretation of the ancient legends concerning black dogs. And once more, it has been Christianized or Demonized, whichever you will, into modern mythology. All we have, we have inherited from the past, sometimes renewed and reborn by virtue of our own creative spirit. As we elves say: Nothing real is ever lost, nothing false endures.

Black dogs are often associated with death and seeing one, like hearing a Banshee or seeing the Bean-nighe, can indicate one's impending demise. Sometimes, black dogs are said to run with the Wild Hunt, tracking down their prey, in the manner of a fox hunt surely. In association with that consider the multi-headed Cerberus, a black dog that guards the underworld in Greek mythology. Also, note Anubis, the dog headed god of the dead in Egyptian lore (his head is black). Further, examine the lore concerning the Cŵn Annwn of Welsh lore, the hounds of Annwn, the land of the dead or otherworld, who specifically are said to run with the Wild Hunt. Which, in this case was led by Arawn, king of Annwn, or sometimes said to be led by Gwyn ap Nudd who is seen as the king of the underworld and alternately the king of the fair or faerie folk according to later medieval lore.

Again, pay attention to the blending of the legends of Faerie as a realm and the underworld of the dead, the Underworld and Otherworld becoming almost synonymous and in time becoming associated with Hell or the demonic realm that is said to be a fiery kingdom beneath the Earth as Heaven is said to be above it. Well, we do have a molten core to the Earth and all things that once were get covered up in time by settling dust (and let's face it, by epithelial tissue that we constantly slough off), sinking down toward the center of the Earth and fiery extinction and then released, coming to the surface again as molten lava (cremated, we might say, or trial by fire?), as the ongoing world continues to change and thrive on the surface (and, we expect, eventually in space).

Also, make note of Garmr or Garm in Norse mythology who is seen as wolf or dog that is linked with Hel (the goddess of the underworld of the Norse), from which we get the title

Hell for the infernal realms, and this dog is also associated with Ragnarök, which Christians like to call Armageddon. Garmr, like Cerberus, guards the gates of the underworld or the world of the dead who are, in this mythology, consigned to Hel's realm for their lack of courage in life or dishonorable behavior or for dying without a sword in their hand. Unlike the Christians, the ancient Norse, Danes and related tribes who went Viking, which was essentially culturally sanctioned rape, murder and theft (like most modern wars) didn't value absolute obedience so much as having *balls*.

As an aside, we might note that while in Western cultures we usually associate death with the color black and wear black garments for mourning, funerals and such, in Asian cultures they associate death with the color white and don white clothes for their funeral rites. Thus, samurai characters that we might see in movies committing seppuku or ritual suicide (which we in the West used to call Hari Kari) wear white garments to do so (plus the blood shows up so much better that way).

Would that indicate that death dogs, if they had them in Asia, would be white dogs not black dogs? (Would Asian goths wear all white?) We do know that there is a lunar or moon white dragon in Chinese lore that is associated with death. This offers us the link between the Moon (rather than the Sun, which is generally thought to represent life) with death, the occult, the astral and psychic realms, the Between and the otherworldly as indicated by the major arcana card of The Moon #18 in the tarot, in which there are usually two dogs howling or baying at the Moon. These are not usually portrayed as black dogs, perhaps for artistic reasons, but they should probably be so.

The black dog is also associated with the Barguest (bar - guest? See *Abbey Lubbers, Banshees and Boggarts: An Illustrated Encyclopedia of Fairies* by Katharine Briggs) that is seen as being similar to a Banshee, perhaps because bar-guests, dogs, wolves and banshees all tend to howl or wail at the moon or the night sky and quite often this leads to someone's death, often in modern times in a drunken auto accident, the Wild Hunt too frequently having become turned into a pub crawl. Although, Barquest is also sometimes said to be translated as Barn-ghaist or barn spirit in reference, perhaps, to protective farm dogs (see *The World Guide to Gnomes, Fairies, Elves and Other Little People* by Thomas Keightley) who howl at any strangers who happen to wander near and will chase after them if released.

And yet, dogs can be the most loyal of creatures. Yes, violent if raised that way, and definitely aggressive if they think you are endangering someone that they love but utterly loyal to those who take care of them and love them. So, being part of the Wild Hunt, being hunting dogs tracking down their prey, is an easy association to understand for dogs, but why are they in the legends of so many diverse cultures guarding the Gates to the Underworld? And, why is it that they are not guarding it, if we are to believe the lore, from the individuals, the ghosts, demons and specters that abide there as though they are prison guards keeping the inmates trapped within? But rather, as legend seems to have it, they guard the gates from outsiders seeking to intrude into the underworld, the world of the fae or the dead. Although, it is true that prison guards do that as well, keeping unwanted people both in and out. What is it that the black dogs are protecting?

We expect that they are guarding the otherworldly realms of the Between, where our powers manifest fully and those who are passing through are moving on to a new incarnation, and do not need to be drawn back into the life that they previously had, as much as those of us who loved them might wish to do so. Death is a door going only one way in and one way out. We have to let those who have passed into that realm go on, just as we can't keep our children, children forever, as much as some of us tend to treat them that way. Although, most of us who are parents will probably always see them as being our beloved wee ones. They will eternally be our children until, in fact, we pass through the Between, reincarnate in the course of time and possibly become their children or grandchildren. And this may explain why some children are inclined to nurture and treat their parents with such loving care, as though they, in fact, are the actual adults in the family situation. Children may not have much knowledge or experience of the world they are born into but they often display a wisdom and an intuitive understanding that belies their youth.

It is important to raise our littles so they might go free and direct their own lives, making decisions for thems'elves and be responsible for their own actions. So, too, we must release those we have known but who have journeyed on, usually of necessity, into the Between so they may develop according to the needs and potential of their own spirits. In other words, it is important that we let them go so they may progress and mature into the powerful spirits they were ever destined to be.

The Spell:

Oh, Banshee, don't wail for me
For I will join you soon
And we shall dance in circles round
And howl at rising moon

Arvyndase:

Tra, Bånshe, ba'kon helz fro el

Fro El yon lyl le qun

Nar eli van far ter dalsoli ond

Nar yalu zan luftdas tarsa

Pronunciation:

Trah, Banshee, bah'cone heal-z fro eel

Fro Eel yone lil (as in lily) lee que-n

Nair e - lie vane fair tier dale - so - lie oh-nd

Nair yeah - lou zane lou-ft - dace tair – sah

Chapter 23:

Passing On, Passing Over, Beyond the Veil, Kicking the Bucket and Giving up the Ghost

*Y*ou may note that modern people, and we expect people in the past as well, often used euphemisms when speaking of death. Some people might say that this is because we are afraid of death and certainly most of us are a bit hesitant and reluctant, to say the least, to die (and there good evolutionary reasons for this fear of death as well as magical and spiritual ones [see our book *Faerie Unfolding*]). But it may also be that many of us are superstitious about evoking death by speaking directly of it (knock on wood), having the feeling that teasing Death or tempting Fate is often less than wise.

But this idea that we should be afraid of drawing Death's attention by speaking of it directly rather contradicts the notion that is popular in magical mythology that if we know a thing or a person's true name we gain power over them. At the same time, Death's true name is Life and when we come to understand the truth of that we do begin to comprehend it and gain greater understanding of it and power over it.

However, many of the expressions that are used concerning death and dying seem to us as being more accurate and explanatory than merely using the term death, as though using that word actually defines what the process really entails. This is rather like saying the stars come out at night when, in fact, they were always there, merely obscured by the light of the sun or daystar. For the word Death, in our opinion, tells us very little really other than that the body of a current incarnation ceases to function properly to the point of having a cardiac event (All death of the material body is ultimately a cardiac event. See *The Lazarus Effect: The Science That is Rewriting the Boundaries Between Life and Death* by Sam Parnia), which forces the spirit to go elsewhere to manifest. You might say most of us are eventually evicted from our current bodily housing, even as we attempt to cling to it desperately, and must seek another abode to house our spirits.

As an example of such euphemisms, we sometimes say that the individual has passed on. Passed on to where? Well, heaven to some people or hell or, as we Silver Elves believe, to the Between and from there to another material manifestation or one that is more etheric but still more physical than the Between or more expansive because while it is more etheric seeming, it is also manifesting in fourth dimensional reality, which thus gives it a wider range of being and experience and a more comprehensive life.

This is rather like the difference between someone who never leaves their home town (like Sam in *The Lord of the Rings* never having ventured very far from Hobbiton, until he goes on the journey with Frodo, first to Rivendell and then to destroy the One Ring) and someone who is able to travel all over the world (more like Gandalf and Aragorn). This doesn't mean that the individual who never leaves their small town cannot be happy, but the individual who can travel the world surely has a greater field of experience and most likely a better understanding of the world and what is in it, overall. We Silver Elves know our own experiences in traveling here and there about the world has increased our awareness greatly. So those who graduate to living in four (or more) dimensions have a wider view and perhaps a greater understanding of the nature of Life and the Universe.

The word death often seems to imply that the individual utterly ceases to exist in any form, despite beliefs in heavenly realms, whereas passing on indicates a potential evolution and perhaps graduation to a new and better incarnation or, at least, a continuance of life in another form. Certainly, that is what is hoped by most of us, although surely some people look forward to oblivion and the end to the emotional turmoil that the world often entails or an end to physical suffering in the same way that many of us look forward to falling asleep at night, particularly when we are really tired.

And, truly, whether an individual who has died was promoted or perhaps demoted, as we might view things, eventually they will fulfill their destiny. Dead-ends or demotions, which is to say an incarnation in a less evolved form or a more difficult and limiting life due to karma, represent temporary setbacks. Always in the long run, we move toward the natural fulfillment of our spiritual being.

In a certain sense, we are passing on quite literally. We are passing on everything we leave behind to our descendants or whomever deals with our remains, including our soiled clothes washed by the Bean-nighe. And since we are, by means of the process of incarnation, potentially our own descendants, we are passing on what we have achieved in the world to ours'elves and those around us, just as we pass on our spiritual achievements from one incarnation to the next, as long as we don't let those talents and abilities atrophy through disuse and neglect.

Still, what do they say about learning to ride a bicycle? Once you learn you can always easily pick it up again? Although, being able to ride for any distance without panting may take a bit longer. The basic technique is remembered by our subconscious and bodily memory but execution of the technique may need a bit of a touch up. We remember how to do it but may not have the muscles or energy to do it so well at first. Rather like a baby learning to crawl, stand and then walk again. So, too, our spirit body remembers certain things that aren't passed on to us by the Collective Unconscious, which is the instinctive knowledge that our physical or genetic body provides (according the theories of Carl Jung). The body, which is to say, our ancestry and genetic lineage has its own secrets to reveal, separate, usually, from our spiritual, light or energetic body. Thus, once again, we are shaped by Nature, Nurture and also Spirit (our individual evolutionary progress), which is a higher and more esoteric manifestation of Nature.

In political and sometimes artistic and business circles, they are known to refer to this process of passing on as the individual's legacy. This is to indicate what the individual has accomplished in life and passed on to posterity that will hopefully make the world a better place for future generations. In our own case, we Silver Elves often hope that in future lifetimes we will come across our own books to help us awaken to our true elven natures once again. We certainly write these books with that possibility in mind. We seek to help our kindred awaken both in this and in upcoming incarnations but we also hope that in doing so those awakened elfin will pass on our culture to help awaken us in a future incarnation.

Passing over has similar connotations, although, what is it we are passing over? In Norse lore, it would be the rainbow Bifrost bridge that spans from Midgard (Middle Earth or Middle World or this material realm) to Asgard the materialized but ephemeral realm of the gods or Shining Ones. Although we elfin are more likely to and desirous of going to Alfheim, the world of the elven and then back to a life of manifestation in this more physical realm as we seek to create Elfin upon the Earth or the more materialized planes of being. In other words, we seek to manifest Elfin in what most people conceive of as reality. This is our mission; this is our *elf quest*.

Passing Over sounds like we are passing the mashed potatoes or the cream for the coffee or something. Or, perhaps, passing over a speed bump. Is death a speed bump on the road to Elfin? Or is each incarnation a speed bump? Of course, what is usually meant is that one is passing over to the other side. The other side? The other world? One is passing into the Faerie Realms of the Between. Two sides of the same coin that is Life, the material and the ethereal realms, or form and spirit, and the

Between is the edge around them. We might say that form and spirit are like the difference between a house and a home. A house is a structure that a person, persons or a family lives in. It is the *living in* that makes it a home and we are the elfae that live there, filling it with our spirit.

Witches speak of Standing Between the Worlds, which is to say being conscious in the realms of the Between or between the world of material consciousness and the realms of etheric awareness where our magical powers are greatest, in order to evoke the spirits, and in that way being able to enter the Between while our physical bodies are in trance states for short periods of time, and without permanently abandoning our body and therefore entering those realms without having to die.

And this is, in its way, similar to shamanic journeying on the astral planes by using our astral form or bodies of light to navigate that world. We walk among the spirits, commune and communicate and sometimes bargain with them in our spirit bodies or ethereal forms and then we are still able to return to our materialized bodies to which we are connected, according to some esoteric lore, by a fine silver thread.

For our own part, we Silver Elves don't believe there is a silver cord that links us to our physical bodies when we are astral traveling. But rather that there is an esoteric energetic link, rather like the connection between us and those we love or have loved, that keeps us attached to the body until it can no longer maintain its organic wholeness and begins to separate into its constituent parts, the energy of the body returning to its essential form while the code that delineated its structure is carried on by others. In the same way, our computer can break down totally but our data is still stored elsewhere and the design for making that particular computer, both its hardware and software, still continues to exist.

The code for our bodies is carried in DNA. We came into existence and consciousness once, why not again? And again, and again? Our spirits live, with or without material bodies to manifest within, although as we say the material world, which, due to gravity, tends to slow down time so we can get to the details of life, is helpful for evolving. Bodies are rather convenient for doing certain things. Otherwise, our lives would be like movies or dreams where we leap from one moment to another, skipping all the in-between events. Of course, that might sound marvelous to some folks who find the ennui of life intolerable and is perhaps the experience of alcoholics who tend to lose time due to their inebriated states.

Sometimes, people speak of going Beyond the Veil. The Veil is an indication that the Universe is a whole and all things are connected. We may look at Life and Death as opposites, or the worlds of the Living and the Dead as being different, but the idea that the dead are on the other side of the Veil or in this world but unseen, is a hint that the world of the disembodied spirits is right here with us only covered by a Veil or Mist through which only those with psychic, faerie or elf sight can see. It is as though individuals in the Between are manifesting as Ultraviolet or Infrared Light, only on an even more subtle frequency. Existing therefore as a light or energy that we don't, for the most part, have the technology to see as we do with Ultraviolet or Infrared light. Perhaps it is the realm of the quarks? We elves are certainly quirky and eccentric people.

People who relate to faeries as entirely otherworldly and ethereal beings (and generally refuse to acknowledge our manifest elfae existence), are also looking beyond the veil, using their psychic powers or faerie sight (they are sometimes referred to as Faerie Seers), and often their imaginal facilities (sort of the night vision goggles for the faerie worlds), to view the more ephemeral beings of that (our) world. See the book *Summer With the Leprechauns: A True Story* by Tanis Helliwell; *The Magic of Findhorn* by Paul Hawken; *The Elves of Lily Hill Farm: A Partnership with Nature* by Penny Kelly; *Fairies at Work and at Play* as observed by Geoffrey Hodson; *Meeting the Other Crowd: The Fairy Stories of Hidden Ireland* by Eddie Lenihan; and *Forty Years with the Fairies* by Daphne Charters, which all proport to be factual encounters with ephemeral elfin beings through the use of faerie sight of clairvoyance, although we find some of these books rather slow reading for our tastes.

Also, for a more how-to book on this subject check out Ramsey Dukes' *How To See Fairies: Discover Your Psychic Powers In Six Weeks*, although we admit this is our least favorite of his books and we enjoy his books on practical magical theory and its practice a whole lot more. They are often quite brilliant.

For our own part, we Silver Elves often consider the dragonflies, butterflies and moths as being faerie folk, only of a more materialized and less anthropomorphized form. We are not inclined to demand that all elfae folk be in humanoid bodies, as some folks seem to do. It is elvish spirit that is most indicative of elfin folk, not a particular form. Dragonflies may just look like insects to other people but we see faeries, conscious beings in otherworldly bodies, when they flit about us. We know they are alive, that they have their own form of consciousness and their own needs, directives, urges and desires in the world. We don't demand that everything Elfin and Faerie be humanized, the mere idea flies in the face of Faerie's essential magic in the first place, but we appreciate when people like Tolkien acknowledge and foster our humanoid manifestations.

The faerie spirits that inhabit what most people would consider to be insects, make do with the bodies that are available to them, just as we other elfae folk make do with what is available to us in utilizing humanoid bodies for our incarnation into the material realm. There are many spirits seeking manifestation in this world and quite a few of them, like individuals desperate for love, marriage or sex, seize whatever or whomever they come across first that will have them or are open to them.

On the other hand, it is possible that unlike those faeries who incarnate into humanoid bodies, those that choose to live the life of the butterfly, dragonfly or moth simply refuse to live a life without their wings. We're not sure entirely what elves who are utterly intent on having pointed ears would do, perhaps have lives as cats, although most of us in humanoid bodies make due with prosthetics and a few have surgery to give them pointed ears. And, yes, there are a few we Silver Elves have known who happened to incarnate into a body that naturally, and wonderfully to our minds, had actual pointed ears.

The Veil, in this case, is not a physical thing but represents our own capacity or inability to see certain things, such as radio waves or gamma waves that exist but cannot be picked up by our ordinary senses. There are whole dimensions of existence that are invisible to our perceptions. Like a person walking around with a veil over their face, you can sometimes sort of see them but not distinctly. Our notions of the other side of the veil therefore are, in most cases, hazy at best. The perception of this world for most people is rather like someone who has colorblindness. There are simply things that most people cannot see.

And since nearly everyone's experience in the Between is unique to their particular spirit and consciousness and to the current level of their evolutionary development, then it is hard to be exact about such things anyway. Plus, for most of us, the journey through death removes most of the memories (the majority of which weren't that germane to our spirit anyway) of our previous life and the passage back into incarnation, back across the veil, shields most of us from remembering our experience in those realms, as well, just as we tend to forget most of our dreams.

Kicking the Bucket is another common expression and along with that people have Bucket Lists of things they wish to do before they die. Some theorize that the expression Kicking the Bucket may come from people being hanged from a tree limb while forced to stand on a bucket or barrel that was then kicked out from under them. But, whether this is true or not, we, nor apparently anyone else for that matter, don't actually know.

For our own part, we suspect that Kicking the Bucket may be related to hypnogogic jerks, also called myoclonic jerks, that occur just as a person is falling asleep and from our point of view the person is 'kicking' out of their body and into the astral planes. We suspect that in many cases the same sort of jerk or kicking occurs when the person is in the process of permanently kicking out of their current body and moving on, passing on, passing over to the realms of the Between and eventually on to a new incarnation. For sleep is like death, as dreams are similar to the Between states of consciousness.

And then we have Giving Up the Ghost. This is a curious expression because it sounds like you are giving up your ghost or spirit (assuming in this way that our material body is our real being) when, in fact, it is the spirit or specter or ghostly being, our energetic or light being that is our true s'elf that is giving up the body it was inhabiting and it was using as a vehicle for manifesting and moving through the world. It might be better expressed as giving up the body and the illusionary life that one was leading and mistook for reality rather than giving up the ghost, for it is really our spirit/ghost that is ridding its'elf, at least temporarily, of our physical body and all the limitations it imposes upon us and going forth in our astral body and/or mental body into the realms of absolute possibility.

On the other hand, when you consider that the material world is just a glamor over the energetic nature of reality that is spirit and consciousness, then perhaps the ghost really is the material body that looks real and solid but is actually a conglomeration of atoms energetically combined for a time due to electro-magnetic forces and the powerful will of our spirits to manifest.

The Spell:

Beyond the veil so dark, unseen
Oh, light that shines both bright and keen
Be like the stars at night and glow
Of Elfin true my heart to show

Arvyndase:
Hyrlon tae fanj re das, murtenïn
Tra, lun dij glislu aso ilu nar reb

Te sylar tae mélli zan sol nar lums

U Êldat lod el'na bom va teke

Pronunciation:

Her - lone tay fane-j ree dace, muir - teen - in

Trah, loon dye-j glice - lou a - so eye - lou nair reeb

Tea sill - lair tay mell - lie zane soul nair looms

You L - date load eel'nah bow-m (rhymes with foam) vah tea - kee

෨

Chapter 24:
Animism, Nature Spirits, and Teraphim

We elves are basically, and for the most part, animists (although every elf has the responsibility to decide for their own s'elf what their spiritual beliefs are [see our book *The Elven Way*]). This is to say that we Silver Elves believe that Divine Magic exists in potential in all beings and in all of manifestation. Everything is evolving toward the realization of that Divine, or magical we might say, potentiality. All of life is in motion. We are developing as spirit/spiritual beings and as energetic beings but so are the animals and even the elements of the Periodic Table of Elements, particularly the radioactive elements, which are still clearly in a powerful transitional phase of their development. Most of them are relatively young in a sense and still deeply immersed in the process of becoming.

All of life is in the process of becoming and transforming. Even the stars are born, live and then die, only to be born again later. They send forth their light until their energy is depleted, their abandoned bodies collapse into themselves becoming black holes and then begin to collect light, matter and energy again. E=mc2. Mass, which is to say matter and energy, are the same thing, really.

And yet, not only is spirit (which some folks would call soul) evolving but also, as indicated by the elements, the physical world and our material bodies, or the material energy that composes our bodies and the forms themselves are evolving as well. Our DNA can change and that is what we are doing as we pass from one incarnation to another increasing our mastery over ours'elves, and through that our mastery over our bodies and the material world. Our choices, which is to say our actions and our magic, helps alter who we are. But our bodies are also mutating and evolving. We are learning through experience and so is every cell, atom and molecule in our bodies.

In that way, we elves are somewhat different from most people in that we see the spirit realm as the true realm of being and the material realm merely as a shadow or reflection of it that has taken shape around the energy of spirit. Most people think the material realm is the basis of all things, even though they often claim to believe in an afterlife in heaven or hell, but we know that the physical plane is merely transitory form that we are learning to shape or sculpt, we might say, according to our will through our intentional and habitual actions and through our many incarnations. The world is spirit, but spirit shaped in particular ways according to the vibration and frequency of our energy.

We need not accept things as being as they currently are forever, as though all things are inevitable and our lives are predetermined. We do, however, need to accept reality as it appears to us if we are to change it toward our vision through our magic, which is to say our actions, our behaviors and our lives. For we have the power and, we Silver Elves feel, the obligation to strive to make things better in this world. Those who don't do so wind up living in worlds that others have created for them. Still, ours is not the only magic or vision in the world or in the universe and learning to enact our magic in harmony with others is key to fulfilling our dreams and our wishes.

The question is sometimes asked *do animals have souls?* To which many religions would reply that they do not, positing the notion that only Men (and women, under them) have souls. Again, let us point out that what they would call soul we Silver Elves call spirit and all living things have spirit, for this is why they are alive in the first place. Soul, to us, is our link and connection, usually through feeling, intuition or psychic sense, to the Universe and to other beings. So, we Silver Elves not only see animals as having spirits, which is to say conscious life energy, but they, like us, also have souls or a soulful function with an ability to connect to the world around them with feeling and intuition.

But what about rocks? Or what about houses, statues and other objects, such as Jesus on the Cross that so many Christians wear or have in their houses and churches? Or the flag of one's nation that people regard with such devotion and will even turn violent if they think someone has insulted it or been rude to it? (Be cautious how you treat some people's favorite symbols, those with less rational intelligence may get dangerous if you make fun or degrade their favorite icons or their beliefs.)

Or what about the acute angled seven-pointed Elf Star that we elves and faery folk (that the faeries like to call the Faerie Star) often wear to adorn ours'elves and that we use to indicate to our kindred, whose paths we might happen to cross, that we are elfin? We wear it as a sort of secret signal, although we are not attempting to keep it secret, usually; it is just that few people outside of our elfae communities have any idea what our elven star and its wondrous magic represents to us. Although, it is true some elfae folk are still hiding their elfin identity in the closet, or woods or whatever.

Actually, most people we Silver Elves have come across who aren't acquainted with the Elven star as a symbol of our culture and happen to notice that we are wearing one and make a comment about it, usually take a quick glance and assume it is the Star of David that Judaic folk often wear. This is somewhat like the fact that when Zardoa wears his green *Kiss Me I'm Elvish* tee shirt, people often simply glance at it without really looking and assume it says 'Kiss Me I'm Irish' and start talking about their Irish ancestors. But then many of the fae folk were, and are, of Irish descent, so such individuals may not be that far off, having unconsciously made the right connection even if they hadn't actually bothered to really see what was on the tee shirt. Faerie or Sidhe spirit may run in the blood of many of the Irish and many of the tales, legends and lore about we fae folk come from Ireland and the British Isles, overall, so it's not such a far leap to make.

From our elven point of view, all organic beings have spirits. All inorganic or artificial structures, such as crystals or houses, or statues, etc. are merely physical forms that are capable of housing spirits in the same way that our bodies house our spirits, die and disintegrate when we abandon them withdrawing our lifeforce or life energy from them, and then they become lifeless as an organic whole. They are still quite active as they rot and disintegrate into their constituent parts and energies that our spirit held together. But then, where does the Life go but on to other manifestations.

We suppose there may come a time, as in some science fiction stories, when we will be able to get a new body, just like getting a new car when we can afford one; but that is merely a technological understanding of the power of glamor really and more particularly the ability to shape-shift. We are, in fact, merely changing one form for another (which we do from one incarnation to another, anyway, and as we grow up and age, changing the cells in our bodies). When we reincarnate our body will be different but our spirit remains the same, except in so far as we have actually evolved and hopefully matured through our previous incarnations.

Artificially created things, on the other hand, things like statues, are still composed of energy but the individual parts or cells are not functioning as a whole in an organic way. The atoms that constitute a statue are rather like a group of strangers who may work together in a factory but have no other real connection of any sort.

Yet spirit exists everywhere so that even houses, restaurants and particular areas or regions, have their own ambience or spirit, or can have one, just in the same way that a crowd of strangers working together could become united by a common cause (such as factory workers unionizing) and begin to act as a group. The spirit of houses, places and such, however, is often a greater spirit (as a national identity holds the greater spirit of a group of people) that abides in a structure and gives it a vibrational frequency.

A stone, rock or house or whatever becomes, in that sense, like a somewhat passive radio station or one that merely broadcasts a repetitive signal as sometimes happens in apocalyptic movies. One might be able to destroy the house, tear it apart or burn it down, but that doesn't destroy the spirit, the vibrational energy, which, like ours'elves merely moves on to a new place of habitation or hovers in the area where the house existed changing in time as other events take place there.

This is also the idea concerning nature spirits. Nature spirits are energies that exist in and express themselves through particular areas of Nature, including the elementals. Note that faeries and sometimes elves are seen as nature spirits who tend the flowers and other growing things, as though they were the gardeners of the etheric realms. So, it is that we have sun spirits, trees spirits, moon spirits, fire spirits, air spirits, water spirits, earth spirits, spirits of a particular region or area and so on. The spirit of a forest is an example of higher spirits. Spirit is everywhere, which is to say, everything is energy and all things that give off or radiate energy are spirits, yet the energy it gives off is also spirit. Life is spirit. And energy can neither be created nor destroyed, it can only transform its state of manifestation, which is to say, it can only alter its form.

Seers, such as Geoffery Hodson, *Fairies at Work and at Play*, see the faeries tending the growth and development of the plants, but at the same time they understand that the faeries are the spirits of the plant. The plant is the material body of these faerie spirits. We Silver Elves were once speaking to Kathleen Harrison, who had been married for a time to Terence McKenna (known for his study and books as an ethnobotanist, mystic and psychonaut) about some tobacco plants we'd been gifted in a magical way (see our book *Eldafaryn*). She told us a story about talking to some shamans in South America about the tobacco plant (which is sometimes called the grandchild of the spirit world [see *The Cosmic Serpent, DNA and the Origins of Knowledge* by Jeremy Narby]) and asked them about the spirit of the plant. The shamans told her the plant was the spirit. She actually already knew and understood this to be the case, but she wanted to be clear about what they were telling her. The plant was the living body of the spirit, just as our spirits manifest through our bodies.

This same sort of idea is associated with enchanted rings, swords and other objects imbued with magical powers. A spirit or energy is inhabiting the object, which is why such magical swords or rings are often given names. Usually, such objects are said to be enchanted by a particular person, a witch, wizard, enchantress, or other magic wielder but nearly everything we own and have for a long time tends to absorb our energy automatically. Just as the things we touch get the oils from our skin, our fingerprints and so forth upon them. Thus, caretakers and curators who are in charge of the preservation of ancient books and art usual wear white gloves to touch them to keep the soils and oils from their skin from damaging these precious and usually rare objects.

This, as we pointed out in an earlier chapter, is the basis for shards, or energetic echoes of spirits who have experienced traumatic events, often of a person dying by violence, in a particular place. The spirit moves on but the energy echoes for a time in the objects or places that surrounded them when the event took place. The enchanted object, on the other hand, bears the idea of a more active spirit living within it, usually;

which would be more like the idea of a ghost or specter than merely a shard or echo of existence. The enchanted object denotes active magic rather than the sort of static and repetitive energy of a shard.

We know for a fact that water, for instance, absorbs electromagnetic energy. It is also thought by some that it can absorb emotional and thought-form energy as well. See Masaru Emoto *The Hidden Messages in Water* and other books, which are seen as pseudo-science, but then so is the existence of we elven, both as materialized and ethereal beings. In fact, the existence of the Scythian folk upon which so many elfin fae legends seem to be based (see Laurence Gardner *Realms of the Ring Lords*) were also thought to be mere myth until about a hundred or so years ago when some of their burial mounds were discovered. Crystals can also absorb and radiate radio waves, which is why crystals are so often valued by energetic healing practitioners as well as by magic wielders of various disciplines.

The point is that we energetically effect the world around us and it can, in turn, effect us as well (mostly through our soul function, which is to say feeling energy on various levels from touch to smell to intuition). When we become conscious of this we can use our lives to transmute the world about us on the astral and mental planes of being through the power of our will and intention and thus serve to manifest Elfin upon the Earth, which is our goal, mission and heartfelt wish.

So, it is that we Silver Elves have a home filled with over 500 teraphim (see our book *Eldafaryn*), which is to say statues of elves, faeries, pixies, brownies, menehunes, gnomes, gargoyles, dragons, fauns, unicorns, a few hobbits (although we tend to think of hobbits as a type of gnome or brownie) and even a few sweet trolls who accompanied us back from a trek to Finland and Sweden. And over time, other elfae spirits come to join us so that the number of fae spirits that live with us, taking shelter in statues as teraphim, gradually increases.

The statues thems'elves are just empty forms (static energy) but because of their form they radiate the idea of the Faerie and Elfin worlds, and in our minds and imaginations they become houses for spirits to live in (like Thai spirit houses or even churches, temples, mosques, shrines and other places set aside for the Divine Magic to manifest), and therefore with us. Spirit lives everywhere, in everything, some of it in organic forms, some in inorganic forms, some in biological bodies, some in artificially created bodies but all of the world is spirit manifesting, which is to say all the Universe vibrates and hums with energy on various frequencies.

The Spell:

Spirit that surrounds us
In every shape and style
Awaken to our magic
Attend us all the while

Arvyndase:
Tari dij åbondlu eli
Ver lotym nalf nar fås
Vasa va eli'na êldon
Naker eli wyl tae jern

Pronunciation:

Tay - rye dye-j ab - ond - lou e - lie

Veer low - tim nail-f nair fahss

Vah - sah vah e - lie'nah l - doan

Nay - keer e - lie will tay jeer-n

ತಿ

Chapter 25:
Fallen

allen is a 1998 movie starring Denzel Washington and John Goodman about a fallen angel or spirit that can occupy (as in the form of possession) the bodies of other people, being able to hop in and out of bodies quickly and easily simply by touching them. Of course, being a demonic spirit, he often does criminal things but this happens mostly in the way that people with anti-social personality disorders act, which is to say without any real feeling, compassion or remorse and accepting themselves as the only authentic arbiters of what is right and wrong. Right being, from their point of view, whatever it is they wish to do and wrong being anyone that stands in their way.

We could say this character does evil things because he is demonic but we expect it would be better and more accurate to say that he's demonic because he does wicked things. Otherwise, he'd be angelic in a more Seelie way. Contrary to the idea that some people are born evil (although lifetimes of wicked deeds may predispose a person to such actions), we elves and other magical people see the world as being a place where choice and will matter and one can nearly always choose a better way. Although, this character, like most sociopaths, doesn't see the things he does or the choices he makes as being evil, merely that he is doing what he chooses to do because he has the power to do it.

This is really the same attitude that many Men have concerning other creatures in Nature, including the trees, as well as the oceans and all creatures in it, the atmosphere and the Earth itself, that other's lives are insignificant and they can be killed without a second thought, merely because they are in the way or because these men just feel like killing them or for the *sport* of it, the pure joy of going about and killing other creatures (often putting their stuffed heads on their wall and calling it a trophy as if they've done something astounding). And then feeling quite superior and 'manly' because they shot a creature with a high powered rifle from a safe distance, often from hiding, sometimes even from helicopters. Even shooting creatures such as elephants and giraffes that would never even bother anyone else if they were just left alone to mind their own business.

In this case (*Fallen*), however, this sense of species superiority and privilege is extended to include members of the human race. But this is also what racists and homophobes often do as a means of excusing their behaviors when they brutalize and/or kill those whose race, religion, nationality, lifestyle or sexuality are of those they don't approve of. They view these others as being lesser beings of little power and thus of no significance, plus these others are simply different from them, which they take to be an indication of inferiority in and of itself. And people being different, to the ignorant, is nearly always a source of fear and paranoia and ever a good excuse, as far as they are concerned, for oppressing people.

Like many vampires in stories, this angel in *Fallen* and other such characters look down upon normal human beings as being inferior (since they are less powerful) and thus also regard them as natural prey. This is a basically an Unseelie point of view, in our opinion. And rather like children, such beings simply do what they wish to do often without much, if any, thought about the consequences for others who are insignificant to them, and many times (in the case of children or teenagers) without any consideration about the consequences for themselves, either. They feel no sense of guilt, have no conscience (as the old folks would say, but we seldom hear this expression used anymore) and consider themselves as being freer, more powerful and above others because of this.

Curiously, this unquestioning confidence in themselves and their own self-importance (the same is true of people who suffer from Narcissistic Personality Complexes) often lends them a certain charismatic quality, especially among those who are inwardly uncertain of their own personal worth or who are of more modest intelligence and are looking for a strong and confident leader or savior to follow and idealize.

In the case of the antagonist in the movie *Fallen*, this character can only die if the body he currently is in dies while he is at a certain distance (like a mile or something) from any other body to jump to and inhabit. Although, from our point of view, this descended Unseelie Shining One, would merely cease to be able to descend into or remain in the material realms and thus would have to deal with those more powerful Shining Ones that exist upon its natural realm of manifestation. This is perhaps why it is seeking so desperately to remain in the physical world so he can be a big frog in a small pond, as the saying goes, rather than under the influence of far greater spirits in the more expansive dimensions of the Shining Ones.

Like many demonic stories, *Fallen* is a story of possession (or serial possession) only instead of staying in the same body and doing crazy things while strapped to a bed and having priest throw holy water on the possessed body while chanting prayers in Latin, the spirit roams freely; at least until it is caught and imprisoned. In fact, in the beginning of the movie, this being is possessing the body of a man that went on a killing spree, while being possessed by this spirit, and is waiting to be executed. Which doesn't entirely make sense, since he can jump effortlessly from body to body, so we don't know why he decided to spend time on death row instead of just finding another body immediately and continuing with its demented activities. But like zombie movies, we don't want to overthink this.

Still, it does make us wonder why in such stories as the *Exorcist* the spirit is trapped in the body it possesses, letting itself be tortured, spewing vomit and obscenities at the priests while taunting them with knowledge of their deepest darkest secrets (let us not even ponder what those might actually be). It could instead easily pretend to be normal for a short while and then go off and do whatever it wanted once more as most people with anti-social personality disorders do when they learn to mimic the feeling expressions of the normal folk around them in order to pass as normal, being a wolf in sheep's clothing, as the saying goes. But then, as we said, it doesn't do to overthink such things, particularly if you just wish to enjoy the movie and sometimes (perhaps often) you have to suspend your disbelief for a while.

Yet, the whole idea of possession by an outside spirit speaks to the notion that we are spirits inhabiting bodies. If, as the materialistic point of view goes, our bodies are our true s'elves or are the primary force for making us who we are then how could any outside spirit inhabit our bodies? Of course, germs and viruses invade our bodies, and we might look upon demonic possession as merely the invasion of a sort of virus, only a virus of an esoteric rather than exoteric form, a sort of psychological or emotional and mental virus, sort of like a computer virus that happens to affect the software but not the hardware. For our spirits are the software (and the electricity), while our bodies are the hardware of the humanoid computer that we inhabit.

We, therefore, might consider the same idea in terms of Dissociative Identity Disorders (once called Multiple Personality Disorders) where more than one personality inhabits the same being and takes turns being conscious. Sometimes, these beings are aware of each other, but often the primary consciousness, or the normal or host personality, we might say, is utterly unaware that there are personalities other than it, except that it experiences lapses of time and memory loss. Although, those other or sub-personalities, are often aware of each other (see the movie *Split* or read the DSM 4 or 5, or whatever edition they are on currently when you read this book, about this disorder).

From our Silver Elves point of view, these personalities are a number of different spirits that are sharing the same bodily form, often in a somewhat disoriented or disorganized fashion. For therapists in dealing with those who suffer from this disorder, the whole idea usually is to help integrate these personalities, make them aware of each other, so they can function as one being, much in the way that a squad in the military or some team, say a Navy Seal Team, trains to function as a complete unit.

But again, the question is, if the body and its biochemical structure absolutely determine who we are as individuals, how can we have different personalities that are unrelated to each other in the first place? Although, most of us do have different personalities, depending upon whether we are angry or in love or happen to be with this or that person, just as we have different facial expressions. And just as we often argue with ours'elves in our minds when we are uncertain what to do or we experience an inner conflict between reason, logic and practicality on the one hand, and our powerful desires and urges on the other. Who exactly are we arguing with when we debate within ours'elves? Carl Jung theorized that we are ultimately all on the path to psychological integration of our beings. So we are arguing with the different aspects or spirits that constitute our being that is seeking an eventual harmony among them and, in a sense, the creation of a greater being.

Still, these inner conflicts are generally seen as varied aspects of one's being not as completely different beings, as is the case in Dissociative Identity Disorders, in which the personalities are often at odds with each other and struggling for dominance of the body and of the conscious mind and when one of the personalities comes to dominate the conscious mind and thus has control over the body, it sometimes forces the other personalities to sleep, you might say, in the subconscious. And we can see this in normal human beings sometimes as well, when individuals do things that they are ashamed of or wish to deny and remove from their consciousness the fact that they ever said or did such things in the first place in a sort of blindness concerning their own behavior.

Sharing a body may be somewhat like sharing a house or an apartment or a room. You've got to learn to live with your roomies or go find your own abode, which is to say find a body of your own in which to live in. Most peoples and countries experience this sort of divide between its liberal and conservative populations. If they fail to reach a basic harmony among themselves, or at least a mutual tolerance, the nation often devolves into civil war or the dominance of one group over the other(s), with loss to the nation overall, particularly as it often neglects, oppresses and by doing so loses the genius and inventiveness of some of its members. This so often happens in countries that strongly oppress women or various other minorities resulting, in the course of time, in that country falling behind other countries that embrace the intelligence, inventive genius and wisdom of all of their citizens.

The Spell:

Descending down into bodily form
I find a place that is safe and is warm
Patient I wait for the life that is right
And where my bright spirit will easy take flight

Arvyndase:

Gadandas dab verva miwåla qum
El låc na al dij da del nar da rov
Remar El her fro tae ela dij da mard
Nar ern el'na ilu tari yon hamath rud fosd

Pronunciation:

Gay - dane - dace day-b veer - vah my - wah - lah que-m

Eel lock nah ale dye-j dah deal nair dah rove

Re - mare Eel here fro tay e - lah dye-j da mare-d

Nair ear-n eel'nah eye - lour tay - rye yone hay - mayth rude foe-sd

಄

Chapter 26:
Forgiveness and Sin Eaters

*I*n the introduction to *The Golden Bough: A Study in Comparative Religion,* sometimes called *The Golden Bough: A Study in Magic and Religion* by Sir James George Frazer, the author says that magic as a common practice came before all science. Magic was, in his opinion, the first science, or the precursor to science (also to theater, religion, chemistry, medicine, astronomy and much else) only a science that seemed to include the astral, mental and etheric realms as well as the material realms of Nature. A more encompassing understanding of the Universe, in our opinion, than the materialistic point of view that is the zeitgeist of the current age of the Kali Yuga.

Although, being a scientist of his time, Frazer did not acknowledge the validity of these shamans including the astral, mental and etheric realms in their considerations and thought that early magical science was mistaken in its understanding of the world and the universe and that the early thinking of these magic wielders was based upon superstition rather than scientific discovery. The educational psychologist Jean Piaget said that *magical* (by which he meant superstitious) *thinking* is typical of children between the ages of two and seven before they reach the age of reason. Thus, aboriginal peoples are often viewed by more sophisticated societies as being child-like in their understanding of the world, although we think their understanding of the world and Nature was more direct and simply included things that industrial cultures do not comprehend. They may have been childlike in certain ways, but they also had the inherent wisdom and purity of many children (see the television series *Green Frontier*, also called *Frontera Verde,* to see the conflict between these world views).

Therefore, if we accept the idea that the early shamans were also the original scientists, more or less, we might assume that when one made a mistake in one's magic in aboriginal times, just as one might make a mistake in a laboratory experiment in modern times, one didn't ask anyone for forgiveness. In casting forth spells that failed, one didn't beg Nature to forgive one nor did one appeal to some deity to do the magic for one, as you might ask someone taller than you to get something from a high shelf that you can't stand on your tiptoes to reach.

We expect that the magician, sorcerer, shaman, witch, wizard or magic wielder merely tried their incantation or spell working again (if sHe survived), altering the spell to be more effective and striving to do it better, observing the results of hir (his/her) efforts (since sometimes things fail but not entirely), honing hir data and continually refining his or her experiments as a good scientist should.

Somewhere, we, the human (or humanoid) race overall, went from doing magic directly, to having others do magic for us and this developed into religion and the notion of a subservient relationship to higher and more powerful beings. We began to implore the higher spirits, some doing so under the notion that they were gods, to help, guide and watch over us, and we also developed the notion that we must appease them, make offerings to them and seek their forgiveness if we have done wrong.

Witches, shamans and magic wielders were then cast to the side, often becoming those who lived in the forest away from the mass of their tribe who had mostly turned to demi-gods to aid them, except in cases concerning things that the priests wouldn't approve people having done and then they'd seek out the local witches (see Alice Hoffman's novels *Practical Magic* and the *Rules of Magic*, for just such witches in the modern era) to do spells for them or for some herbal treatment.

However, when things have inexplicitly gone badly, such as a failed harvest or a plague, some priest then tells us god is punishing us for doing evil things (such as not tithing enough, or being too liberal, being gay, or whatever it is they don't happen to like or condone) and for not following God's will (as delineated by the priests) or violating some taboo or religious social custom that the priests made up (inspired by their god, they tell us) in order to control us and make themselves seem powerful and important and to ensure their social position and financial security.

Do we Silver Elves seem somewhat scornful and skeptical about priests, ministers and such? Well, only some. We have known some in that profession that really are superior beings who have devoted their lives to helping others and one cannot help but feel a certain power emanating from them due to the advanced nature of their characters. But, alas, they are few and far between and many seem to be but avaricious conmen while others are well meaning fools.

At the same time as priesthood developed, the idea of chiefs and leaders, who then became warlords and eventually kings and emperors, came into being as well. And with that also came the idea that these leaders were appointed by the gods (the Divine Right of Kings), and we then began to have to beg them for forgiveness when we disobeyed them as well, for their will was God's will. At least this was so according to them and according to the wealthy individuals who supported them in order to stay rich and in power and often by the priestly caste if they wanted to stay in power alongside of them.

And with all this came the specialization of labor, the development of social hierarchies, the accumulation of wealth to families of individuals and the notion that those who are wealthy and more powerful are better and superior than anyone else and are so because they are beloved of the gods. Which has a certain logic to it after all, if you believe your life and luck are gifts from the Divine and that all things come from the Divine then certainly success in life would be Divinely ordained as well. Although, we might ask what gods are these who seem to favor those who lie, cheat and enslave others in order to accumulate wealth and power?

In the early days, our ancestors (us in past incarnations) would kill a cow, goat, horse, or even a human being to plead with their particular chosen or inherited demi-god to forgive them for any supposed violations of their dictates. Notice that in the Old Testament of the Bible, Abraham was ordered to kill his son and offer him up to his god to prove his loyalty and, while reluctant, he was willing to do this to show his absolute obedience. And why not? Since it was his god making this request, He could kill Abraham's son anytime He wanted to anyway so there was no way to save his son if his god wanted him dead. That's just logical.

Only, this tale reminds us of one of those stories about Nazis where an SS officer gives a person a gun and tells them to shoot other prisoners or they will die themselves or alternately he will kill someone they love, like their child, if they don't do so. Just a bit of a cruel mental and emotional torture, really, from a bully in power delighting in his superiority over others. But what a wonderful Biblical story created to convince people how they better do whatever it is that the priests tell them that their god wants them to do or else suffer accordingly (and suffer, anyway, if you actually wind up having to kill your child, unlike Abraham who was told to stand down at the last moment).

And, if you live long enough, unless you are the luckiest person in the world something always goes wrong in life, sooner or later (for Nature and Life move in cycles of development, see the *I Ching*), and when it does the priests and preachers say it was because so and so didn't do what he was told or acted in a way that they didn't like or which violated their dictates, such as dressing differently than they were told to do or, for the elves, not dressing at all. The gods made us naked but apparently don't want us to show our fabulous bodies to each other, except in private, and only then under strictly controlled circumstances.

Which reminds us of our time at military school (which was run by nuns) and, of course, if there had been magazines with naked women in them, most of us elf, pixie and other boys would have been delighted, although the nuns would have gone nuts and punished us severely for having and looking at them.

That punishment surely would consist of stress positions or beatings we were forced to endure from time to time for violations of the rules but also would include nearly interminable lectures, which were sometimes even worse than the physical torture.

Yet, they would let us have *National Geographic* magazines to read and look at in which there would be, on occasion, photos of bare breasted tribal women in Africa, which apparently was okay because they were black and not white folks, or maybe because they were aboriginal folks instead of women in the modern world, although we couldn't for the life of us understand the difference (women's breasts were women's breasts as far as we were concerned), but we were none-the-less appreciative of this incongruity in their logic and not about to bring their inconsistent reasoning to their attention.

In the course of time, the Catholic church developed the idea of the confessional and regular admission of sins and doing penance for any infractions of church law and policy, which was, according to them, a reflection of God's will. In time, as capitalism began to develop, they began selling indulgences (you can sin for a price) carried on these days by the fact that those who can afford good lawyers can often get away with doing illegal things that poor people cannot. Although, Martin Luther, a German priest, took exception to this church practice and the Protestant Reformation began.

Still, the idea remains that you can't get to heaven if your god doesn't forgive you for this, that or the other thing or things that you did. Note, that in communist countries, they had people writing self-criticisms (about how they weren't being communist enough and were too selfish and individualistic, instead of sacrificing for the party, which is, according to them, the people), which is pretty much the same thing as confession, only your penance is usually hard labor and it is the *party* that forgives you or not. Communism is a social and political doctrine but it is essentially still a religion and a monotheistic one at that, which doesn't tolerate any competitive beliefs as it is deemed as the One True Faith or Way, Glory be to Marx, Glory be to Lenin and/or Mao.

In some places, this idea of needing forgiveness (or going to hell otherwise, or among the communists being shot or imprisoned for life [some sources claim that China has killed prisoners to harvest internal organs—read about the Falun Gong prisoners]) developed into the practice of having a sin-eater consume a ritual meal after a person had died so that they would take on the sins of the recently deceased. And, hopefully, they would have another eat their sins after they died (somewhat like putting items on layaway or using a credit card). This practice has been particularly associated with Wales and the Welsh culture.

However, we might note that in Mesoamerican civilization, the Aztec goddess of the Earth, Tlazolteotl, who was the goddess of motherhood and fertility as well, could also redeem those who confessed their ill deeds to her and she would then cleanse the individual's soul (or spirit) by, it is said, *eating their filth.* Not entirely unlike the tale of the Bean-nighe washing the clothes of those about to die.

Now, if we return to the original idea of magic, before the development of religion and with it the idea that we must appease the spirits or confess our sins to them about violating this or that taboo, we come to the idea that, as much as we certainly should apologize to the Earth for all that we have done to it, it is not forgiveness we need but rather an acknowledgement to ours'elves of what we have done wrong and due to that an alteration of our behaviors. We need to change the way we deal with each other and the planet and all the creatures and beings upon it, not beg some god's or goddess' forgiveness for violating what became, in time, arbitrary rules and taboos many of which were originally in place in order to protect us. The Earth has no use for our confessions, only the transformation of our attitudes and actions toward ones that create a sustainable future for it and us and all others.

Such taboos, in our experience, usually begin for practical reasons, although they are often carried on long after their usefulness has passed. We don't really need forgiveness so much as evolutionary development of our spirits and our souls (which reflect the way we interact with each other). When taboos become merely a part of a culture or belief system and children and others who question why such prohibitions exist in the first place are ordered to shut up and do unquestioningly as they are told (because I said so, that's why), the taboo loses its link to practical reality and becomes meaningless, mere habit and tradition without purpose other than control. This is rather like those individuals who go to church, synagogue or mosque merely for social appearances and approval.

We have, through time, gotten farther and further away from Nature and from our essential magic and it behooves us to purify ours'elves and our relationship to Nature if we are to proceed into the future developing advanced material bodies in which to manifest. We are in the process of gradually becoming X-Men/Women, mutants of an advanced human species in form and increasingly conscious and intelligent and intuitively and soulfully aware as elfae and otherworldly spirits.

Still, the idea of the sin-eater does bring up the question about whether we can take on another's sins, or carry the burden of someone else's karma, at least in part, for them. This idea of the sharing of sins derives surely, or certainly in part, from the fact that whole families were and are still in some places, such as countries where narco-trafficking dominates, punished for the violations of certain rules by one of its members. If the individual is disloyal or betrays the cartel the whole family might be killed for his transgressions.

This is actually the whole idea surrounding the notion that Jesus died for our sins that Christians often proclaim as a matter of faith. This doctrine holds that Jesus suffered death to expiate the sin upon all of Mankind due to the original transgression/sin committed by Adam and Eve. Somehow, all Mankind was held responsible for a violation committed by their earliest ancestors. Which, again, has some truth to it in that the mistakes, neglect and failings of our ancestors do often confront us in the present. But then, we are our ancestors, or at least some of them, and what we inherit from them is usually our own doing.

And such a notion can be also seen in which a king or other leader vanquishes his rivals and then kills that individual's entire family so that no descendants can arise later to act against him. Which is not all that different from the Chinese, in relatively modern times, executing dissidents and then sending their family the bill for the cost of the bullet, since the parents clearly raised the individual the wrong way, which is to say that they somehow didn't teach their children to obey society and thus its rulers unquestioningly like good little communists.

This reminds us once more of when we were at military school and all of us there would be punished at times because one or two individuals transgressed. We expect that they thought we, as fellow students, might use peer pressure on such individuals to behave but, really, most of us just resented what we thought was the stupidity and the unfairness of punishing everyone for the misbehavior of a few, especially when their bad behavior had nothing to do with the welfare of the community overall.

And, yet, as far as karma and Nature goes, it is not a matter of sin or forgiveness. It is about our behaviors, and if we don't change them, we continue to do the things that led to that karma in the first place. Still, we can share karma in a certain sense. We can love individuals as they re-incarnate (usually as our children). We can raise them to be better people and the love that we hold for them and the positive action it produces will in some way serve to ameliorate their karma. And it is quite possible that we can, sometimes, if our love is deep enough, suffer in our own lives so that those we love will not suffer quite so much in theirs.

Yet, once again, we each still bear the real burden of changing the way that we live and we each will need to go about our lives and our interactions with others in more positive and harmonious ways so that we might create a better world for ours'elves and our others and manifest Elfin thereby. The greatest power we have for relieving our own and other people's karma, which is to say suffering, is to be better people ours'elves.

The Spell:

I carry you deep in my heart
Will help you from the very start

And ever on as we advance
Upon the path that we do dance

Arvyndase:
El deca le dorae ver el'na bom
Yon loth le an tae lefa altu
Nar vari ton tat eli kreon
Repton tae tål dij eli ba far

Pronunciation:
Eel dee - cah lee door - ray veer eel'na bow-m
Yone loath lee ane tay lee - fah ale - two
Nair vay - rye tone tate e - lie kree - ohn
Reap - tone tay tahl dye-j e - lie bah fair

࿇

Chapter 27:
Day of the Dead and Santa Muerte

The Day of the Dead or Día de Muertos is celebrated in Mexico and by those of Mexican heritage (and also by those of other cultures who have become intrigued by this festival). It is, in its way, a combination of Halloween and All Souls Day, also called All Saints Day that the Catholic church created to replace Halloween, much good that did, in the same way that it created Christmas to replace Yule. Christmas was a more effective transition for most people, many even believing that Jesus was born on December 25th when, in fact, the factual data seems to indicate he was born around June or July. But saying his birth is just after Winter Solstice aligns Jesus with the traditional rebirth and return of the gods of light and the increasing length of days and of the coming spring.

The Day of the Dead takes place over several days from October 31 to November 2. This holiday involves family and friends gathering to pray for and remember those they loved who have died and, as in the case of this book, to help those transiting the Between to progress on their spiritual journey. Death, thus, in the Mexican culture is seen as a natural part of the life cycle. This festival gives individuals a chance to celebrate with those who have passed on and whose spirits are thought to awaken on this day to share in the festivities. Not all cultures have a morbid fear of death nor consider it to be the absolute end of the human being or even a journey to another world such as heaven or hell with no connection to Earth life anymore until the end of the world. Some embrace death as a part of life and include the dead in their hearts and ongoing lives and incarnations.

This, we expect, is pretty much how the ancient Celtic tribes viewed things, as a world of spirits that have their own realm but still can visit us in this world from time to time. Although, the Celts, like the Vikings, imagined that their tribes might continue feuding with each other in that other world as they were, at times, in this one and if you were killed in the otherworld, you'd be reborn again on this side of the veil (see the 2014 documentary *Boudicca: Warrior Queen of Ancient Britain* narrated by Liam Dale).

It is thought by scholars that this holiday (The Day of the Dead) originates back at least as far as the Aztecs and to a festival that they held, which was dedicated to a goddess they called Mictecacihuatl. Originally, this festival was thought to take place in August until the need to harmonize it with Christianity took place, which therefore associated it with the Christian idea of All Saints Day or All Souls Day and, by extension, with Halloween.

Note that the Toraja people of Indonesia, for whom the dead are treated as if they are merely sick for several days after their spirits have left their body, offer food, drink and tobacco to the dead body, since the spirit is regarded by them as being near the body for up to five days and may absorb the essence of these objects. Every three to five years, these people dig up the dead again, clean them and give them new clothes. Talk about honoring the ancestors!

For these peoples, and others around the globe, the dead, or spirits who have passed on, still exist as part of their lives. This is not unlike, in its way, the idea of reincarnation, only reincarnation places less emphasis on the importance of the body and more on the spirit of the individual and its ability to descend into the material realms again. However, the practice of the Toraja people in digging up and re-clothing the body is not entirely dissimilar to our Silver Elves practice of inviting spirits into our statues as teraphim and genius loci. The body, human and otherwise, is a place for the spirit to abide in but the abode should not be mistaken for the spirit itself. If one of our statues should fall and break, the spirit doesn't die, it just goes on to find another habitation.

And we should consider that it is DNA, our genetic material, that determines our physical existence. Determines what our body looks like, the color of our hair, eyes, skin and so on and its immunities and weaknesses and other physical aspects. And we need to remember that our DNA is carried in the human species overall. We bear each other inside of us, just as your parents bore your DNA in their bodies, and if they are currently alive, still do. Only about 2% of our DNA encodes proteins to build our bodies, the rest is called junk DNA, although actually we think it is a cosmic library we carry of DNA that isn't directly related to our particular body but bears instructions for other bodies, which is to say for the rest of humanity and for beings manifesting in this world.

Your DNA and ours is approximately 99.9% similar to any other person we may happen to come across anywhere on this planet (while the difference between the human and the chimpanzee genome is about 1.2%). If we are to believe that the material form, or DNA really, is our essential being as materialists suggest, then we have to understand as well that we live in each other. Which is to say that the blueprints for our material form is carried in the human race, as is the all of life upon this planet.

Still, these practices and rituals that honor the dead and incorporate them into people's lives make it clear that some people understand that the death of the body is merely a change of the spirit's abode. They still consider the spirit to be alive in a more ethereal way and they still interact with those they love and carry on a relationship with those who, in their minds, no longer have functional human bodies but who still exist in this world or, at least, exist here sometimes, visiting from the other worlds, as faeries and fae folk were often thought to do according to many of the legends and tales of our elfae peoples.

The name Nuestra Señora de la Santa Muerte means Our Lady of Holy Death. This being is frequently called Santa Muerte or Saint Death or Sacred Death and is a female deity and folk saint in Mexico and Mexican-American folk religion. This saint is not officially recognized by the Catholic church and is, in that way, somewhat like St. Christopher who is the popular saint that protects travelers but no longer has any official church recognition.

While Santa Muerte is a personification of death, she is also associated with healing, with protection, and with an easy passage into the afterlife or the Between states. The Catholic church canonizes some saints, but the common people canonize others. It is, in its way, rather like the difference between movies that win Academy Awards but that few people see, and those movies that are never even close to being nominated for any award but which masses of viewers flock to and adore, watching them over and over again (*The Lord of the Rings* movies did both those things, winning awards and having a devoted fan base).

It is likely that this Saint symbolizes the merger of pre-Columbian cultures that held a reverence to certain death gods and goddesses with the doctrines of the Catholic faith, which was imposed upon them by the Spanish conquest of those lands. These gods could be found among the Aztecs, the Maya, Mixtec (a less well-known Mesoamerica people) and other tribes. The worship of this being is especially prominent during, but by no means limited to, the celebration of the Day (or days, really) of the Dead festival.

This syncretizing is not unlike that of Baron Samedi (or Saturday, thus Saturn) who is one of the loa/spirits of Haitian Vodou. He is a loa of the dead and is also called Baron

Cimetière (cemetary), Baron La Croix (of the cross, thus crossroads), and Baron Kriminel (criminal) and is associated with the Catholic Saint Martin de Porres.

While Saint Death is seen as being a female saint or deity currently, in some cases this spirit was originally a male figure. Like the popular figure of death in modern Western cultures, her statues often have her holding a scythe. Also, note the association with Kali, a goddess of death in Hindu culture, who often holds blades and severed heads in some of her hands (like most Hindu gods she is frequently portrayed having many arms and hands, since most Hindu deities seem to be multi-taskers).

Like Nuestra Señora de la Santa Muerte, Kali, who is noted for being the destroyer of the wicked and evil, was also worshipped by criminals in the form of the thugee or strangler cult of India, thus worshipped by thieves and murderers. So, also, Nuestra Señora de la Santa Muerte, is appealed to in order to bless and to protect ones'elf or one's loved ones from death, but also evoked by some folks in order to curse others unto death.

As a side note, we once had a Mexican woman who came to us for lessons in witchcraft and magic. One time, she told us that a woman she knew had stolen about $200 or so from her and she wanted to curse her for doing so. We explained to her that she could, of course, curse this woman but a curse was really calling a person's karma down upon them in a more hasty fashion than it would usually be expected and that in cursing someone, one was also declaring to the spirits of the Universe that one didn't mind having one's own karma examined, since all magic returns to the sender. So, we asked her if she had ever stolen anything of significance, and was she really sure she wanted to quicken karma for the other person and therefore for herself and she told us that, on second thought, she'd forbear from cursing the woman and would just let karma take its time.

We can, of course, curse people. But again, all our magic comes back to us magnified, at least three-fold it is said by the witches, although for elves it is often seven-fold. And we should ask ours'elves, what is it we really want in a situation. We could wish a person to die, appeal to Santa Muerte with a death curse, but all that would do, if it did in fact work, is kill the person, which is just a temporary solution to the problem and they would surely come back into our lives in another incarnation and plague us again with an even stronger attachment to us due to the curse/magic that would connect us.

In the long run, what we elves wish is for people to become enlightened. So, we don't curse people, we wish them to be illuminated, for it just so happens that in doing so greater enlightenment then comes to us while they are faced with clearing away whatever karma bars them from illumination. This is a sort of elf trick, of course, but it works. We are not directly calling their karma upon them, but, of necessity, it comes anyway. Some men claim that you sometimes have to be cruel to be kind, but we elves say that most often you need to be kind to be cruel.

Because the Catholic church does not acknowledge or approve of this folk saint of Death, Santa Muerte, then her worship is usually carried out in private, although that is not always the case. People sometimes have altars to her in their homes or at some secluded location, however, there is also a public shrine to her in Mexico City. She seems popular as a figure among criminals, as one might expect, and those in prison (who are not always criminals), but she is also seen by some as a protectress of gays, bisexuals, and transgender people and others who are seen to be outcasts from normal society, which would include, in our estimation, we elfae folk as well for we are ever The Other Crowd.

One might think that the connection between criminals and gay folk a bit odd, since criminals are often socially conservative, racist, and frequently look down on gays (unless they are in prison, in which case they often practice it but claim it is the person they rape who is gay, not themselves), but criminals often view themselves as being outlaws, with all the cultural, folkloric and even adventurous and romantic connotations that being an outlaw holds and outlaws are also, by definition, traditional outcasts from society. Among we Silver Elves, one of us is descended from a family whose surname comes from an Irish word for 'outlaw' and others of us come from a lineage of actual outlaws who fled Scotland and also Wales to avoid prosecution.

From our Silver Elves point of view, Nuestra Señora de la Santa Muerte would be one of the Shining Ones that looks over the transition process as we travel through the Between from one incarnation to another. It is good to have friends in high places, but then we elves seek friends everywhere.

The Spell:

Oh, spirits great of the Between
Guide me through the realms unseen
Awaken my own spirit bright
To find my way into the light

Arvyndase:

Tra, tarili ralt u tae Vyrlan
Foren el joul tae êldli murtenïn
Vasa el'na os tari ilu
Va låc el yer verva tae lun

Pronunciation:

Trah, tay - rye - lie rail-t you tay Ver - lane
For - reen eel joe - yule tay eald - lie muir - teen - in
Vase - sah eel'nah ohss tay - rye eye - lou
Vah lock eel year veer - vah tay loon

ও

Chapter 28:
Sitting Shiva with Shiva

Sitting Shiva (which is Hebrew for the number seven) is a Jewish practice of sitting together to mourn the passing of a loved one. One sits Shiva for seven days usually, thus the name. Shiva is also the name of a Hindu god (one of the Holy Trinity, we might say, composed of Brahma, Vishnu and Shiva), who rules over destruction and transformation. Thus, when those of Jewish faith Sit Shiva for the dead they are really Sitting Shiva with Shiva.

Sitting Shiva is a practice of mourning to honor someone's passing and deal with one's own sense of loss over a loved one who has died. The Buddhist discourage one from overly mourning the dead since this tends to keep their spirit clinging to the vicinity of its previous body, but it is difficult not to feel some loss when one's beloved parent, child, spouse or friend has left one's life for a time to eventually pass into a new incarnation. Even when one's children move away to college some parents feel sad, and when a friend, whom we may never see again, relocates across the country we cannot help but feel a certain loss. So, when a person we love passes from this incarnation into the unknown, it is nearly impossible not to feel a bit of emptiness.

It is true that in mourning we are, temporarily, keeping the spirit of the deceased near us, but obviously it cannot return to its previous body and will eventually have to move on to a new one. In mourning, we are actually calling the spirit back to us in another incarnation and the stronger our feeling of loss the greater the attraction will be.

Prayers are often said for the dead to aid them, and the dead are often well spoken of (don't speak ill of the dead, as the admonition goes) to encourage them toward a better incarnation (and to prevent their disfavor), and people often say to them the things they feel that they should have said when they were alive and regret not doing so. They may feel it is too late to say these things to them, but it is not. Their spirit still hears their words and, most of all, feels their intention at making amends and reconciliation, as this book and *The Tibetan Book of the Dead* attest. All of this helps the spirit pass into another life, which is to say it helps it to return into this world in a new incarnation or pass on to a higher dimension of reality.

It is true that sometimes our feelings of loss also involve the fact that we were materially dependent upon someone and feel helpless in the world without them. But it is also the case that it can be difficult to find the right person for us in this world and when that person has gone many of us experience a devastating sense of emptiness as though our heart has been sucked out of our body. We are unlikely to find anyone like them again in this particular incarnation (although we will surely meet them again in another incarnation). Thus, people who have been very close for years often die within a short time of each other, going forth from this world to rejoin each other in new incarnations.

The Buddhists would urge us to consider the person's spirit and encourage it to go on toward complete enlightenment, which is to say avoid being reincarnated into this less than perfect world, and surely it would not hurt to have friends in high places, have friends and former loved ones among the Shining Ones who would certainly help to guide us in our own continuing development as spirits if they don't, in fact, forget us as the bliss of these higher realms overwhelms them as it certainly may. In some ways, they are like someone who becomes famous and is totally involved in their new social environment and acquaintances and forgets, at least temporarily, their old friends and the world of their upbringing.

But we Silver Elves will not tell you to suppress your mourning. There are times when one cannot help but grieve and those are the times that really count anyway. We simply suggest that in Sitting Shiva with Shiva remember that our connection to our loved ones never ceases really and we will surely see each other in other incarnations on this or other planes and dimensions in the future where we shall, in time, manifest Elfin.

The Spell:

By each point of the elven star
I call out through my soul
To touch your spirit where it might be
And make you safe and whole

Arvyndase:
La cha lynt u tae êldata mêl
El koar zes joul el'na der
Va fost le'na tari ern ter tri te
Nar kord le del nar loj

Pronunciation:
Lah chah lent you tay l - day - tah mell
Eel co - air zees joe - yule eel'nah deer
Vah foe-st lee'nah tay - rye ear-n tier try tee
Nair cord lee deal nair low-j

༄

"Mayhaps the essence of the difference between the philosophies of the elves and that of men is this: Men think there is nothing more permanent than Death. While we elves think there is nothing more transitory."
—The Silver Elves

The Elves Say: "Death is just the sleep of a lifetime."

Part Two . . .

Dealing with Reality and the Practical
Application of Spells for Aiding in the
Transition through the Between

"WHEN SOMEONE PASSES FROM THEIR BODY, THE ELVES GUIDE THEM THROUGH THE GREAT FOREST TO ANEW LIFE IN FAERIE.". .
. . . . .

Introduction two/too and
possibly to... Elfin

I t is nearly impossible to know exactly what you will encounter in the Between since our experience there depends greatly upon our own inner being and consciousness, especially our subconscious being, our right brained symbolic consciousness that manifests in dream states and during the Between. However, the general principles and developmental stages are rather universal so we have fashioned the following spells and admonitions of guidance so that we might aid anyone who is transiting the realms of manifestation.

We began writing this book at the end of November of 2019 and are now in the midst of the worldwide Coronavirus Pandemic. None of us know if we will survive this period or not, but surely sooner or later we will pass from this world into the Between. To date the death toll from the pandemic has passed 300,000 globally. We are using the daily spells presented here in Part Two of this book to assist all those that pass over during this time to make the transition peacefully. And if we Silver Elves have also passed over by the time you are reading this book, would you be so kind as to perform the daily spells for us, as well as for those you know and love who have passed over/on. It doesn't matter if the deceased is still in the Between or not, even if one has already reentered the world in a new body, or passed on to the higher realms (which seems unlikely for us Silver Elves since we still have dharma and surely some evolutionary karma here), it would still be helpful to our spirits if you enchanted these spells. We, for our part, send elfin blessings for you and your life and thank you in advance for your kind efforts and your magical actions on our behalf. Touch this page now and elfin starlight will enter your mind and heart and awaken a magic that has been secreted in your unconscious waiting to be released your entire life.

These spells are linked to the Elven Star and its seven points and seven intersections or interstices (so 14 in all) and the energies they represent. They are designed to be spoken over 14 days (one spell each day) as you contemplate or more importantly feel (if you knew and have feelings for the individual you wish to guide) the person on whose behalf you are casting the spell. You might wish to set up a temporary magic table, what most people call an altar, with photos or items reminiscent of the individual(s) for this purpose. These spells relate to energies of the 14 realms of manifestation: The Red Diamond World, Blue Wave World, Realm of the Wondrous Yellow Orb, Realm of the Rainbow Bridge, Emerald Green World, Orange Glowing World, Royal Purple Mist Realm, Lavender Lotus World, Deep Green Forest World, Golden Light of the Shining Realms, Silver Realms of Moonlight Being, Realm of the Amber Orbs of Translucent Wonder, Opalescent Realm of Radiant Being, and Pure Clear Realm of Radiant Light.

If, in fact, the person you are striving to guide through the Between has been dead for some time, it is best if you begin this process when you have had a dream about them or suddenly find yours'elf strongly feeling or thinking about them. Again, it doesn't matter how long they have been dead, the magic will still reach them and aid them in their evolutionary journey. However, if they have died recently, it is often best to wait four or five days to begin this spell so they will have time to loosen their connection to and lose interest in this world as the call of the other world grows stronger and they begin to move on into the Between.

Each stage of the Between represents evolutionary and developmental progress. However, just because one has risen to, say, the fourth stage, it doesn't mean one isn't still developing ones'elf in regard to the aspects of the lower stages, just that one has obtained some mastery, at least, of those stages. Even the Shining Ones are still evolving and dealing with some of the lower aspects of being, which is why sometimes those who have evolved to a certain level can fall or descend again to another level to master it more thoroughly. And it is important to understand that in a certain sense evolutionary development is like a spiral. We keep dealing with the same issues on higher and higher levels, which means more and more subtle levels of being, just as one might learn basic arithmetic and then geometry, and then say calculus, trigonometry and so forth and yet, one is still learning mathematics.

What the Elves Say: **"Elves can live a very long time and in good health, but when a body does begin to fail, we never say we are dying; we say instead, "I'm shedding."**

"The only time is now, which is eternally transforming. The place is here, which is everywhere."
—Old Elven Knowledge

"We elves are immortal, not because we live forever, but because we share in the Life Divine."

Elves listen

"We listen to the people
We listen to the trees
We listen to the stars
That whisper on the breeze
We listen to our hearts
We do this most of all
And we listen to the dance of death
That comes about in Fall
We listen to the seeds in Spring
As they heed life's new call
And springing up remind us
Of the Faerie Ball
They summon us to rise as well
And holding hands renew
Our journey on the Elven Way
Toward all that's bright and true."

Chapter 29:

Enchantment for the First Day, Point One on the Elven Star

$\mathcal{L}$isten to my voice, Oh, noble elfae one, ... (and/or say the person's name and think of them and/or feel their presence), and heed well the blessings I send unto you. After having slept for a time, you are now awakening into the **Red Diamond World** and you now remember that you are immortal and shall live forever. You knew this previously but had forgotten this truth. While this realization might bring you joy, it may also produce fear in you for the great unknown still looms before you. And everything now seems overwhelming and you are washed away with the tide of the life energy going swiftly you know not where faster than you can think or imagine. Do not resist this flow. There is no need to do so and no purpose in doing so.

However, if you have hated anyone in your previous life, any person or group of people, those individuals will now appear before you, mighty in their visage, threatening in their being and their rage against you, and you will tend to forget that you are an immortal being once more and fear for your survival.

If you flee from them you will reenter the material world seeking incarnation as quickly as possible in whatever portal opens and you will likely be born in the grimlen world among those who live their lives with hate in their hearts and you will be trapped for another life attempting to free yours'elf or be carried away by senseless and unthinking animosity your entire existence there, living in a hell world, often without realizing you are doing so. But this is not at all necessary and you can relinquish your enmity at any moment and fly free.

And heed well, oh, immortal one, these beings that threaten you now are but part of your own being. You need not fear or hate them, for in doing so you are only fearing your own powers and hating part of yours'elf, baring yours'elf from further realization, limiting your enchantments and trapping yours'elf without realizing you are doing so.

Relax. Touch your heart, as I now touch mine, and extend your hand to them in peace, as I extend mine to you, and go on farther into the Between. Be not born again yet, there are better worlds ahead of you and greater powers still to realize.

Now say this chant with me:

"I do not hate

I do not fear

I embrace mys'elf

And all who are near

We are one in our hearts

And that is quite clear

As the way before me opens."

ॐ

Chapter 30:

Enchantment for the Second Day, Point Two on the Elven Star

Heed now my voice, oh, noble elfae one, ..., you have now entered the **Blue Wave World** and are awash in pleasure. All pleasure will come to you. All the food you wish, all the sex you desire, all the drink or drugs or whatever it is that you hunger for are now all yours as much as you wish with no end nor any limitation.

However, none of this will fulfill you. You will never feel satisfied. No matter how much you eat you will still feel empty. No matter how much sex you have, you will still feel lonely. No matter what alcohol or drugs you imbibe you will never get intoxicated. This is a world of illusion, bereft of real content. If you continue to consume you will return again to another material body and spend your life among the goblin folk struggling with addiction to this, that or the other thing, ever greedy for more and never feeling you have enough, ever stuck in insatiable yearning and craving no matter how much you get.

Smiling spirits will come offering you all you desire, acting friendly but seeking to addict you. Heed them not for they are but your own hunger seeking satisfaction in ways it can never come. Smile, but move on declining their proffers. They are but your own desires seeking to fulfill themselves and drag you back down into the world to do so. If you look closer, they will appear like demons beneath their glamour but they are not that either, they are but cravings unsatisfied that have yet to understand the effective means of achieving what they truly desire.

Know this, oh kindred ours, you need nothing outside to fulfill yours'elf. You are complete within yours'elf, whole and wondrous and all that you need resides in your own being. Pause. Seek not pleasure in empty things but go on farther in the Between for there are greater worlds awaiting you, increasing powers and ecstasy unlimited.

Chant this incantation with me:

"All I need exists within
I pause and wait then start again
Pleasure postponed increases strong
My powers now my whole life long
All I need will come to me
And by that truth I shall be free
And abide forever in ecstasy."

ॐ

Chapter 31:

Enchantment for the Third Day, Point Three on the Elven Star

isten well, oh, beloved elfae one, ..., you have entered the realm of the **Wondrous Yellow Orb** and now feel a surge of confidence and power. You realize that you are a great one, with tremendous power and knowledge, and wish to pursue your goals with passion and ferocity. You look outward and feel such immense energy that you may now decide that you are meant to set the world straight, to be the Master of the Universe, and seek to dominate the worlds based purely upon your own power and sense of right and the way you think things should be or have been told and have accepted that they should be.

But, heed this, beloved and powerful one, power alone does not make right, and while all knowledge is available to you, you do not know all things. Positive thinking is good but not absolute. It needs to coordinated with the rules of Nature and the Universe. If you proceed on strength and will power alone you will arouse resistance, and other dominators will arise to crush you, seeking just as you do to Master the World. If you battle them, you may be cast down, or you may even conquer them, but still others will arise and eventually you will fall beneath them and tumble back into the world again, born among the Unseelie folk and lower men, ever struggling to assert yours'elf and dominate the world and those around you, stuck in perpetual conflict, arousing hate and paranoia and descending even further to even less advantageous incarnations.

Might does not make right, and s'elf confidence is not the same as reason. Seek not to Master others but to Master your own s'elf and do that lightly and with a caring and tender heart. Be not harsh unto yours'elf, nor unto others, and you will pass on from this realm to the farther realms of the Between and in doing so rise even higher, gaining ever more potent powers and obtaining all that you desire with little effort save that which it takes to make yours'elf a better being and to help others do the same.

Incant this charm with me:

"I feel so strong and powerful
And certain in mys'elf
All I need will come to me
Love, and wealth and health

No force I need to make this so
Nor any to convince
The Universe supports my will
Will do so ever hence."

≈

Chapter 32:

Enchantment for the Fourth Day,
Point Four on the Elven Star

arken, oh, royal elfae one, ..., you have entered the **Realm of the Rainbow Bridge** and will be faced with many choices. Up to now you have relied on pure feeling and an inner sense of your own power. Now, you confront the greater Universe where power is not enough and facts and reason and the laws of Nature on its various levels are seen to prevail. You need to understand to proceed. You need to know to understand. Here you begin to reason, and in mastering logic you may feel superior to those who have yet to develop this tremendous power. You have entered the realms of the higher men and the gnomes, those great preservers and lovers of knowledge, and this is the beginning of wisdom.

But look not down on those beneath you, irrational and ignorant beings that they may temporarily be. Remember, you were one of them at one time and the Shining Ones reached out to aid you and you were uplifted. Know compassion for those who are not as evolved as you, still struggling to arise. They will try to overthrow you in their ignorance, unaware that this will just bring about their own downfall, but have sympathy, even while you seek to reason with those who are, as yet, incapable of reason, and be firm with them in a kind and courteous way for they need guidance and gentle direction even while they reject your advice. Dispassionate truth will eventually prevail.

Do not argue with them and become entangled in their passion for that will merely drag you back into the world of the Unseelie. Nor become so coldly above them that you are like a child pulling the wings off insects to see what will happen, or a scientist utterly uncaring about the cruelty they enact upon their subjects with no regard for the feelings of these beings at all and excusing what they do as being done for the higher good. Develop your logic but do not divorce yours'elf from feeling and intuition. These powers need each other to be whole. Otherwise, you will be born into the world where people value knowledge over love and will feel bereft your entire life but probably never acknowledge that this is so, denying love altogether, calling it but a trick of biochemistry. You will never find your true love this way.

Gently now, take the next logical step, when you feel it is the right time, move on to that subtler world, where greater powers yet await you and frasority abounds.

Feel this spell as we chant it together:

"Clear as day I see the truth
The facts speak plain to me
My intuition just informed
By all that I do see
I do not flatter those above
Nor scorn those there below

Through my life compassion lives
My kindness I do show
The vaster world to know."

ॐ

Chapter 33:
Enchantment for the Fifth Day,
Point Five on the Elven Star

Welcome, magnificent elfae one, ..., to the **Emerald Green World** where you are greeted warmly and recognized by all about you and showered with praise. Your skills have developed to the point where you have obtained a certain level of fame. And you feel proud of yours'elf and filled with a sense of accomplishment, success and s'elf validation, but let this not make you arrogant, for all beings are destined to become a great success and all will be recognized in time for their momentous contributions to the whole. This is the world of the Fae, and of higher men, but normal folk seldom venture here and usually only for a short period in their youth. It is too far afield for them, and far apart from the paved paths of their world. Here they fear to tread save for brief periods.

If you let this feeling of great importance you now experience go to your head, you will suddenly have a sense that you are falling from a great height and descend into a new incarnation to live this life of fame. That is not a bad thing, but it is limited, oh, noble one, and less than you can be. You are greater still than you or others yet realize.

Always give credit where credit is due. Encourage those beneath you to develop their skills and joyfully share the spotlight with others who are arising and seek fame and recognition in their own lives. Give it to them and this will serve you well. Like the fae of legend, be a patron of the arts and encourage the creative spirit in all beings, uplifting them and increasing their skills and talents.

It may just be that you will find fame to be a fleeting matter that comes and goes and has no real substance to it. It may be that you grow tired of people coming to you with their hands out ever seeking something from you even while praising you. They just wish to be close to you and like unto you, touching you in the hopes that the magical Law of Contagion will uplift them through contact and association with one as great as you.

If you despise them for this, you will eventually fall to the first realm of grimlins. If you become enticed by the rewards of fame and become absorbed in a life of pleasure and luxury you will in time drop back to the second realm of the goblins. If you heed not others and think you know everything better than everyone else, you will tumble back into the realm of the Unseelie, heedless but determined. If you retreat, feeling like you are standing naked before a crowd embarrassed, you may descend to the fourth realm and seek a life of knowledge, contemplation and solitude, but there is nothing wrong with doing this once more if you retain a sense of compassion for others less developed than you.

But, beloved, why not go on further into the Between where even greater powers await you and deeper knowledge still to gain and behold. Leave fame to others, unless it serves your destiny and higher purpose, for it is like the moon, ever changing cycles, becoming full and then emptying again and will be ever so. It but reflects the sun and bears no true light of its own. It is a shadow standing out but it is not the thing that casts the shadow.

Spell this with me:

"Fame is but a tool for me
A means to do my art
I dedicate my life to style
In public and apart
And ever I do strive to be
Better than I've been
In what I do and in mys'elf
And for my loving kin."

శ

Chapter 34:

Enchantment for the Sixth Day, Point Six on the Elven Star

Blessings, great elfae one, ..., listen well to me as you enter the **Orange Glowing World** and know magical power profound. If you descend to the world now you will know true power in the world either high or low depending upon your development, but power still and great authority. If you use that power to promote factionalism and arouse hate against others, as some do, you will fall again to the first realm of the grimlins. If you wallow in the pleasure that power inevitably brings enticed by luxury, you will in time descend to the second realm of the goblins. If you use your power to lord yours'elf over others and are arrogant to them, you will become a martinet in the third realm, an authority that none respect. But if you use your power well, you will rise ever higher and learn that service is the duty of all with position and privilege and in serving well will rise even higher still. Power, beloved, is a tool not a destination.

This is the realm of the mighty fae, Seelie lords and men of strength and will power. It is the realm of the great magicians and the lower masters but it bears with it the danger of losing touch with those that one is empowered to serve and if that happens one will feel trapped despite all one's power, feel helpless even in one's arrogance and one's sense of superiority, will feel bound up and unable to act, and will retreat to the fourth realms seeking refuge in knowledge in order to be alone or go to the fifth realm to experience fame, which will draw people to you and possibly further temptations.

Use your power well, oh, magnificent one, and you may journey on to the seventh world where a great choice awaits you and you may ascend even higher still.

Chant this with great feeling:
"Mighty power great is mine
Above the common world I find
All I wish doth come to me
Except the urge to fly 'way free
And yet in serving I will see
The Path goes ever on."

❧

Chapter 35:
Enchantment for the Seventh Day, Point Seven on the Elven Star

What glory, bright elfae one, ..., risen now to the heights of worldly manifestation, you now see that all is service and you are free to manifest in any body you choose to fulfill your quest, your destiny and your mission on the Earth plane. Person of power? Person of knowledge? Artist great and immortal? All paths are open to you and in all that you do you shall serve the greater good as well as serve each individual and yours'elf. Rich or poor, high or low, famous or unknown, choose what life you will for all you do serves to make yours'elf and the world a better place for everyone.

This is the **Royal Purple Mist Realm** and what you do with your life is totally up to you but light will shine from you touching all that you encounter and all will be blessed to have known you. This is the realm of the great Seelie elfae and of evolved men and women and of the great masters of the world. Here all serve side-by-side endeavoring ever to enlighten the world and to manifest Elfin on that material plane and unite the higher realms with the lower, infusing materiality with spirit and magic, for this is our vision, quest and mission.

Here you will dream of a new dawn. Here you will sense love flowing from your heart to all others and because of that, love will come to you freely again and again. Here you will find your true companions on the path and together you shall bring light unto the world. Here you will truly begin to manifest Elfin in that world and make magic real through your life and all your actions.

However, beloved illuminated one, you are not obligated to descend into the world at all anymore. This is a free choice for you and if you wish to forego Earth life and go on to the higher, more expansive dimensions you may do so. You may always return if need or desire or purpose dictates. If this is the case, be patient and seek not reincarnation. If duty doesn't draw you back to the world, or those you love dearly no longer need your aid and you would evolve to the more ethereal realms, then pause here for a moment for the next world opens before you and you may join the Shining Ones as one of them.

Deign to say this spell with me, oh great one:

"Upon the world I cast my gaze
Down on through the Purple Haze
Upward through the Purple Rain
To the world that has no pain
I make a choice based on my heart
And once again I make a start
Up or down I now depart
Magic doth surround me."

ॐ

Chapter 36:

Enchantment for the Eighth Day, Between points One and Two on the Elven Star

Greetings, noble Shining One, ..., you have entered the **Lavender Lotus World**, and are awash in pleasure. Unlike the second world where nothing you consumed satisfied you, here even the tiniest bit of any food or drink or touch fills you with ecstasy and you need nothing more than a dab of anything. The realms are Glorious and all is awash in magic.

You are new here, and naturally filled with the joy of having ventured into the Higher Realms of Faerie and need do little more at first than relax, enjoy yours'elf and get your bearings. Here is the true Rapture and you are aware that you can now create your body to be or seem utterly as you desire. Create your own form. Change it again, like someone trying on clothes from their closet or in a shop. You may appear exactly as you wish.

And in time, which is different now, so in your own time, you realize you can now fly or levitate, if that is your will. You have the power to inspire others in the world with your thought forms. Especially those who are connected to you of old will be inspired by you, or those who call out to you for aid and it may be that they look upon you as a sort of god, but it would be unwise to fall for this illusion. You are more advanced than they, surely, but still evolving. Be like a loving parent unto them or a kindly and caring elder sibling.

Here you may develop the power of great healing. Shed your healing light upon those of us still struggling and inspire us to live our lives in enlightened and wondrous ways spreading healing in our own lives and by our actions.

Stay in this realm as long as you desire, mighty elfae one, or return to the world if you will to serve or would learn even more or go on further for there is still much to understand and worlds even greater to explore.

Listen now to my evocation:

"Oh, Shining One, so great and true
Remember me (us) in all you do
Reach out your heart
Stretch out your mind
So greater worlds I (we), too, will find
And rising through the planes I'll (we'll) be
One with you as you are with me (we)."

&

Chapter 37:

Enchantment for the Ninth Day, Between points Two and Three on the Elven Star

harken, wondrous elfae one, ..., you have flown into the **Deep Green Forest World**, where everything thrives and grows abundantly. Here is life ever prosperous. Here you will attract others of your kind, whose vibration complements your own and you shall form vortexes of magic and power so you may work together, in swirling love, made for each other and destined to accomplish mighty things in harmony.

In the material world, your vibrations will be felt and soulmates will come together, groups will be formed, cults will arise and elfae folk will seek each other out striving to discover on their own plane what you have created on this one. Smile upon us, and beam your joy to us so that we, in our realms, shall align unto you and rise toward Elfin Manifest as we do so.

Here you will surely need some time to luxuriate in the ecstasy of total union as you observe how the Universe creates itself and how all comes to be through the manifestation of consciousness and mind. There is no hurry, for there really is no such thing as time. All is now and has ever been and you realize you have always been here but didn't always realize this was so. Thus, we are one with you and you with us and together we shall spin our magic and marvels will flow forth.

Remember, you can always return to the material realms if you have purpose in doing so. It will be limiting in a sense, that is true. You will be like a master violinist playing a great sonata on a cheap violin, but still, you are a master and no one can take that away from you.

Or, you can move on, when you are ready, to finer realms still.

Enchant this spell with me:

"We are together
Now and forever
This has always been
Our magic united

We heal what's divided
Bright Elfin we shall win."

๛

Chapter 38:
Enchantment for the Tenth Day,
Between points Three and Four
on the Elven Star

heed my voice, oh, elfae one, ..., mighty and great are thou as you enter the **Golden Light of the Shining Realms** and realize you have the power to be utterly as you desire, to create your own realities but know in doing so that this is, indeed, your own creation. Never forget that we are making real our own minds, for to do otherwise is to become trapped within the illusions we have created and fall back into the material world unwilling, forgetful of our immortality, entangled in our own imaginations.

Energy is a blank canvas, paint your world upon it as you will. Energy is unformed clay, sculpt it as you wish. Consciousness is silence until we speak, choose your words carefully, for your word will become reality for yours'elf and for others. Be kind and generous in the worlds you create and aid others to realize their own unique being. The Universe is Infinite and there is no limit to what you can create.

Here you will find telepathy is the norm and all to whom you are connected will know your thoughts and intentions immediately. We will be of One Heart and One Mind and yet unique within ours'elves. Joyfully together, our shared thoughts and feelings will create pleasure in all who are a part of us, for we are one being, individual, united and each fully one unto ours'elves. This is the mystery of our being and it will vibrate down through the dimensions that are directly related to us and our frequencies will harmonize for the benefit of us all. Elfin manifests in our hearts and minds and in the realms we create through our lives.

Live here in utter joy and peace for eternity, one with us who are manifesting Elfin on the material planes of being, or proceed even further, if you will, for there is still much to know and understand.

Bright the magic we enchant together:

"Our Eald we make

Unto the worlds

Where we may all abide

Together we are one with you

A flowing of the tide

And as unto the Universe

Our magic thoughts we hurl

Our Elfin banner bright we raise

With pride we do unfurl."

ॐ

Chapter 39:

Enchantment for the Eleventh Day,
Between points Four and Five
on the Elven Star

Oh, wondrous Shining One, ..., you elfae bright, enter now the **Silver Realms of Moonlight Being** and know that you are a master of the root races, can create your own race of beings and guide them through the worlds to fulfillment of their uniqueness. For they are part of you, as our toes and fingers are a part of us, and in seeking the best for them, you seek the best for yours'elf and the worlds become a better place for all.

But remember, beloved illuminated one, that if you forget you are a part of the Universe, your creation will not thrive as well as if it is united with Nature vast and infinite, and in harmonizing your people with other peoples they shall have all the Universe to explore and worlds infinite to manifest within. Limit us not, oh mighty one, but render unto to us the powers that you have for we are one unto you and will rise to join you as your very own. There are wondrous things to create together in loving harmony with each other, now and forever more.

And when you are ready, leave these worlds unto us as you proceed further still and we will, surely in our own time, follow after, sharing our delight in our mutual admiration and love.

Chanting together we say:

"New peoples we will be
Ever ours'elves and ever free
Ever greater becoming so

Through each other we will know
The love that makes us better still
Until we each we do fulfill
The glory of our being."

੭

Chapter 40:

Enchantment for the Twelfth Day, Between points Five and Six on the Elven Star

ow, beloved Shining One, ..., having found your others, you blend together, merging and manifesting ever brighter worlds of being, born of your union, devoted to each other and to the Magic, creating Art for Art's sake, for the pure joy of creating what is wondrous, and your art is love and delighted elfin being. New dimensions flow from your being and the Universe grows ever wider and greater and there is infinity to explore and create within.

We sense your magic on our plane of being and draw down to us your starlight energy and enhance our magic thereby, becoming greater as we do so and manifesting Elfin upon the Earth by the Light of the Elven Stars. This is the **Realm of the Amber Orbs of Translucent Wonder** and we shall devote ours'elves to the creation of a world ruled by love and guided by elfin starlight and empowered by elvish magic.

You create worlds together. Solar systems and galaxies of being. Yours is one of many multi-verses and we from our world cannot know exactly what you do or how you do it, but we shall in time learn as we become like unto you evolving ever onward into a bright future of starlight being and radiant love. Elfin manifest throughout the Constellations. Magic everywhere. And you, greater still, may move on, when you are truly ready to do so.

Intone this spell with me:

"Worlds flowing
Spiral round
The truth is here
In what is found
Within our hearts
Our beings strong
The elfin love
For which we long
Now manifest within us."

ॐ

Chapter 41:

Enchantment for the Thirteenth Day, Between points Six and Seven on the Elven Star

Oh, magnificent starlight being, ..., we send you our blessings and know that you in turn send us, yours. You have arisen in the **Opalescent Realm of Radiant Being**. Devoted to the Life Elfin, your magic flows from your being and radiates into the worlds touching all our lives, bringing us success and prosperity, healing and ecstasy and urging us ever onward, as we urge you to continue on becoming ever more and greater still, as you were ever destined to be and as we, for our part, shall be as well in our own time in worlds of our creation. You are a multi-dimensional being. You are here and there and everywhere. You are within us and beyond us. Enlighten us as we enlighten others, aid us as we assist our kindred, prosper us as we share our success and help us be better in every way. Illuminate the path that leads to the heart of Elfin, which is your heart and our hearts united.

I listen to this spell as it echoes through the Universe, ringing in my ears like the bells of Elfin:

"Here, now, everywhere
We are as we will be
Manifesting Elfin true
As you do join with we
Together in our yearning
Our Vision thus appears
Becoming real through what we do
We strive on through the years."

☙

Chapter 42:

Enchantment for the Fourteenth Day, Between points Seven and One on the Elven Star

O h, spirit Elfin, bright and true, ..., if you have entered here, the **Pure Clear Realm of Radiant Light**, then you are unique beyond our comprehension, and may be whatever you will be according to your own nature. We trust that you will smile upon us, as we still think of you, and in harmony our magics will be greater still and all will benefit by our union. Blessings unto you and we shall in our own time enter the worlds you create and delight with you therein and manifest our own elvish realms magnificent.

Blessings upon your way, we say:
"We gaze into the light so bright
We cannot really see
But we do trust our hearts to know
That you are ever free
And onward as you do become
All that you will be
We honor you as one of us
As we will come to see."

See you in Elfin, beloved kindred. . . . .

About the Authors

The Silver Elves, Zardoa and Silver Flame, are a family of elves who have been living and sharing the Elven Way since 1975. They are the authors of 50+ books on elven magic and enchantment and the elven way, available on Amazon internationally, and through your local bookstore, including:

The Book of Elven Runes: A Passage Into Faerie;

The Magical Elven Love Letters, volumes 1, 2, and 3;

An Elfin Book of Spirits: Evoking the Beneficent Powers of Faerie;

Caressed by an Elfin Breeze: The Poems of Zardoa Silverstar;

Eldafaryn: True Tales of Magic from the Lives of the Silver Elves;

Arvyndase (Silverspeech): A Short Course in the Magical Language of the Silver Elves;

The Elven Book of Dreams: A Magical Oracle of Faerie;

The Book of Elven Magick: The Philosophy and Enchantments of the Seelie Elves, Volume 1 & 2;

What An Elf Would Do: A Magical Guide to the Manners and Etiquette of the Faerie Folk;

The Elven Tree of Life Eternal: A Magical Quest for One's True S'Elf;

Magic Talks: On Being a Correspondence Between the Silver Elves and the Elf Queen's Daughters;

Sorcerers' Dialogues: A Further Correspondence Between the Silver Elves and the Founders of the Elf Queen's Daughters;

Discourses on High Sorcery: More Correspondence Between the Silver Elves and the Founders of the Elf Queen's Daughters;

Ruminations on Necromancy: Continuing Correspondence Between the Silver Elves and the Founders of the Elf Queen's Daughter;

The Elven Way: The Magical Path of the Shining Ones;

Through the Mists of Faerie: A Magical Guide to the Wisdome Teachings of the Ancient Elven;

The Book of Elf Names: 5,600 Elven Names to Use for Magic, Game Playing, Inspiration, Naming One's Self and One's Child, and as Words in the Elven Language of the Silver Elves;

Elven Silver: The Irreverent Faery Tales of Zardoa Silverstar;

An Elven Book of Ryhmes: Book Two of the Magical Poems of Zardoa Silverstar;

The Voice of Faerie: Making Any Tarot Deck Into an Elven Oracle;

Liber Aelph: Words of Guidance from the Silver Elves to our Magical Children;

The Shining Ones: The Elfin Spirits That Guide You According to Your Birth Date and the Evolutionary Lessons They Offer;

Living the Personal Myth: Making the Magic of Faerie Real in One's Own Personal Life;

Elf Magic Mail, The Original Letters of the Elf Queen's Daughters with Comentary by the Silver Elves, Book 1 and 2;

The Elves of Lyndarys: A Magical Tale of Modern Faerie Folk;

The Elf Folk's Book of Cookery: Recipes For a Delighted Tongue, a Healthy Body and a Magical Life;

Faerie Unfolding: The Cosmic Expression of the Divine Magic;

The Elements of Elven Magic: A New View of Calling the Elementals Based Upon the Periodic Table of Elements;

The Keys to Elfin Enchantment: Mastery of the Faerie Light Through the Portals of Manifestation;

Elf Quotes: A Collection of Over 1000 Ancient Elven Sayings and Wise Elfin Koans by The Silver Elves About Magic and The Elven Way;

The United States of Elfin Imagining A More Elven Style of Government;

Elven Geomancy: An Ancient Oracle of the Elfin Peoples for Divination and Spell Casting;

Creating Miracles In the Modern World: The Way Of the Elfin Thaumaturge.

The Magical Realms of Elfin: Answers to Questions About Being an Elf and Following the Elven Path (Volume 1 of our question and answer series, of which The Manifestations of Elfin is Volume 2);

Elven Psychology: Understanding the Elfin Psyche and the Evolutionary and Esoteric Purpose of Mental Disorders;

The Elves Say: A Collection of Over 1000 Ancient Elven Sayings and Wise Elfin Koans by The Silver Elves About Magic and The Elven Way, Volume 2;

The Complete Dictionary of Arvyndase: The Elven Language of The Silver Elves;

Sticks and Stones, Feathers, Charms and Bones: An Original Oracle of the Elfin Peoples of the Ancient Future;

Elf Tribes: The Silver Elves' Guide for Finding Your Magical Kind and Kin and it's companion book;

Faerie, Fae and Otherkin: The Silver Elves' Guide for Finding Your Magical Kind and Kin;

Elven Hedgewitchery and Found Magic: Using Art-Making for Evoking Elfin Magic and Living the Elven Way;

An Elfin Book of Trees for the Elven Druid: The Ogham of the Elves Using Elvish Wizard Script;

The New Dawn of Elfin: Answers to Questions About Being an Elf and Following the Elven Path, Volume 3; and

Elves, Faeries, Fae and Otherkin Tribes: More Descriptions of Otherworldly Folk.

The Silver Elves have had various articles published in *Circle Network News Magazine* since 1986 and have given out over 6,000 elven names to interested individuals in the Arvyndase language, with each elf name having a unique meaning specifically for that person. If you wish to know more about The Silver Elves, you can read pages 100 to 107 in *Circles, Groves and Sanctuaries*, compiled by Dan and Pauline Campanelli (Llewellyn Publications, 1992), which contains an article by them and photos of them and their home/sanctuary as it existed at the time. They are also interviewed and mentioned numerous times in *Not In Kansas Anymore* by Christine Wicker (Harper San Francisco, 2005) and in *A Field Guide to Otherkin* by Lupa (Megalithica Books, 2007. Also, an interview with The Silver Elves is included in Emily Carding's recent popular book *Faery Craft* (Llewellyn Publications, 2012*)*.

The Silver Elves understand the world as a magical or miraculous phenomena, and that all beings, by pursuing their own true path, will become whomever they truly desire to be. You are welcome to explore their website at **http://silverelves.angelfire.com**, visit their blog site at **https://thesilverelves.blogspot.com** on the Elven Way and also their blog site on Elven Lifestyle, Magic and Enchantment at **https://silverelves.wordpress.com**, and join them on Facebook with the names as "Michael J. Love (Zardoa of The SilverElves)" and "Martha Char Love (SilverFlame of The SilverElves)."

You are also invited by The Silver Elves to come join them in some of their elven and magical otherkin Facebook groups where you will find the elven-faerie-fae otherkin community interacting and sharing the Elven Way:
The Magical Books of the Silver Elves —
https://www.facebook.com/groups/539205916250397— And if you would like to find out more about our Silver Elves books on The Elven Way, please do join us! We have discussions about our Silver Elves books as well as about Elven and Otherkin philosophy, elven lifestyle and the Elven Way and

everything Elfin. If you have read our books and would like to discuss them with us, this is the place to come join in the discussions and share with us your responses.

Elf Witches of the Mystic Moon —
https://www.facebook.com/groups/806583242768352

The Elven Way —
https://www.facebook.com/groups/165938637423212 —A group for all our elven kin and friends to gather and share in discussions about The Elven Way and elvish life.

Elven Life and Magic —
https://www.facebook.com/groups/629491797123886

Elvish Magical Chat —
https://www.facebook.com/groups/307775362744491

The Faerie Circle —
https://www.facebook.com/groups/1025483294180077

Faerie Craft —
https://www.facebook.com/groups/395403367195312 — This is a group to share and advertise your elven and fae artistic creations.

I Heart Elven Magic —
https://www.facebook.com/groups/2215672296

Silver Elves Embassy —
https://www.facebook.com/groups/206231890276255

United Otherkin Alliance —
https://www.facebook.com/groups/328253710566869
This is an alliance for Otherkin/ Therians, where elves, faeries, dragons, kitsune, gnomes, hobbits, merkin, pixies, brownies, nymphs, driads, niaids, valkyrie, vampires, devas, fauns, unicorns, animal kin and all manner of Faerie Folk gather and come together! This group is open to anyone who wishes to be part of a congenial group of Otherkin.

Feasting With the Elves (come join us, we are just having some fun sharing elven recipes and healthy eating) — https://www.facebook.com/groups/597948240617006

Devayana: Buddhism, Vedic, & Asian Spirituality for Elves and Fae
https://www.facebook.com/groups/devayana

Nature & the Unseen Realms with the Elves & otherkin. A spiritual journey —
https://www.facebook.com/groups/196916350335537

Have you always wanted to hear elves speak in Arvyndase, the magical language of The Silver Elves? Come listen! The Silver Elves just published their first You Tube video in their new The Silver Elves channel. And they would love it if you would please subscribe, like and comment! **https://youtu.be/unUkxT9QbNE** .

Realities of Elfin: **"Even death cannot make us forget our elven lovers."**

"The waters of the Eternal Spring of Elfin don't make one immortal; they enable one to see that one *is* immortal."

"Some folks think they are speaking to the Dead. We elves know there are no dead, there are only those who have transformed."
—Ancient Elven Wisdom

"The path of the Elfin never ends for it is the Way to Immortality."
—Ancient Elven Wisdom

Printed by Amazon Italia Logistica S.r.l.
Torrazza Piemonte (TO), Italy